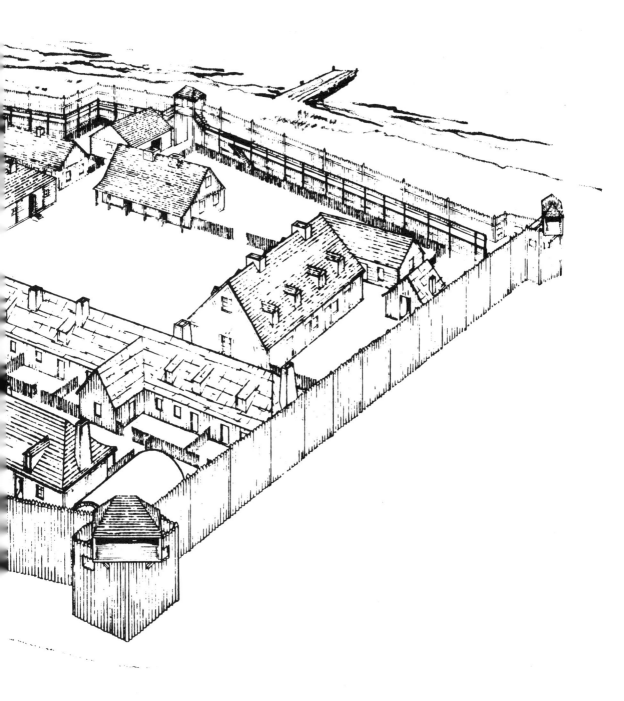

At The Crossroads

Michilimackinac
During The
American Revolution

by
David A. Armour
and
Keith R. Widder

Mackinac State Historic Parks
Mackinac Island, Michigan

Copyright 1986

Mackinac State Historic Parks
Mackinac Island, Michigan

First Printing 3000 copies
Revised Edition 2000 copies
Third Printing 1500 copies

Printed by
John Henry Co.
Lansing, Michigan

ISBN 911872-24-8

Cover: Portrait of A. S. De Peyster   — Burton Historical Collection
Portrait of Sir John Caldwell   — F. E. G. Bagshawe
Drawing of Fort Michilimackinac   — Victor Hogg

Contents

To:

Eugene T. Petersen

Maps

Lexington Green   April 19, 1775

Introduction

In the gray light of dawn on April 19, 1775, a column of British soldiers marched onto Lexington Green. On the opposite side a thin line of local militia awaited them. Major John Pitcairn halted his red-coated troops and called on the American colonials to disperse. People began to move and to shout. Suddenly a shot rang out, and billows of smoke covered the field as British regulars exchanged blasts of musket fire with the militiamen. When the shooting stopped, eight colonials, all dead or dying, lay on the Green. No one was certain who fired that first shot, but it did not really matter. The American Revolution had begun.

Among the British soldiers were men of the Tenth Regiment of Foot. Only a few months before they had been stationed on the Upper Great Lakes, some at Fort Niagara, Detroit and Fort Michilimackinac. After spending two years in the wilderness, they were eager to return to England. During the summer of 1774 soldiers of the King's Eighth Regiment came to replace them, and the 477 men of the Tenth finally assembled at Quebec.

But instead of boarding ship for England they found that, due to disturbances in Boston, they were not going home. On October 6, 1774, they embarked and almost a month later sailed into Boston Harbor. In Boston they discovered hatred and hostility towards the English government and heard rumors of American preparation for an armed revolt. As winter gave way to spring, spies reported the amassing of munitions at Concord, about twenty miles from Boston. On April 19th the Tenth planned to nip a potential uprising in the bud. Instead war exploded in their faces.

Distribution of His Majesty's Forces in North America. 11th June 1775.

Regiments	Companies	Where Quartered	1
Royal Reg of Artillery	5	At Boston, One at Montreal & Lakes, One at Quebec, One at East & West Florida	
17 Light Dragoons		At Boston	
4th Foot	10	At Ditto	
5th	10	At Ditto	
10th	10	At Ditto	
18	8	At Ditto, Two at Kaskaskias Illinois Country	
22	10	At Ditto	
23	10	At Ditto	
35	10	At Ditto	
40	10	At Ditto	
43	10	At Ditto	
44	10	At Ditto	
45	10	At Ditto	
47	10	At Ditto	
49	10	At Ditto	
52	10	At Ditto	
59	10	At Ditto	
63	10	At Ditto	
65	6	At Ditto, 3 at Halifax Nova Scotia, 1 at St Johns & Placentia	
1 B. Marines	10	At Ditto	
2d do	10	At Ditto	
7th Foot	10	At Quebec	
	4	At Niagara	
8	3	At Detroit	
	2	At Michilimackinac	
	1	At Oswegatchie	
14	9	At St Augustine, a Detach'd of 100 Men ordered to Georgia, And a Detacht of 70 Men & the Compy at New Providence ordered to Virginia	
	1	& a Detacht of 1 Drum'r & 95 Rank & file at Castle William	
16	10	At Pensacola	
26	9	At Montreal, Small Detachments at Three Rivers, Chambly & St Johns	
	1	Taken by the Rebels at Ticonderoga	
64	10	At Castle William	

Thos Gage
Commdr in Chief

2

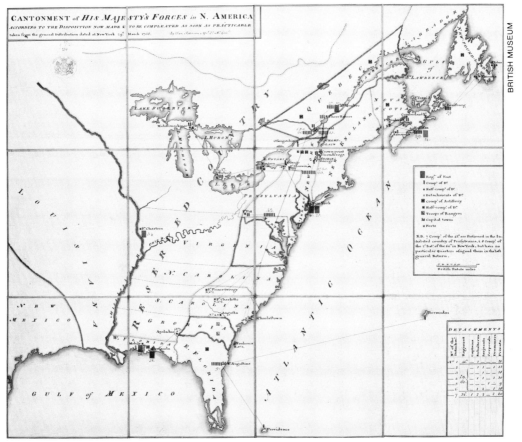

Map showing the location of British soldiers in North America on March 29, 1766. By 1775 most of the troops had been assembled in Boston.

When Great Britain defeated France in the French and Indian War, she acquired vast new lands in North America. To guard against French or Indian insurrection, Britain maintained garrisons throughout Canada. The furthermost post in the Upper Lakes was Fort Michilimackinac, five thousand miles from London on the outer fringe of the British Empire.

Michilimackinac was a crossroads. This fortified trading village of only a few hundred winter residents was the center of a complex fur trading industry which reached far north of Lake Superior, west across the Mississippi River, south into the Illinois Country and along the wooded shores of Lake Michigan. Michilimackinac was located at the juncture of Lakes Michigan and Huron, where the vast network of lake and river routes in the northwest converged.

Travelling to Michilimackinac were urbane British officers, thousands of Indians from many nations, French-Canadians, a scattering of free and enslaved Blacks, and aggressive English, Scottish and French businessmen. The lure of furs brought them to the Straits. Here they traded or transhipped their merchandise. Most came only for a brief stay; a few resided year round. Attempting to maintain a semblance of order on the rough and tumble frontier was a small garrison of British troops.

Shock waves from the shots fired at Lexington and Concord reverberated to the Upper Lakes. Most of the French and Indian inhabitants of the Michilimackinac region were not part of the revolt, but rebel promises, threats, and military excursions forced them to take sides or attempt neutrality. The war created economic disruptions which affected many who did not even understand the political reasons for the conflict.

Michilimackinac remained loyal to the Crown, and the Revolution forced the military to reconsider its defense. A number of raids were launched to keep the Americans at arms length, but in 1779 a crucial decision was made — the community was indefensible and must be moved. Over the next two years the people were uprooted and the fort and town were transferred to Mackinac Island.

The commanding officers were faced with difficult decisions and awesome responsibility. Arent Schuyler De Peyster and his successor Patrick Sinclair had to pacify, cajole, lavish with presents, and threaten the Indians to keep them at peace with each other and loyal to the Crown. At the same time the commandants had to supervise the trading community, which included many unscrupulous men whose only concern was profit.

This task drained the emotional and physical energy of both Major De Peyster and Lieutenant Governor Sinclair. In 1779 De Peyster departed with his honor intact, but Sinclair was not so fortunate three years later.

T he Revolution's impact on Michilimackinac has remained largely untold. American historians writing about the Revolution in the Old Northwest have been fascinated by the success of George Rogers Clark and have usually focused on his efforts to displace the British in the Illinois Country. Maps depicting the "Revolution in the West" frequently find Michilimackinac too far to the north to include.

While much of the story is told through the experiences, attitudes and judgments of De Peyster and Sinclair, we have attempted to present the community as a whole. Unfortunately most of our subjects did not leave written records. Consequently we were forced to rely for the most part upon papers left by British officials, merchants, and traders. This made it extremely difficult to assess the motives and points of view of Indian chiefs, warriors and their families, voyageurs, poor French residents, Black and Indian slaves, and the King's enlisted men. Despite this handicap, we have tried to portray their life at Michilimackinac during the Revolutionary War years.

Arent Schuyler De Peyster

5

I.

Arent Schuyler De Peyster Arrives at Michilimackinac

As he watched the white sails of a schooner draw near Fort Michilimackinac, a blue-coated royal artilleryman rammed a charge of gunpowder down the barrel of a six-pound iron cannon. He touched a smoldering linstock to the vent and sent a cloud of smoke and a boom over the deep blue waters of the Straits of Mackinac. The concussion shook the wobbly wooden gun platform.

The salute was heard by Captain Arent Schuyler De Peyster and two companies of the King's Eighth Regiment of Foot aboard the approaching ship. On this day, Sunday, July 10, 1774, they craned their necks to see the stockaded fur trading village which would be their new home.[1] The schooner *Dunmore* dropped anchor four hundred yards off shore beside a bobbing batteau. Captain De Peyster climbed down the ship's ladder into the rocking, thirty-foot boat. Rowed by soldiers from the Tenth Regiment, the batteau, slapped by waves, headed toward shore. Reaching the stony beach several of the oarsmen jumped into the cold water and dragged the boat onto land.

Lining the shore were the soldiers of the garrison and most of the town's inhabitants. Children chased barking dogs while their mothers waved and talked excitedly in French. Flintlock muskets fired shots into the air to welcome the new commandant.

The person most eager for the arrival of the disembarking troops was Captain John Vattas. For the past two years he had worried about the safety of this isolated post. Eager to return to civilization and England, he had been waiting impatiently since spring for his replacement.[2] Now relief had come. As he watched his men tug the batteau, he was pleased with the way the vessel slid smartly up the newly constructed rollers which protected the boat's flat bottom.

The 38-year old Arent Schuyler De Peyster had been born into an aristocratic Dutch family in New York City. His lineage reached back to the time the city was called Nieuw Amsterdam and through his mother, Catherine Schuyler, he was linked to prominent colonial families in New York and New Jersey.

When he was only sixteen years old, he first crossed the Atlantic to London. Soon after the French and Indian War erupted, he received an Ensign's Commission in William Shirley's regiment in New York on April 30, 1755. Two years later De Peyster purchased a lieutenancy in the King's Eighth Regiment. After serving in a number of campaigns in North America, he soldiered in Germany before returning to England. On May 16, 1768 he embarked for Canada. Promotion was slow in the post war years, but he attained a captaincy on November 23, 1768. Until he was ordered to Michilimackinac, his duty centered in Montreal and Quebec.

Snow was falling as De Peyster departed from Quebec by batteau on May 4, 1774. Proceeding up the St. Lawrence, he stopped briefly at Montreal and then crossed Lake Ontario aboard the schooner *Ontario* to the Niagara portage. At Fort Erie, located at the eastern end of Lake Erie, he boarded the *Dunmore*. Crossing Lake Erie he stopped briefly at the thriving village of Detroit and then continued up Lake St. Clair and along the western shore of Lake Huron to Michilimackinac and his new command.

Accompanying De Peyster was his wife Rebecca, his *"chere compagne de voyage."* They were inseparable. The daughter of Provost Blair of Dumfries, Scotland, she was a vivacious woman and skilled dancer who had trained under Monsieur Pique, a French dancing master in Edinburgh. Childless, she was devoted to her many pets. She missed her spaniel, "Dapper," recently killed when soldiers pushed him out of a third-story window in the Quebec Artillery barracks. Her current favorite, a chipmunk "Tim," delighted his mistress by whirling in circles.

Although it had been difficult to leave her friends in Quebec, the trip west had been exciting, highlighted by a view of the "Falls of Niagara where, laying on her breast, she drank of the water as it fell over the precipice."[3] Michilimackinac was a long way from Dumfries, but Rebecca would find many who spoke with a Scottish brogue.

As he stepped ashore, De Peyster saw the fort's eighteen-foot gray cedar pickets just a few feet from the water. Bastions jutted out on each corner, and a sentry house perched above the entrance — the water gate. Indian birchbark canoes and wigwams dotted the beach to the east. Behind them, stretching for several hundred yards, rambled a village of nearly a hundred bark-covered buildings that traders used as summer residences and shops. Eight miles to the northeast across open water forest-covered Bois Blanc Island, Round Island, and the green hump of Mackinac Island rose above Lake Huron. Directly north across the four mile strait, a line of low hills formed the northern shore. Completing the circle, De Peyster glimpsed St. Helena's Island on the western horizon where the straits disappeared into Lake Michigan.

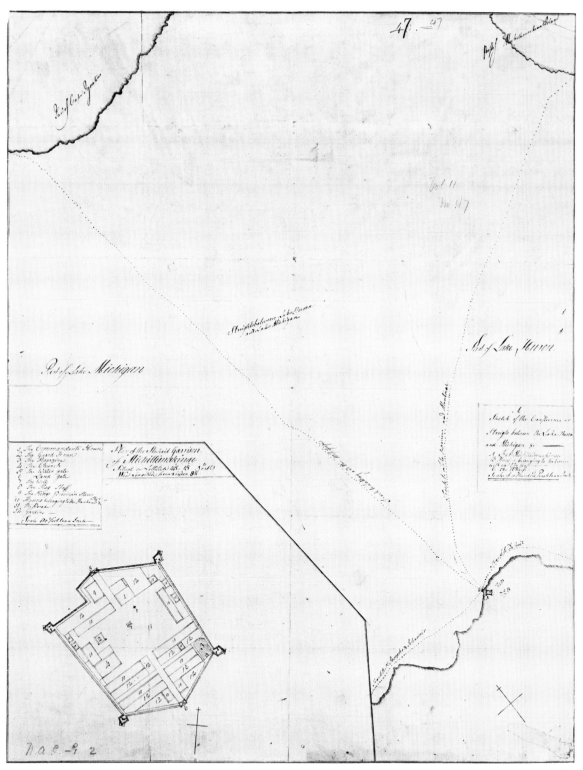

Michilimackinac in the 1760's –

West of the fort, sand dunes reached to the forest edge along a shallow bay which afforded scant protection from winter storms.

The Commanding Officer's House

A red-coated sentry smartly saluted as the two Captains strode through the water gate into the three and a half acre enclosure. On their left the refurbished commanding officer's house, constructed in the French style of vertical logs, was to be the De Peyster's home. Vattas occupied two downstairs rooms while other officers lived in the remaining two. The rooms were small measuring only thirteen by fifteen feet, but there were two garrets upstairs.[4]

While his baggage was carried into the fort, De Peyster and Vattas reviewed the troops mustered in stiff lines on the King's parade ground facing the commanding officer's house. De Peyster, a firm believer in tight discipline, carefully examined each man's weapons and uniform. Having finished the inspection, Vattas pointed out the few buildings which belonged to the King. From their vantage point on the edge of the parade ground they could look in both directions down the Rue Dauphine. This street, only 350 feet long, connected both entrances to the fort and divided the village in half. Directly across the street, facing east, stood the single story soldier's barracks. In 1769 men of the Sixtieth Regiment of Foot had hewn the timbers and assisted a carpenter crew brought especially from New York to build

The Soldiers' Barracks

this horizontal log structure. Seventy-two men could crowd into the barracks. At the north end of the street beside the water gate was the new King's provision storehouse in which the commissary kept military supplies and the soldiers' food. Completed only a year ago, the storehouse had been difficult to construct because stone for the foundation had to be brought several miles. Except for the soldiers' privy in the northwest bastion and a few other small plots of ground, the lands and buildings inside the palisade were privately owned.

De Peyster and Vattas turned and strolled south to the cross street called Rue de la Babillier on the east and Rue Diable on the west. On one side of each street were several row houses. They faced the five-foot picket fences which enclosed the rear gardens of the houses. Owned by French and British civilians, a few houses were rented to soldiers and officers because the King's quarters were inadequate. Several merchants had shops in the front room of their homes.

Behind the barracks, the Church of Ste. Anne de Michilimackinac, built in the 1740's of clapboarded logs, was the focal point for French Catholics living in the Upper Great Lakes region. Here they were baptized, married, and ultimately buried. Attached to the north side of the church was the bark-roofed priest's house. The building was unused, however, because no priest had resided there since 1768. Connected to the southeast corner of the rectory was a blacksmith shop where iron implements were made and repaired. Tucked between the priest's house and the barracks, the post guardhouse sheltered the soldiers on guard duty and contained a cell to lock up unruly soldiers or an occasional criminal.

Church of Ste. Anne de Michilimackinac

As they approached the land gate, Vattas pointed to the grassy mound of the powder magazine. Located in the southeast corner, this semi-subterranean rectangular building was constructed of pine logs covered with cedar bark shingles. The flat log roof was heaped with sod to protect it from flaming arrows or artillery shells and minimize the danger from accidental explosion.[5] Soldiers up in the bastions and sentry box over the fort entrance could shoot along all sides of the walls in case of attack. Fifty yards outside the land gate the post stables sheltered a few horses and cattle, and citizens tended small gardens.

During the next three days Vattas explained to De Peyster the post commandant's responsibilities and introduced him to the community.[6] One of the first men De Peyster met was John Askin, a prominent 35-year-old trader and post commissary. Askin, an Irishman, resided at Michilimackinac because he realized that it was the strategic center of the western trade.

Traders from Albany, New York, where Askin first entered the fur trade, came westward on the Mohawk River, worked their way up to Lake Ontario and followed the coastline of the lakes through Niagara and Detroit, finally arriving at Michilimackinac. Usually they transported their cargoes in batteaux or small sailing vessels. On the other hand traders from Montreal had a choice of two routes. They could proceed up the St. Lawrence River to Lake Ontario and then follow the same course as the Albany merchants or use the quicker and shorter northern route via the Ottawa River, Lake Nipissing, the French River, Georgian Bay, and then on to Michilimackinac. From this post they dispersed to distant points westward or returned home with a load of last winter's furs.

For over a hundred years the French and British had contested control of the Straits of Mackinac and the Upper Great Lakes fur trade. The French first occupied the northern shore of the straits in the 1670's. When a few English fur traders from Albany ventured to the straits during the 1680's, they were captured and taken to Montreal. Shortly after 1700 the French moved to Detroit from St. Ignace in an effort to block the spread of British influence. About 1715 they returned to the straits and erected a fort on the southern shore because the Ottawa village had moved there from St. Ignace in the interim. During the next forty-five years the French and British fought bitter wars for control of North America, and Indian warriors from Michilimackinac fought beside their French allies. In 1760, following capitulation of Quebec and Montreal, the French surrendered Canada, and Michilimackinac passed to Great Britain.

Alexander Henry

As a result, British traders surged westward to take advantage of the lucrative Michilimackinac trade. In 1761 Alexander Henry from New Jersey was the first English trader to venture into the interior, and Askin followed three years later. In the beginning local Chippewa and Ottawa, never defeated in battle, were suspicious of their former enemies. Only the timely arrival of the troops of the Sixtieth Regiment spared Henry's life. Other merchants, such as Henry Bostwick and Ezekiel Solomon, owned houses in the fort at the time of De Peyster's arrival.

Both Vattas and Askin bluntly told De Peyster that his duties as Indian Superintendent would require his utmost skill, patience, and diplomacy. Each summer thousands of Indians led by their chiefs came to receive presents from the King. They also brought furs, corn, and game to trade with the local merchants for blankets, clothing, powder, shot, rum, and trinkets.

The Indians, essential to the fur trade, could be dangerous. Vattas reminded De Peyster that eleven years before, during Pontiac's Uprising, local Chippewa had surprised and captured this fort. Here outside the land gate, the Sac from Wisconsin and the Chippewa had engaged in a spirited game of *baggatiway*. On a pre-arranged signal the ball was thrown over the palisade. Captain George Etherington, the Commander, permitted the braves to retrieve it. Instead of fetching the ball they grabbed weapons from beneath their women's blankets and swiftly killed sixteen soldiers. None except Lieutenant John Jamet had a chance to defend himself before being overwhelmed. One trader, Tracy, was killed; the remaining Englishmen were captured. Only the intervention of the local Ottawa kept these captives, including Henry, Solomon, and Bostwick, alive.[7] A year later when the British re-occupied the fort, they remained wary of the Indians and watched them closely. The leader of the attack, the Chippewa Chief Matchekewis, lived during the summer in a village at Cheboygan, sixteen miles southeast of Michilimackinac. Over the years he had come to realize the advantages of remaining on good terms with the British King.

By chance Matchekewis happened to be visiting the fort so Vattas introduced him to De Peyster. With flowery rhetoric Vattas emphasized the Chief's great influence among the Chippewa residing at Thunder Bay and Saginaw. De Peyster and Matchekewis, who were nearly the same age, greeted each other with mutual respect.

De Peyster also met the important Ottawa Chief La Fourche, now nearly sixty years old.[8] He made his home at L'Arbre Croche thirty-five miles southwest along Lake Michigan. His village had once been located a short distance from the fort, but in the early 1740's the community moved to L'Arbre Croche to find more fertile lands for

The Priest's House and Blacksmith Shop

their corn fields. These Ottawa, the band of Chippewa who lived on Mackinac Island, and the Chippewa from Cheboygan, frequented the fort. De Peyster promised to meet in formal council with both Chiefs within a few days.

For the fur trade to prosper, the Indians had to be at peace with each other. Inter-tribal war diverted the Indians from hunting and placed the isolated traders in peril. When disputes arose, it would be De Peyster's job to find a solution.

Vattas related an example from last autumn when a band of Sioux and Fox warriors attacked and killed a party of Chippewa gathering wild rice on a creek near the Menominee River.[9] According to Indian tradition retribution or satisfaction was required, yet it was the superintendent's duty to find peaceful resolution without further bloodshed.

Much of the violence associated with the fur trade was caused by the wide and undisciplined use of liquor by both Indians and whites. For the traders rum was an ideal commodity since it was easily transportable and could be watered down by adding tobacco and spices. Liquors clouded the mind of the user so that he lost the power to bargain effectively. Some unscrupulous traders cheated intoxicated Indians, and drunken engages fought among themselves or with Indians. After two years of watching alcohol's demoralizing impact in the Indian community, Captain Vattas felt strongly that the quantity of rum used in the trade should be restricted.[10]

By mid-July most traders had reached Michilimackinac.[11] De Peyster realized that one of his problems was to maintain order among the thousands of undisciplined summer visitors. Vattas assured him that the noise and brawling would be ended by a long, cold winter. Before the straits froze over, the summer callers would return hundreds of miles to their wintering places. All commerce stopped until the warm April sun melted the ice. Life functioned on an annual cycle dictated by the seasons.

The destructive impact of alcohol on the Indians as depicted by Peter Rindisbacher in the 1820's.

Robert Rogers was well liked by the Indians at Michilimackinac.

This country with its lure of riches brought together a parade of ambitious people. None was more remembered than Robert Rogers of the Rangers, a hero of the French and Indian war. As Commandant during 1766 and 1767, he enlisted James Tute and Jonathan Carver to search for the ''Northwest Passage,'' a shortcut to the Far East's riches. The mission failed, leaving Rogers deeply in debt. Falsely accused of treasonably plotting with the Spanish, Rogers was arrested and taken in shackles to Montreal for a court-martial. Captain De Peyster was a member of the court which declared Rogers innocent. Rogers' memory

Artillery.
1778.
Rail
F v Germann

A Royal Artilleryman drawn in 1778 by Friedrich von Germann.

10th Regiment silver officer's buttons excavated at Michilimackinac.

lived on at Michilimackinac, particularly among the Indians who held him in high regard because he treated them with respect and was not miserly with his presents.

Rich copper deposits along the southern shore of Lake Superior also held promise of wealth. Alexander Baxter, financed by English investors, had come to extract these precious metals. Alexander Henry, Henry Bostwick, and Jean Baptiste Cadot joined him as partners. Several attempts were made to mine, but the experiment was a failure by 1774.[12]

The Commandant was plagued by the shortage of troops particularly skilled Royal Artillerymen. Vattas had only one bombardier and two matrosses* to service his cannon. In the spring James Lewis, a matross, while boarding the schooner *Chippewa* at Detroit bound for Michilimackinac, fell overboard and drowned. John Bennett, his replacement, arrived at Michilimackinac on May 27 and drowned on the same day when his canoe overturned.[13]

After three days of briefings, Captain Vattas turned over his command on Wednesday, July 13, to Captain De Peyster.[14] Dreaming of England, Vattas and the soldiers of the Tenth Regiment boarded the waiting *Dunmore* leaving De Peyster to struggle with the problems of the frontier.

*A matross was a gunner's mate who assisted in loading, firing, and sponging cannon.

BEAVER HUNTING in CANADA.

II.

The Natives and the Fur Trade

As Captain De Peyster walked along Michilimackinac's dusty streets and sand swept beach, he was jostled by some of the traders, voyageurs, and Indians who had congregated at the Straits of Mackinac. This small community of a few hundred souls was over-whelmed each summer by several thousand visitors; some stayed a few days, others a couple of months. They came to exchange furs or food for the traders' goods. It was also a time for play, and revelers' shouts punctuated the cool summer nights.

De Peyster was particularly interested in the many Indians who constantly arrived by birchbark canoe. They camped along the beach, and some even brought along portable bark or rush covered wigwams. Many of the braves came with their wives and children and occasion-ally their dogs. The Chippewa from the west side of Lake Huron and both sides of Lake Superior, and the Ottawa living along the east shore of Lake Michigan, were most numerous. Sac and Fox made the long voyage from western Wisconsin and Illinois, while the Menominee and Winnebago had a shorter trip from the La Baye [Green Bay] area. Even a few Sioux visited the post from their far-off lands west of the Mississippi.

On Saturday, July 16, De Peyster held his first council with the stately Chippewa Matchekewis. Dressed in a ruffled shirt and wearing a tricorn hat, the Chief assured the Captain of his loyalty to the King. Matchekewis also expressed sorrow that he had led the war party which captured the fort in 1763. De Peyster was relieved that this fierce warrior had become a firm ally.

Next the Captain met with La Fourche. He, too, promised fidelity, but he then presented De Peyster with his first lesson in Indian affairs. The Ottawa Chief held out a wampum belt which he had recently received.

The economy of Michilimackinac was built on furs.

The belt, composed of cylindrical purple and white clam shell beads, was the medium of Indian diplomacy. Whenever nations exchanged communications regarding peace or war, their words were accompanied by strings or belts of wampum. Likewise the French and British had adopted this practice whenever they held council with Indian chiefs. Since the Indians had no written language, a wise man in each village remembered the exact wording of these speeches. Each year he recited them, thereby reminding the chiefs of their international commitments.[1]

La Fourche explained that he believed the belt in his hand came from the Mohawks in New York and probably represented plans harmful to the British. Later that same day a courier brought a verbal message from the trader Louis Chevallier at Fort St. Joseph [Niles, Michigan] that the Potawatomi residing near there had received large belts from some Delaware warriors.[2] The Delaware and Shawnee in eastern Ohio were stoutly resisting the advance of Virginian frontiersmen into their hunting grounds along the Ohio River Valley. They were seeking allies to fight the Virginians led by Governor Lord Dunmore. Though La Fourche and the Potawatomi refused to aid the Ohio tribes, De Peyster realized that they could swiftly turn against him if they were threatened by advancing settlers or unfavorable British policy. To ease La Fourche's mind De Peyster told him that he was certain Sir William Johnson, head of the British Indian Department in the Northern District, would prevent the Mohawks from raising mischief.

Before La Fourche departed for L'Arbre Croche, he asked De Peyster to rescind the order prohibiting traders from selling large quantities of liquor to the Indians. La Fourche wanted several barrels of rum for his village so that he would not have "the trouble of fetching the Kegs so often." When De Peyster replied that he did not have authority to allow this, the Chief begged him to petition General Thomas Gage, Commander of the British forces in North America, to change the policy. De Peyster responded that since the regulation limiting rum consumption benefited the trade it was unlikely to be modified.[3]

Approximately one thousand Ottawa including 250 men lived at L'Arbre Croche and Kishkacon.[4] During the summer women cultivated corn, beans, peas, and other vegetables on the surrounding fields. They planted corn by dropping five kernels into each hill hoed in the ground.[5] When crops were plentiful, they traded the surplus. John Askin and other merchants from Michilimackinac depended upon Indian corn to feed their canoeists each year. Agriculture was strictly women's work as was the production of bulrush mats, birchbark rolls, cedar bark strips, and tanned hides to make wigwams. These coverings were attached to a frame of saplings bent to form a dome. A hole left in the top permitted smoke from the cooking fire to escape. The women also constructed birchbark makuks, sweet grass baskets, and other containers.

While the women tended the fields and watched their children, the men hunted or fished and remained alert to protect their band. During the summer Ottawa warriors frequently took to the warpath, and the

A wampum belt collected by De Peyster

An Indian decked for war with a scalp. Drawn by George Townshend in the late 1750's.

Ottawa had a long history of fighting with tribes to the west and south.[6] Throughout the first half of the eighteenth century they had joined the French in wars against the Fox, Chickasaw, and even the English.

Usually a war chief organized a small war party to make a swift raid against an enemy. In order to recruit a band, he built a bark lodge and hung inside it a belt of purple wampum painted red with vermillion. Any warrior wishing to join the party entered the wigwam, smoked tobacco, and drew the wampum belt through his left hand. By so doing, he symbolized his enlistment in the raid. Young men welcomed the opportunity to take up the hatchet, for bravery in battle brought them praise and respect.[7]

La Fourche, a veteran of many campaigns, remembered one incident in particular. His sister Domitille had married Augustin Langlade, a French trader. Their son Charles Langlade, born in 1729, was only ten years old when the French recruited the Ottawa to attack the Chickasaw to the south. La Fourche credited the success of this mission to the presence of the boy. Charles, a favorite of his uncle, acquired great influence among the Ottawa and other western nations. When the British conquered French North America, La Fourche and Langlade accommodated themselves to the new regime and eventually became staunch supporters of the English.[8]

Chippewa mode of travelling in winter

Once the crops were planted, the men took their families to Michilimackinac to receive presents from the King. The Indians gave furs to the Commandant, and expected an abundance of goods in return. By these exchanges both groups demonstrated their bond of friendship. Most of the items dispensed by De Peyster were practical. Stroud and moulton cloth, blankets, shirts, thread, pork, and flour were popular. Flints, gunpowder, and ball and shot enabled the warriors to hunt. He doled out tools and utensils such as knives, screws, awls, needles, and kettles. Trinkets, tobacco, vermillion, and rum were usually provided.[9] Broken muskets and dull axes and hoes were repaired at the fort blacksmith shop. La Fourche's people had become dependent upon a steady flow of European trade items. Sometimes this rankled them, but the guns, cloth, kettles, and knives made their lives easier.

Before autumn the Ottawa returned to L'Arbre Croche to gather their crops. Both the post commandant and the merchants hoped for good yields since they purchased any surplus. When the harvest was over, the Ottawa dismantled their wigwams and headed southward for their annual winter hunt. The village dissolved into small family units, each having its own traditional hunting territory.[10] Most paddled down the Lake Michigan shoreline to the Grand River and beyond. Upon arrival at their camp site, the women erected the warm bulrush wigwams and prepared for the cold winter. The men spent their days hunting and fishing. Hunting provided food and also their main income — pelts. Using snares, traps, spears, and muskets they collected as many beaver, muskrat, raccoon, and other pelts as they could. Without furs the hunter could not purchase the goods he coveted.

Some traders such as Pierre Hurtibise and Pierre Cardinal spent their winters among the Ottawa and Potawatomi living near the eastern and southern shores of Lake Michigan. There they purchased furs from Indian families. When warm weather returned, Hurtibise and Cardinal paddled back to Michilimackinac to sell their pelts.

With the early spring thaw the Ottawa returned north to make maple sugar. Using an ax or a gouge a single family tapped hundreds of trees when the sweet sap began to run. They drove a wooden spile into the trunk and caught the dripping sap in a birchbark basket. The sap was boiled in larger brass kettles. Women carefully stirred the thick syrup as it was reduced to brown sugar. A necessary part of their diet, each family stored sugar in large birchbark makuks which held up to fifty pounds; they traded what they could not eat.[11] When sugaring was finished, they returned to L'Arbre Croche to plant the new year's crops.

Many traders wintered with the Indians in order to purchase prime furs. Drawn by Mrs. M. M. Chaplin.

Indian maple sugar camp by Seth Eastman

Although the English and Scottish traders out of Montreal controlled most of the money in the fur industry, the vast majority of employees were French. Most of the local French traders, such as Laurent Du Charme and Ignace Bourassa, who owned houses at Michilimackinac used them only in the summer.[12] During winter they took their wives and children to far away places such as the St. Peter's [Minnesota] River, Des Moines River, Illinois River, or north and west of Lake Superior. Not all the *hivernants* or winterers were French; a number of English traders, including Alexander Henry, Henry Bostwick, Ezekiel Solomon (the Jewish merchant), and Peter Pond from Connecticut, spent some of their winters among the Indians collecting furs.

In July Peter Pond and his flotilla returned from their winter's stay on the St. Peter's.[13] De Peyster and the community enthusiastically welcomed Pond and the French Canadian voyageurs as they paddled their loaded *canots de maitre* toward the beach. Their safe arrival was cause for celebration as old friends were re-united and new acquaintances made after a hard winter of work, loneliness, and suffering.

One could not mistake the French speaking Canadians dressed in their multicolored shirts, sashes, leggings, and garters. Most were short and extremely strong, dark complexioned with dark hair. They accepted their work's burdens with little complaint and boasted of their ability to paddle endless miles and carry two or three ninety-pound bales on their backs at each carrying place along the river routes. Yet, the contented puffs of tobacco smoke coming from their pipes often belied a sordid past for many had fled creditors or law enforcers from lower Canada. Sometimes encouraged by dishonest employers, they cheated and misused the Indians.[14] Not uncommonly, their exploits resulted in injury and death.

Camped along the lake, they cooked their usual meals of pork or fat and corn over open fires. Along with this they ate biscuits.[15] Most of their energy, however, was reserved for merrymaking. During the days or weeks at Michilimackinac many dissipated their year's wages in reckless abandon. Often intoxicated by rum or wine punch, they shouted, sang, argued, and fought. When they were bored in camp, they strolled to the village or fort to try their luck in games of chance or billiards.

Voyageurs camping on the beach. Drawn by Frances Ann Hopkins

Running a rapids in a Montreal canoe

Amid the revelry, Peter Pond and fellow merchants transacted serious business. Happily, he discovered that Felix Graham, his partner from New York, had brought enough merchandise to Michilimackinac for next winter's expedition. Pond, buoyed by a very profitable year, bought out Graham's interest in their partnership. His pile of furs was sufficient to pay for last year's goods and a large per cent of this year's cargo of twelve canoes.[16] Pond and Graham still imported by way of New York, but this trade was fast coming to an end. Non-Importation agreements protesting Parliamentary policies and the quicker northern route from Montreal made competition too stiff for New York merchants who were shifting their business to Montreal.

By July most of the Montreal canoes had arrived. Each merchant had obtained a license in Montreal stating his destination, quantity of goods, and the names of his crewman. Joseph LeClair received the first license on March 25, giving his destination as "Grand Portage and to winter in the North." In 1774 a total of seventy-nine canoes were authorized to make the trip to Michilimackinac.[17]

Montreal merchants bought their birchbark *canots de maitre* at Trois Rivieres and moved them up to La Chine as soon as the ice let loose in the St. Lawrence. Here they loaded them with ninety-pound bales of merchandise and kegs of rum, powder, and shot.[18] Each bale contained an assortment of goods ranging from clothes and blankets to beads and butcher knives. As many as sixty pieces of cargo fit into each canoe, which measured up to forty-feet long and six-feet wide, plus a forty-pound bag for each of the eight crewmen. The most skillful voyageurs steered in the bow and the stern; they received three hundred *livres* for a trip to Michilimackinac and back, twice the other paddlers' pay. Put in charge of a brigade of three or four canoes was a guide called a *bourgeois* who was responsible for its entire contents.[19]

The canoes set out for Michilimackinac early each spring. With good weather, they could make the journey in a month. The man in the bow had to be alert to avoid rocks that might puncture the thin bark. As they paddled, the voyageurs entertained themselves singing lively French songs that helped them paddle together. Every hour the guide ordered a short rest allowing each man to light up his clay or stone pipe. All along the way mosquitoes and black flies pestered them relentlessly. Before the trip was completed, the men unloaded their canoe and carried it and its cargo over thirty-six portages through mud and rugged terrain. Although usually good humored, the Canadians could sometimes be heard to mutter, "C'est la misere, mon bourgeois."[20]

During the summer of 1774 at least thirty-two of these canoes were destined for the growing trade beyond Lake Superior. Alexander Henry was headed for Sault Ste. Marie; Etienne and Alexis Campion, for Lake Nipigon; and Benjamin Frobisher, for the Grand Portage, all of whom passed through before De Peyster's arrival. Other traders were still at Michilimackinac or on their way. As they came in, the Commandant checked their licenses and became acquainted with them.

Stone pipe excavated at Michilimackinac

De Peyster was impressed by the huge quantity of merchandise these entrepreneurs moved this year. The totals approximated:[21]

800 barrels and kegs of rum, brandy & wine	50 barrels of lard, ham, butter, etc.
32,000 pounds of gunpowder	20 kegs of pork
37,000 pounds of ball and shot	2 kegs of salt
800 fusils [trade muskets]	12 bags of flour
640 bales of merchandise, dry goods, etc.	200 pounds of biscuits
106 bales of tobacco	40 cases of axes and ironworks
48 bales of kettles	

The trade extended for hundreds of miles beyond Lake Superior north to Lake Nipigon and northwest through the rugged wilderness of Saskatchewan. Because of great distances, it was impossible for one crew of men to make the complete journey from Montreal. At Grand Portage on the western end of Lake Superior at the mouth of the Pigeon River the *hivernants* met the traders from Michilimackinac and exchanged furs for merchandise and food. They soon returned to their small outposts. Bitter cold and snow hampered fishing and hunting, and at times they averted starvation only with food supplied by Indians. When Indian families and bands brought their furs to the traders, both parties tried to strike a profitable bargain. But the Indians found trade goods expensive. It might take as many as twenty beaver skins to buy a trade musket, ten skins for a stroud blanket, three skins for a one-pound ax, or one skin for one-half pint of gunpowder.[22] At winter's end the trader baled his furs, loaded his twenty-five-foot-long *canots de nord,* and headed for Grand Portage. There the furs were shipped to Michilimackinac and on to Montreal.

De Peyster realized it was essential that the fur trade prosper. If not, it meant economic disaster for merchants all the way to London. The industry's financial structure was tied together with a long line of credit. The Michilimackinac traders were indebted to the larger

Montreal trading firms who in turn purchased their goods from London pledging the value of the following year's furs.[23] Hence anything that interfered with the Indians' ability to hunt freely caused serious trouble. This economic reality placed a great burden upon De Peyster. Through diplomacy, force or threats, he had to keep the western Indian nations from fighting either the traders or themselves.

In early August a Lake Superior trader reported the alarming news that the Sioux and Chippewa again were killing each other. The traders' safety was seriously threatened. Immediately De Peyster convened the merchants to inform them of this danger. Frustrated, he explained that there was little he could do to restore peace in that distant land. He urged the traders to use their influence to help him bring about a settlement.

De Peyster ordered six large wampum belts prepared — three for each tribe. He composed speeches to accompany the belts and gave the belts for the Sioux to Peter Pond and the others to the Lake Superior traders. The carriers were instructed to ask the Sioux chiefs to come to Pond's post on the St. Peter's and the Chippewa chiefs to those in the Lake Superior country. There interpreters would recite the Commandant's speeches and present the belts. Pond and the others were to bring the chiefs to Michilimackinac next spring for a large council.

De Peyster wished Pond and his counterparts well as they embarked on their winter's expedition. They pushed their provision laden canoes into the straits and paddled away to an uncertain rendezvous.[24] De Peyster, Askin, and those left behind could only hope the mission of peace would be successful. They anxiously awaited the return of Pond and his companions.

The red ensign flies over Michilimackinac today.

Anticipating the arrival of the warring chiefs next summer, the Commandant was embarrassed that he had no British flag to fly over the fort. Captain Vattas had borrowed one from a boat master who now wanted it returned. De Peyster wrote to Lieutenant Colonel Samuel Cleaveland, the Commander of the Royal Artillery at New York, asking that a large red ensign be sent. He stressed it was "absolutely necessary to return the compliments to tribes of Indians when they come on matters of any consequences to the Government."[25]

After the traders departed, De Peyster directed his attention to repairing the fort, and his men had a lot of work to do. Before spring he wanted to replace the rotted gun platforms. Some of the cannon also needed new carriages. The outside work would soon be difficult to do for the crisp October air signaled that winter was not far away.

III.

The Community

*Medal of Ste. Anne,
the patron saint of
the voyageurs.*

Brisk winds churned the straits' heavy, gray water into angry waves on Sunday, November 6. Peering out the northeast bastion, Captain De Peyster shivered as the cold southerly gusts whistled through the cracks between the pickets. At noon torrents of rain began to pelt the community. Suddenly, the Captain and sentry watched in amazement as the lake level rose rapidly and threatened to wash away all canoes and batteaux on the beach. Quickly De Peyster ordered his troops out into the storm to save the King's vessels. With great difficulty, the rain drenched soldiers secured the boats and rescued most of the winter's firewood supply stacked outside the palisade. They did not have time to prevent the destruction of all the privately owned small craft. Having advanced thirty-six yards inland, the water receded below its previous level within an hour after the storm calmed.[1]

De Peyster felt helpless before nature's fury. The violent seas meant that no more vessels could be expected from Detroit until spring, for soon the straits would be frozen. Winter was now upon Michilimackinac and its residents prepared for its harshness and isolation.

When the storm subsided, the soldiers returned to their barracks to put on dry clothing. Extra logs were put into the iron stoves to warm the chilled men and to dry their wet uniforms. Red coats, white breeches and shirts, black felt tri-cornered hats, and linen stockings hung about the rooms. Each soldier purchased his own uniforms and food from his daily wage of 8d [pence], thus he gave particular care to his clothing. Lying on his bunk, waiting for his overcoat to dry, Private James Barker pondered the future as he mused about his duty at Michilimackinac.

The lonely sentry beat

Despite the blustery weather, the barracks offered a comfortable shelter and home. Each of the four twenty-foot-square rooms had berths and racks for at least eighteen men. White woolen blankets, marked with the King's broad arrow, and linen sheets covered the straw-filled mattresses on the wooden bunks. Two men slept side by side on each bunk, sharing blankets and body warmth. Weapons and clothing were neatly kept on the racks assigned each man. Small rugs covered parts of the cold floor. A tallow candle, placed in an iron candlestick resting on a wooden table in the center of the room, provided the only light at night. During the day windows admitted sunlight.

Two large chimneys with fireplaces on two sides divided the building. Barrackmaster John Askin had provided sufficient iron pots, trammels, tongs, and kettles for the men to prepare their meals over the open fire. Each man received a daily ration of a pound of flour, a pound of beef or salt pork, slightly less than an ounce of butter, a cup of peas, an ounce of oatmeal, and a gill* and a half of rum.[2] At times this monotonous fare was enlivened with fish or wild game. During summer fresh vegetables gave a welcome addition to this bland diet. Since nearly all provisions came from Detroit, the first vessel each spring was eagerly anticipated. As the stores dwindled at the end of the winter, the commissary at times was forced to issue partially spoiled salt meat.

*A gill is equal to one-fourth pint.

Michilimackinac was a dull post, particularly in the winter. For the soldiers most tasks were monotonous, if not laborious. Every soldier took his turn at guard duty. He walked sentry beats in the bitter cold, guarded prisoners in the guardhouse, and controlled passage in and out of the fort.

When De Peyster sent out a few soldiers to cut hay or firewood, many returned with sore muscles. The fort had been occupied for sixty years and the nearby trees had been long since cut down. Now it was necessary to go miles away to find enough firewood. Large quantities were needed for it took 17½ cords* to keep one room warm during the winter.[3] Stockpiles, cut and stacked in the summer, were hauled over the ice sometimes as far as thirty miles. When timbers, boards, or pickets were needed, the soldiers found themselves at the end of axes and saws. Private Barker and his fellow soldiers shoveled snow that sometimes drifted nearly to the top of the palisade. During the summer the troops shoveled sand to keep the shifting dunes at a respectable distance from the fort.

When time and weather permitted, the drummer beat the drill call. Assembled on the parade ground, the men practiced the manual of arms and marching. De Peyster, a stern disciplinarian, expected his troops to be well drilled. He loved to watch his men parade, and he could shout out commands in his rough voice with the best of drill sergeants. Standing tall and erect, he was the very picture of a commanding officer. Although these maneuvers instilled a sense of discipline and teamwork, most men hated them. Yet, they responded when the sergeant yelled:[4]

> "Come, stand well to your order,
> Make not the least false motion,
> Eyes to the right,
> Thumb, muzzle tight,
> Lads, you have the true notion.
> Here and There,
> That the *Kings* boys may be found,
> Fight and die
> Be the cry
> Ere in battle to give ground."

*A cord is a pile of wood measuring eight-feet-long, four-feet-high, and four-feet-wide.

British soldier's were frequently recruited from the dregs of English society.

Most enlisted men joined the army for life and came from the lower classes of English and Scottish society. Often they were prone to vice and carelessness. When they broke the rules, discipline was harsh. For minor offenses the drummer administered floggings of a hundred lashes or more with a cat-of-nine-tails. Men who disobeyed orders, showed disrespect to officers, fought with fellow soldiers, or were drunk on duty, felt the cut of the lash on their bare backs. While awaiting court-martial, offenders were locked in the guardhouse or, if the accusing officer directed, in the darkness of the black hole. Usually punishment was swift, and though his back ached, the chastised man was soon back on duty.

Soldiers did some hunting and fishing, but generally not for sport. Fishing through the ice was dangerous, but soldiers, traders, and Indians would trudge over a mile from shore to prime fishing spots. Many strapped iron spikes called creepers to their feet to keep from slipping and carried heavy iron spuds to cut holes in the ice which sometimes got two feet thick. They set lines over a hundred feet deep hoping to catch trout. Sometimes they lowered nets to take whitefish.

One blustery winter day De Peyster and a sergeant walked out to check on the fishermen's successes when suddenly a storm roared in from the northwest. The ice split and open water appeared between the rapidly widening cracks. The sentry at the fort observed the breakup and reported it to his sergeant. The artillerymen loaded a cannon and fired a warning to their floating commander. Four Indian chiefs ran to the shore, picked up their frail bark canoe, carried it over ice to open water, and paddled swiftly until they reached the stranded men. This courageous act saved De Peyster's life.[5]

Winter locks the Straits in its icy grip.

A few soldiers had families with them. To supplement their meager income their wives usually washed the company's laundry, helped with cooking, cared for the sick, and cleaned the barracks.[6] If married men were fortunate, they rented a room of their own, otherwise the only privacy a soldier's family had was created by a blanket which walled off a corner of the barracks. Should an enlisted man wish to marry, he had to receive his commander's permission. Occasionally a soldier at Michilimackinac wed a local girl, but most remained single.

Anti-war cartoon – 1775 – stressing the plight of the British soldier

For the garrison to function smoothly it was essential to have good sergeants. Sergeant Amos Langdown watched over his men carefully making certain they were properly outfitted and behaved; each day he reported to De Peyster and accounted for each man. The sergeant supervised work details and drilled the men. He was expected to be fair and firm and to follow the Army's directive that he "be feared by the bad, and be loved by the good."[7]

Commanding the sergeants were Captain De Peyster and his subalterns Lieutenant Thomas Bennett and Lieutenant George Clowes. For everyone, both military and civilian, De Peyster was the final authority at Michilimackinac. He could command obedience, but he had to earn respect and admiration. De Peyster, an easy, open and affable man, exercised his authority wisely, fairly, and patiently and won the support of the entire community. Few settlements had such a warm, generous, and competent man overseeing their security. The subalterns, too, were expected to exhibit the same qualities. Unfortunately, they did not always live up to their commander's standards.[8]

34

Officers in the British army came from the middle and upper class. Military service was highly sought after, and commissions were bought and sold at high prices. Usually fathers purchased commissions for their sons to assure them a position of rank and responsibility. Always conscious of class distinctions, the officers kept apart from their men. At Michilimackinac the De Peysters, Bennett, Clowes, and the wealthier merchants such as John Askin formed the upper class. Their parties, weekly dances, billiard games, and teas included only members from their group.[9] Because they had money, they were able to enjoy many of the same comforts of life which they had known in more civilized places.

De Peyster and his wife lived comfortably and found new friends. Rebecca became very close to Archange Askin, John's 25-year-old wife. Archange had grown up in Detroit where her father Charles Andrew Barthe was a prominent trader. Her brother Jean Baptiste had moved to Sault Ste. Marie where he traded in close association with Askin. Such personal relationships were frequently the cement of commercial bonds in the eighteenth century.

John and Archange had only been married for a year, but she already had several children in her household. Like so many other traders, John, or "Paddy" as his friends called him, had formed a liaison with an Ottawa woman from L'Arbre Croche. Three children were born to them. Thus, Archange became the mother of John Jr., Catherine, and Madelaine at the time of her marriage.

Rebecca, Archange, and other trader's wives maintained interest in London styles and had their husbands import dresses, shoes, china, silver, and porcelain of the latest fashion. When they gathered in each others homes to drink tea or chocolate from exquisite Chinese porcelain teacups, they discussed recent news. Within a year nearly any London or Paris book, magazine, or newspaper could be read at Michilimackinac.

A fine English red stoneware teapot excavated at Michilimackinac.

The friendship between De Peyster and Askin grew throughout the winter. "Paddy" loaned the Captain a pair of andirons and two mouse traps. Earlier De Peyster had borrowed one of Askin's calashes, a low-wheeled carriage with a folding top.[10] They spent many hours over the billiard table and chessboard or sitting near the fire exchanging experiences. Interested in literature and arts, the Captain frequently borrowed books from Askin's extensive library. De Peyster tried his literary bent by recording in poetry some of his impressions of life at Michilimackinac.

During winter some of the French Canadians hired themselves out to work for wealthier residents. A few women were employed as domestic servants and some men cut wood, but there was little work available. Used to poverty and boredom, they survived until warm weather when their services were in demand.

At the bottom of society were the Indian and black slaves. John Askin possessed three black men — Charles, Jupiter Wendell, and Pompey — and at various times a number of panis.[11] Indian slaves, called panis, were usually women, young girls, and boys who had been captured by the warring tribes and sold to the merchants. Panis received their name from the Pawnee nation since many Indian slaves had been taken from that tribe near the Mississippi. Females were preferred because they more readily adapted to their new environment and owners.[12]

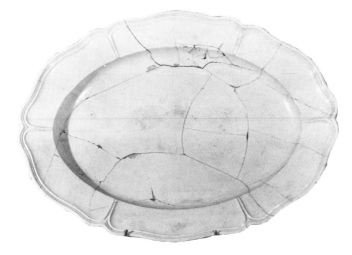

English creamware platter and plate from Michilimackinac.

A rare peek into a French Canadian home by Cornelius Krieghoff

R ebecca De Peyster and Archange Askin supervised busy households. Preparation of meals, particularly for the Askin household, which numbered as many as twenty, took much of their time. Archange and Charlotte, her panis, made stews of beef, dried corn or peas, and potatoes in large iron pots hanging over an open fire.

Charlotte boiled corn in lye, removed the husks, then mashed and dried it. She baked bread in outdoor French style stone ovens. First a fire was built in the oven to heat the stones. Then Charlotte scooped out the ashes and placed the dough inside to be baked by the hot walls. Spices such as cinnamon, cloves, and nutmeg added flavor to many recipes.

Fresh whitefish or trout provided a nourishing variety to many resident's year-around diet. At times hunters brought in venison, partridges, ducks, geese, and passenger pigeons.[13] The Askins and De Peysters supplemented their meals with such extras as loaf sugar, tea, chocolate, and Madeira wine. Many, however, could not afford these expensive imports. Rather they subsisted on a steady diet of sagamity — a thick stew made from parched corn and fish or pork.

Domestic industry was a constant activity. Every spring Askin sheered his sheep and Archange saw to it that the fleeces were washed, carded, and spun into yarn and dyed. On dreary winter days and evenings, she knitted mittens or mufflers. Some of the fine cloth imported by John had to be cut and sewn into breeches and dresses for the children. Most adult clothing was purchased ready made. Throughout the year all excess tallow and lard was saved, for in the spring it was boiled with lye in large kettles outside to make soap. Askin hired Elizabeth Staniford, a soldier's wife, to do all his family's laundry for 8s [shillings] per week.[14]

One needed strong arms to do the ironing with this heavy flatiron.

37

Archange's daughters required love and attention. Mother settled disputes, repaired torn dolls, disciplined disobedient acts, and read stories. Since there was no school here, Archange taught Madelaine to read both French and English and gave her as much mathematical skill as she could from *Wingates Arithmetic*. The Askins sent John, Jr., to Detroit and Catherine to Montreal for their education.[15] Most of the French children received no such training because their parents were illiterate and too poor to pay a teacher.

Archange was also the family nurse and tended to sick children and servants. On her medicine shelf stood numerous bottles of herbs, powders, ointments, and tonics. To aid digestion she might give a dose of Stoughton's bitters, to induce purging — some Glauber salts, for a sore throat — a saloop or sassafras solution, for open wounds — an application of mercurial ointment or healing salve, for a cold — some sage, and for pain — an opium pill. When all else failed, she reached for Turlington's "Balsam of Life," an elixir from London. If her patients did not respond to treatment, she called Dr. David Mitchell, the army surgeon.[16]

Turlington's Balsam came in a distinctive bottle.

Cedar bark was used to cover most of the roofs at Michilimackinac.

In March, 1775 De Peyster noticed a quickening of activity. The French inhabitants were preparing to travel five or ten miles to their sugaries. Each spring entire families went to their huts among the sugar maples and set up camps where they stayed for six or eight weeks. One family could tap as many as eighteen hundred trees. The sweet sap thus collected was boiled down to produce up to one thousand pounds of fine, dry sugar. Traders thought this sugar to be of better quality than Indian-produced sugar and purchased whatever quantities were available.[17]

This year the sap began running earlier than usual because winter had been very mild; the temperature had never dipped below seven degrees above zero.[18] No one complained for the wood piles lasted longer and navigation would begin earlier. Also the warming rays of the April sun enabled De Peyster to get on with needed repairs to the fort.

Rain, wind, dampness, and frost persistently eroded and rotted the exposed wooden structures. During the winter a gale blew down half the palisades of the fort's east wall, and the "Garrison necessary-house," a large outdoor privy, collapsed. The battle against rotting wood was never ending. Some of the traders' houses were propped up with poles to keep them from toppling over. De Peyster considered one dilapidated house bordering on the west side of the powder magazine a fire hazard and tore it down.

If the fort was to be tenable against enemy attacks, its defenses had to be maintained. De Peyster noted a serious danger: Rot had rendered most of the wooden gun carriages unserviceable, and he began constructing new ones. To rebuild stairs and gun platforms, De Peyster bought boards from a local merchant whose sawyers laboriously cut them by hand in the sawpits from hand-hewn timbers. He hired carpenters for complicated construction, and if there were insufficient skilled workmen at Michilimackinac, he imported men from Detroit. Soldiers cut long cedar pickets and raised them to replace rotted poles in the stockade.

Carpenters built a new double gate which they hung on large iron hinges fashioned by the blacksmith. The smith also forged needed pintles, chisels, gouges, punches, and hammers. Masons repaired and built stone fireplaces and chimneys and even molded some clay bricks.[19]

The inhabitants at Michilimackinac ate large numbers of passenger pigeons.

By May 1 the ice was out of the lakes and the days became warmer. John Askin dispatched to Lake Superior his first vessel, the small schooner *Captain De Peyster*, named for his new found friend. Ten days later the sloop *Archange*, named after his wife, followed. Askin had hired LaBoneau, a servant belonging to Monsieur Campau, for ℓ3 [pounds] a month and Peter Ord at 7s a week to assist Pompey in loading rum (imported from Montreal last year), corn, grease, and sugar on these vessels, thus getting an early start in moving this year's provisions. The work was dangerous. Only a week earlier Askin's man, Toon, tipped over his canoe and drowned while returning to shore from the *Captain De Peyster*. On May 11 the schooner *Chippewa* brought additional merchandise from Detroit. The pace of life was quickening as traders came in from their wintering grounds along Lake Michigan.[20]

Two weeks later Ignace Bourassa arrived with the first canoe from Montreal bringing twelve barrels of rum and wine, 150 pounds of gunpowder, three hundred pounds of ball and shot, and seventeen trade guns. A very busy trading season was opening. Before summer ended, 101 canoes came to the straits carrying larger quantities of goods than last year.[21]

Encouraged by increasing trade in the northwest, Askin supplied a growing volume of goods to these traders. This year at least forty-four canoes were licensed to go to Lake Superior and beyond. James McGill, Benjamin Frobisher, and Maurice Blondeau outfitted twelve canoes in a new partnership called the Northwest Company.[22] During the next winter they would meet Alexander Henry, Peter Pond, Joseph and Thomas Frobisher, Charles Patterson, and Jean Baptiste Cadot in the northern Canadian wilds.

When the traders and Indians arrived at Michilimackinac, De Peyster asked them how profitable the winter's hunt had been and if there were any disturbances in the interior. Joseph Fulton, an Indian trader, revealed a terrible horror. Murder occured often in the Indian trade, but Fulton told of the death of at least thirteen persons including his party and an Indian family of nine. Several of the victims even had been cooked and eaten. De Peyster worried about any repercussions this might have in the north country.[23]

Ein Canadischer Bauer.
1778.
F. v. Germann
Kail

A Canadian farmer in a blanket coat smokes his stone pipe.

J ohn Askin also had a farm to maintain. Two years earlier Captain Vattas had given him permission to erect a house about three miles from the fort. This farm gave Askin a sense of permanence in his life at Michilimackinac. He enjoyed watching crops and animals grow, and he kept a careful diary of his observations. Three calves were born that spring, and between April 8 and 13 three sows pigged. Earlier his hens began laying eggs, and the ewes "began to Lamb" in late February. Because of the mild weather, he let his cows outside by the middle of March and one calved in the woods.

On May 6 Askin started sowing peas, oats, and clover. Ten days later he set out his first potatoes. To maintain the thin soil's fertility and increase his yields, he rotated his crops. Near the end of the 1775 growing season, he observed in his diary:[24]

"Thro bracking when Green, rotted Hay or any such Stuff on land where pease & Buck wheat have been, plow it in the month of Sepr Harrow it in the Spring & Plant Potatoes with Y^o Plow without any more dunging.
When Potatoes are dug up in the fall Clover seeds may be sowed.
Oates, wheat, Clover or Turnips may be sowed in the spring on Land where Potatoes were the year before
Buck Wheat may be Sowed the 20th of June on Land twice plowed where Pease have been the year before
Potatoes may be planted on Stuble Ground with Dung
New Ground twice plowed I think best for Pease
Oates May be sowed in old Turnip Ground"

A bone bottle stopper in the shape of a rooster

Askin and most others at Michilimackinac grew a variety of vegetables. They plowed furrows two and three feet apart, placing manure on the bottom. Then women sowed turnips and peas and closed the drills. They also planted lettuce, carrots, parsnips, cabbage, potatoes, beets, onions, squash, cucumbers, and beans. Throughout the summer they hoed weeds, hilled potatoes, and transplanted cabbage and other vegetables.[25]

Homemakers, slaves, servants, and soldiers searched the surrounding woods for blueberries, cherries, gooseberries, currants, strawberries, and raspberries. They also collected medicinal herbs and shrubs. The French brewed beer from the needles of the spruce tree. This common table drink was believed to prevent scurvy. Besides, spruce beer tasted good.[26]

A somber mood hung over the garrison on the morning of June 15, when Matross Lindsey of the Royal Artillery died.[27] Two weeks earlier while preparing to fire a salute commemorating King George III's birthday, the cannon discharged prematurely, and Lindsey lost his arm. The best effort of Dr. Mitchell proved inadequate to halt the infection. De Peyster suspended normal work details so the troops could pay their final respects to Lindsey.

The pallbearers, all privates, carried the body out of the hospital room while Sergeant Langdown and thirteen privates faced the building. Langdown barked: "Rest your firelocks. Reverse firelocks. Rear ranks close to the front. March." When the detail was in position, the drummer slowly beat the muffled sound of the dead march. De Peyster, wearing a piece of black crepe around his left arm, led the funeral party past the barracks through the fort, and out the land gate to the cemetery. Arriving at the grave site, the troops marched into place and awaited the Captain's orders. "Make ready. Present. Fire." Three volleys resounded; ramrods clanked as the troops reloaded their weapons. Turning, they marched back to the fort.[28] De Peyster and Lieutenants Clowes and Bennett collected and inventoried Lindsey's pitiably few possessions and dispatched them to headquarters where they were forwarded to his family.

For over ten years there had been no regular priest or clergy at Michilimackinac. Marriages and baptisms often were postponed until a priest came. For the French Catholics this lack of spiritual guidance and sacraments created a void in their lives. Prior to 1765 when Father Pierre Du Jaunay returned to Quebec, a Jesuit priest had lived either in the fort or at the mission of St. Ignace among the Ottawa at L'Arbre Croche.

A few days after Matross Lindsey's funeral, the Catholics excitedly welcomed Father Pierre Gibault to Michilimackinac. Captain De Peyster, too, was pleased to see the young priest for he knew his visit would be good for the parishioners. Although many English here were Anglicans, they did not object to Catholicism, and the Treaty of Paris in 1763 guaranteed the Canadians the right to practice their religion. Gibault served the French in the Illinois country at Kaskaskia and occasionally made missionary trips to areas without a priest.

June 23 was a special day. The townspeople smiled as they filed into Ste. Anne's Church to witness the marriage of Francois Maurice de la Fantaisie and Marie Anne Cardin.[29] Standing before Father Gibault, the bride and groom, though both of modest means, made a handsome couple. Marie Anne wore a long dress with a full skirt extended by a whale-bone frame. Francois had a knee length coat over a waistcoat and shirt. On his vest was a row of shiny buttons, and large cuffs protruded beyond his coat sleeves. The bride's father, Louis Cardin, had formerly been the notary at Michilimackinac; her mother Constance Chevallier, had died a few years ago. A native of Montreal, the groom now lived at Michilimackinac and worked in the fur trade. As Francois and Marie Anne exchanged vows and listened to the Father's words of advice, friends looked on. Included in the audience were Pascal Pillet, Hypolitte Campeau, Joseph Louis Ainsse — the bride's step-brother, Hypolitte Chaboillez, Jean Baptiste Barthe, Ignace Bourassa, Guillaume LaMotte, and Suzanne Boyer. After the ceremony all celebrated with wine and food.

Ste. Anne crucifix

Four days after the wedding the new bride witnessed the baptism of her 1-year-old godson, Jean Baptiste Bertrand, and his brother, 4-year-old Laurent. Their parents were Joseph Laurent Bertrand and Marie Therese DuLignon. On July 9, Louis DeMouchelle and his Indian wife, Francoise, brought their three children, Bernard, Jean, and Francoise, to the church where Father Gibault baptized them. The next day the priest baptized Marianne and Marguerite Marcotte, daughters of Jean Baptiste Marcotte and his native wife, Neskeek.[30] These trading families were gratified that this sacrament had finally been administered to their children for Father Gibault had not been here since 1768.

Because it was summer, Father Gibault was able to minister to a large number of parishioners. He spent hours in the confessional listening to guilt-ridden men and women relieve their minds and souls of sin. For some it had been five or even ten years since confession or Holy Communion.

Interior of Ste. Anne de Michilimackinac

Flags fly as the western Indians arrive. From Jonathan Carver's Journal

De Peyster and the Chippewa chiefs who had come to the fort with traders from Lake Superior awaited the arrival of Peter Pond and the Sioux chiefs. When Pond's party was sighted, De Peyster immediately ordered up the Red Ensign and salutes to be fired. Everyone at Michilimackinac crowded along the beach and shouted greetings to the Sioux.

When Pond and the chiefs reached shore, De Peyster extended his hand to greet his emissary who, through his interpreter, introduced the Sioux chiefs to the Commandant. The Captain then called for a council with the Chippewa and Sioux to settle their quarrels. As a precaution, De Peyster doubled the guard during the Indian council.[31]

For two days De Peyster presided over the "Grand Council" in the "Grate Chamber." The chiefs spoke forcefully, outlining grievances, and listened intently while De Peyster advised them to respect each other's hunting grounds. He warned that only if peace prevailed would the traders be allowed to go among them. Both sides promised to abide by the articles of peace. The Sioux were not to cross to the east side of the Mississippi, nor were the Chippewa to cross to the west side. They pledged to live in peace as neighbors.

Success achieved, De Peyster ordered a celebration. He presented the chiefs with a keg of rum. The next day soldiers slaughtered a fat ox and roasted it over an open fire. As the smell of the delicious beef drifted down the beach, the Commandant invited the Indians to a feast. For four days Indians, soldiers, and traders reveled together. Finally, De Peyster gave each chief a present and sent him on his way in friendship. War between these two large and powerful adversaries had been averted.[32]

For the present the western nations were at peace, but trouble was brewing in the eastern colonies. American rebels had engaged in open combat with British regulars at Lexington and Concord in Massachusetts, and Fort Ticonderoga in New York had been captured. An intense battle had been waged in Boston, and Williams, Higgins, and young Vernon, three of De Peyster's friends, had been killed at Bunker Hill. Disturbed, De Peyster wondered if this violence would spread to Michilimackinac.

Wampum belts gave solemnity to the councils and helped record the speeches. Drawn by Benjamin West.

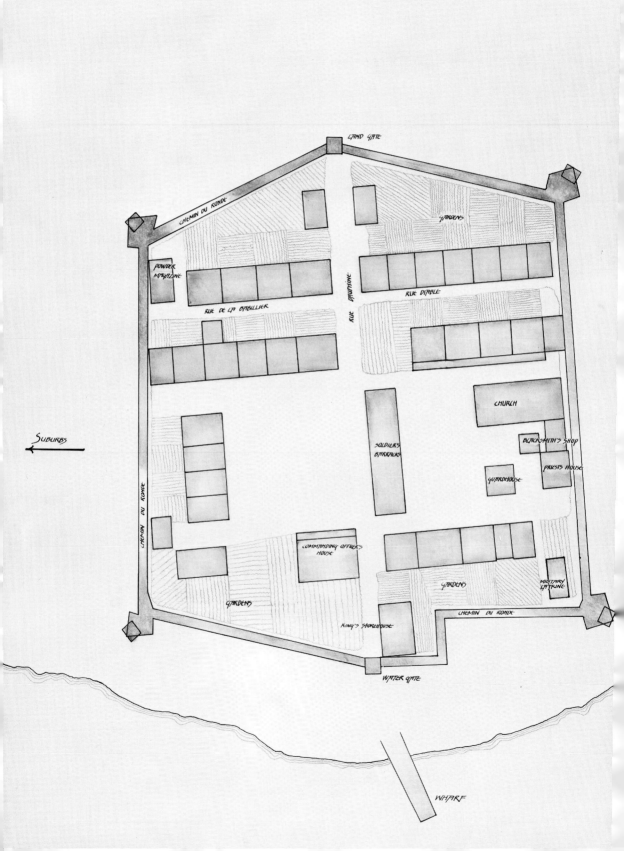

IV.

The Rebellion Reaches Michilimackinac

As Rebecca De Peyster pushed back the curtains of her covered bed, she noticed a bite in the air. It was Wednesday, September 27, 1775. She poured some icy water out of the pitcher, standing on the night table, into a large basin. She washed and dressed. In the next room a warm fire roared, built by her husband before he left to make his early morning inspection of the garrison. While sipping hot tea from her blue and white porcelain cup, the Captain returned. Shivering he threw off his coat and knocked fluffy snow off his black boots. Winter had come early, draping a four-inch white blanket over the fort and surrounding countryside.[1]

Although the snow soon melted, the inhabitants realized that winter's severity would soon be upon them. They could not expect another mild season like last year. Standing on the soggy parade ground, De Peyster observed men chinking cracks in the log walls of their houses and making sure the hinges on their shutters worked properly. The snowfall had stimulated preparations for winter.

At the Askin house on October 3 candles flickered in the early morning darkness. John had aroused Dr. David Mitchell and led him home to attend to Archange, who was about to give birth. Puffing on his long-stemmed clay pipe, John paced back and forth before the kitchen table. The new-born's first cries from the adjacent room brought relief to the new father. With the doctor's permission, John entered the bedroom and gently kissed Archange who proudly presented him their new daughter.

Father Pierre Gibault, the only priest to visit Michilimackinac during the 1770's

Fortunately, Father Pierre Gibault had just returned by canoe from Montreal. Before sunset Archange bundled up the little baby so she could be brought to the Church of Ste. Anne. Here, before her godparents Hypolitte Chaboillez and Felicité Barthe, Father Gibault baptized the infant named Archange after her mother.[2]

Father Gibault impatiently awaited the arrival of a ship from Detroit, hoping to take it down Lake Huron. But when none had appeared by November 4, he determined "to risk perishing on Lake Huron" rather than winter at Michilimackinac. Sad French inhabitants waved good-by as the priest, in company with another man and a child, set out for Detroit in a small birchbark canoe. For twenty-two difficult days these inexperienced canoeists steered through ice, snow, and gusty winds before reaching the safety of Detroit where they spent the winter.[3]

L ocated on the Detroit River, the narrow strait joining Lake Erie and Lake St. Clair, Detroit controlled a key point in the upper lakes commerce. A fifteen-foot high cedar picket "Stockade 1200 Paces in extent" surrounded the fortified town.[4] The curtains sheltered over forty shingled log houses, trader's shops and stores, a church, military buildings, and the Indian council house. Eleven blockhouses and gun batteries provided defense against Indian attacks, but men of the garrison realized that they could not resist an enemy armed with cannon. On the riverfront the British had erected a naval yard to build large sailing vessels.

When Lieutenant Governor Henry Hamilton assumed civil command of Detroit on November 9, he had recently experienced first hand rebel mischief in Montreal. Disguised as a French *habitant*, he had slipped past American forces and paddled up the St. Lawrence River. In his position of Lieutenant Governor, Hamilton brought civil government to Detroit for the first time since the British conquest of Canada. The Quebec Act of 1774 created this new administrative office to help govern Quebec Province. Formerly the citizens answered directly to the military commander. Hamilton also served as Superintendent of Indian Affairs.

Farms extended for thirteen miles to the north and eight miles to the south of the stockade on both sides of the river. Approximately fifteen hundred whites and one hundred Negro slaves lived here. In their fields stretching in narrow ribbons back from the river, farmers grew melons, wheat, corn, barley, oats, peas, and buckwheat and tended sheep, hogs, horses, cows, and oxen. Orchards provided peaches, plums, pears, apples, mulberries, and grapes. Sharing this rich country were several thousand Huron, Potawatomi, and Ottawa Indians scattered in villages along both river banks.[5]

Detroit in the early 1780's

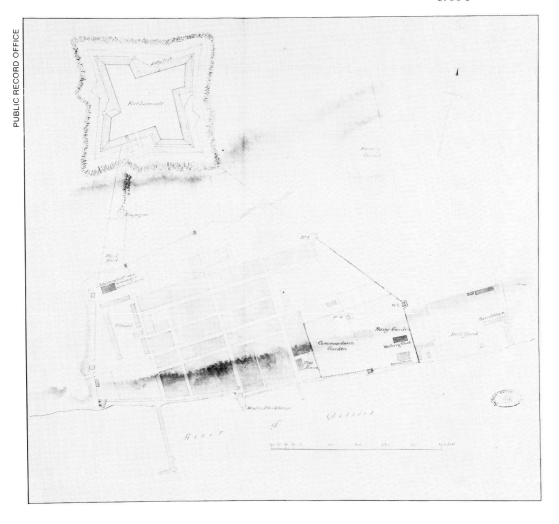

Like Michilimackinac, Detroit's economy revolved around the fur trade. Traders went south into the Ohio country and down the Wabash River to the Illinois country collecting furs from the Miami, Shawnee, Delaware, Ottawa, Chippewa, Potawatomi, and Huron. Frequently these Indians, and some Iroquois, came to Detroit to receive the King's presents.

Hamilton heard bitter complaints from the Ohio tribes that thousands of white men were streaming westward from Virginia through the Cumberland Gap into their Kentucky hunting grounds. In defiance of the 1763 British regulation prohibiting settlement of this wilderness, these frontiersmen threatened both the Indians' livelihood and British authority at Detroit. Resistance to this movement forged a major link in the chain of friendship between the British and the western Indians.

Lieutenant Governor Henry Hamilton

On November 13, less than a week after Hamilton reached Detroit, the American rebels led by General Richard Montgomery captured Montreal creating serious problems for De Peyster, Hamilton, and the fur traders. With hostile forces controlling Montreal, trade goods could not be obtained and the vital link to British markets and industries was severed.

The successful American army moved down the St. Lawrence to attack Quebec. There they joined more than a thousand men, led by Benedict Arnold from Cambridge, Massachusetts, under orders from General George Washington. On the stormy night of December 30 the rebels attacked the fortress of Quebec. Despite heroic efforts, the assault failed before the town's formidable defenses, and Montgomery lay dead.[6]

The Continental Congress meeting in Philadelphia had launched Montgomery's ill-fated expedition. Members of Congress recognized the strategic importance of Canada and hoped to bring the Canadians into the rebellion. Many revolutionaries believed that the French in Canada would welcome an opportunity to throw off British rule. Since only seven hundred regular British troops were stationed in all of Canada, it seemed an easy prize.

Montreal drawn by Thomas Davies in 1762

Congress felt that control of Canada would keep the western Indian nations neutral in the conflict. In June, 1775 John Adams noted that the Indians "seem disposed to Neutrality," and the British had not yet enlisted Indian aid. Adams feared for the frontier settlements if Indian warriors were loosed upon them.[7] Appalled by the failure at Quebec, Adams was gravely concerned that leaving Canada in British hands "would enable them to inflame all the Indians upon the Continent."[8]

When General Washington, without Congress' authorization, sent a force to capture Quebec, he believed that if Montreal fell, British control of territory further west would crumble. Writing to General Philip Schuyler,* the Commander of the rebel army's Northern Department, Washington asked, "If you carry your arms to *Montreal,* should not the garrison of *Niagara, Detroit,* &c. be called upon to surrender, or threatened with the consequences of a refusal?"[9] Rebel success in Canada would mean the end of British rule at Michilimackinac.

Congress also considered launching an expedition against Detroit from Fort Pitt. Located at the confluence of the Allegheny and Monongahela Rivers, the source of the Ohio, this key installation was a dagger pointing at Detroit. Although in September, 1775 there was strong support for a move against Detroit, Congress, believing that winter was too near, postponed the action.[10]

*General Philip Schuyler was Captain Arent Schuyler De Peyster's maternal uncle. Only a few months before coming to Michilimackinac the De Peyster's had stayed at Schuyler's estate on the Hudson River near Saratoga. Now they were enemies. The American Revolution was indeed a civil war.

With Americans entrenched in Montreal, fur merchants there hardly knew which way to turn. It was absolutely necessary that they dispatch canoes laden with trade goods to Michilimackinac as soon as weather permitted. If the canoes did not leave, the traders would go bankrupt and the Indians would starve for their livelihood depended upon European merchandise. Without their necessities, the Indians would likely raid traders in the wilds or attack settlements at Michilimackinac or Detroit.

The Montreal merchants' dilemma was difficult because if they cooperated with the rebels, they would have to answer to British authorities in the event they reassumed power. Desperate, some merchants, early in March, 1776, petitioned Congress to allow them to carry on their Indian trade. On March 20 Congress sent a commission to Canada to convince the Canadians to join forces with the "United Colonies," stressing that "their interests and ours are inseparably united." The commission was given power to establish regulations to ensure peace and order and was to promise the Canadians that their liberties would be preserved. Significantly, Congress allowed the commissioners to grant trading passes.[11] If the Americans still controlled Montreal at the end of the summer, the merchants probably would be unable to send their furs to England and import a new supply of trade goods. But for the moment business could continue, and Michilimackinac's economic livelihood was not seriously interrupted.

Michilimackinac suffered through extreme cold and many snowstorms this winter. Fortunately, dances, card and billiard games, teas, and hunting and fishing expeditions helped pass away the time and provided relief from monotony. On March 15 Marie Anne Cardin La Fantaisie gave birth to a boy who, in the absence of a priest, was privately baptized the same day by his uncle, Joseph Ainsse.[12] The community wiled away winter in local concerns unaware of events in Montreal and Philadelphia.

With spring came shocking news. On May 12 Simon McTavish, a 26-year-old Scottish trader, arrived from Detroit after dodging cakes of ice floating in the straits. He reported to De Peyster the British disasters in Canada.[13] Word spread in a community eager for news as both soldiers and civilians tried to fathom the implications of McTavish's report. Would the King's troops be able to recapture Montreal and drive the rebels from Canada? Would the trade continue? How would the Indians respond to the American successes? Would it be possible to obtain provisions? Was a rebel attack likely at Detroit or even here? These questions gnawed at De Peyster's mind.

Shocked by McTavish's report, De Peyster was impatient for further news. Nearly a month passed before Monsieur Legras, who had escaped from Montreal, and James Stanley Goddard, a trader who had been at Niagara, brought a report of the Montreal merchants' efforts to induce Congress to allow the trade to continue. They were, however, unsure whether any canoes had left Montreal. On June 9 the sloop *Felicity* from Detroit carried word that Montgomery had been killed at Quebec. Even this failed to cheer McTavish who believed it unlikely any goods would come unless the dispute was settled soon or British troops regained possession of Canada.[14]

Amid these uncertainies traders arrived from the interior with the winter's fur harvest. Many from the Mississippi country rode high in their canoes for they had few pelts to weight them down. Fortunately, at Michilimackinac they found some goods in abundance, particularly Indian corn and sugar. A good quantity of provisions had come from Detroit aboard the *Welcome, Angelica,* and *Felicity* for John Askin, James Bannerman, and others. In late May Samuel Robertson, Captain of the *Welcome,* delivered a cargo of flour, corn, bags, thread, pans, locks, knives, fishing line, candles, and bowls to Askin. The *Angelica* brought a pair of oxen to work Askin's farm and haul his goods. Much more was needed, particularly merchandise and rum for the trade and flour and grease to feed the voyageurs.[15]

The Parade of Quebec in 1789. Drawn by Thomas Davies

On Wednesday, June 12, an excited sentry shouted from the northeast bastion that canoes were approaching from the direction of Mackinac Island. As was usual when vessels were sighted, the soldiers and civilians poured through the water gate to see for themselves. Sure enough, several miles away the sun illuminated shiny blades that flashed as voyageurs lifted their paddles out of the water for each powerful stroke. What a sight — the Americans must have granted passes after all. Soon the crowd counted seven canoes heavily loaded with desperately needed trade goods. A loud cheer went up as they reached the beach. This cargo plus £15,000 Sterling worth of merchandise brought from Albany, helped to fill the traders' needs.[16]

Sir Guy Carleton, Governor of Quebec

To aid General Guy Carleton, Governor of Quebec, in driving out the Americans in Canada, De Peyster determined to organize Indian war parties. In early June he dispatched Goddard to La Baye "to beat up for Indian Volunteers" among the Menominee and perhaps the Winnebago.[17]

On June 17, De Peyster and his officers gave instructions to Joseph Louis Ainsse, the Interpreter, who had assembled a party of local Ottawa and Chippewa. He was to lead them along the north shore of Lake Huron to the French River and then proceed to Montreal by way of the Ottawa River. Along the way Ainsse was to meet Goddard and the Menominee. At Montreal Ainsse was to assist Colonel John Butler's drive against the Americans.[18]

When Goddard brought his force of Menominee to Michilimackinac in early July, De Peyster chose Charles Langlade to lead his party. Langlade, a 46-year-old veteran leader of Indians in many military engagements, had helped defeat the young George Washington and General Edward Braddock near Fort Duquesne in 1755. Native warriors did not respond favorably to European discipline, but they respected Langlade, who understood their ways, and they followed his lead when he sang the war song.

On Thursday, July 4, Langlade and Goddard assembled their braves on the beach east of the fort.[19] De Peyster, speaking through Langlade, warned them that if Canada was not freed, the goods essential for their survival would be cut off. He emphasized that the Bostonians, as he called the rebels, only wanted the Indians' land, but their father the King had their best interests at heart. He admonished them to obey Langlade and to refrain from cruelty against their enemies. The chiefs solemnly affirmed their allegiance to George III, then launched their canoes and paddled northeast to try to put down the rebellion.

Unknown to De Peyster and Langlade, a thousand miles away in Philadelphia the Continental Congress adopted the Declaration of Independence. The thirteen colonies proclaimed their freedom from Great Britain, and the break between the colonies and England was complete. The present war would determine whether this division would remain.

NEVILLE PUBLIC MUSEUM

Charles Langlade's coat and sword

*Michilimackinac
as seen from the
northwest*

Two weeks after Langlade's warriors left for Montreal, De Peyster received a letter from Governor Carleton informing him that the rebels had been driven out of the province. De Peyster was to stop his Indian party "provided you can do it without giving them offence."[20] The recall came too late, and on July 19 some of De Peyster's forces arrived in Montreal. Carleton received them, thanked them for their services, and passed out rewards. Explaining that they were no longer needed, he sent the braves back to winter with their families.[21]

Michilimackinac welcomed the news that the British again controlled Montreal. Now the trade could function normally. Before the summer ended, over thirty canoes licensed by Carleton made their way to Michilimackinac, making a profitable year possible.[22]

Not everyone prospered, however. This turn of events cost James Bannerman a considerable sum of money. "I'm afraid I have been taken in this Summer," he complained to his partner William Edgar in Detroit, "I imagined no Goods would have come up, wherefor I made large purchases of Goods, provisions, & Liquors by which I'm afraid I shall lose considerably."[23] But such was the nature of business; the prices of furs and goods fluctuated dramatically. Individual traders and merchants had no control over the London markets or the political and economic events outside the wilderness. This highly volatile business produced quick fortunes and failures without discrimination.

While the Mississippi traders had experienced a lean year, those wintering in the northwest had considerable success. Simon McTavish, returning from Grand Portage in mid-August, was ecstatic over the load of furs he brought down with him. "Our bad success at Detroit," he informed his partner Billy Edgar, "has been in some measure made up by my Jaunt to the Carrying place. We can say with a heart felt Satisfaction, that this Fall we can pay every one their own."[24]

Many of the furs arrived at Michilimackinac in loose unpressed packs. Bannerman and others frequently shipped these to Detroit on board the *Felicity* or other sailing vessels. At Detroit the packs were opened and the furs counted, weighed, and pressed tightly together for transport to Montreal.[25] To conserve space most packs that went to Montreal via the Ottawa River were sorted and pressed into ninety-pound bales at Michilimackinac or the interior outposts.

With the departure of the final canoes another trading year came to an end. This season had been unusual. The secession from Great Britain by thirteen of the colonies meant war might go on indefinitely, and neither De Peyster nor anyone else know how long it would last. If this past summer was an indication of things to come, serious disruptions were likely. Michilimackinac survived its first threat with a minimum of pain, but would its isolation in the interior continue to shield it from the ravages of war?

V.

British War Policy
Takes Shape

Nippy September air kept Simon McTavish alert as he wandered about the streets of Montreal. All around him he could see the scars of the recent American occupation. Many citizens had been plundered three months earlier by the fleeing rebel army.[1] But he was more concerned with his impending voyage to England. Despite the high prices of furs in Montreal this fall, McTavish, hoping to increase his profits, had decided to accompany his pelts to London and sell them personally. "Fortune has proved so kind a Mistress to me for some years past that perhaps I am too Sanguine," he commented to Billy Edgar, "and the Jade may now Jilt me effectually by lowering the Prices of Furrs at home — at any rate I am determin'd to Venture."[2] On October 10, 1776 McTavish sailed down the St. Lawrence accompanied by John Porteous, Benjamin Frobisher, and several other Michilimackinac traders.[3]

A view of Montreal in Canada in the 1760's by Thomas Patten.

With the commercial link between the wilderness and England intact, Captain De Peyster and the Michilimackinac traders anticipated that trade would remain profitable. Yet conditions had changed — the colony was at war and all loyal subjects were expected to defend the Crown and adhere to official restrictions. Politics and economics were closely intertwined, and British officials scrutinized carefully the traders' associations with their colleagues, dealings with Indians, and willingness to obey authority. Disloyalty brought arrest and loss of trading privileges. Montreal merchants cautioned their agents and partners in the west to avoid political disputes with their commanding officers.[4] Even appearances of sympathy to the rebel cause could bring harsh reprimands or punishment. A man could swiftly lose his livelihood.

Silver medals were given to important chiefs to gain their loyalty

THE MUSEUM, MICHIGAN STATE UNIVERSITY

While organizing his forces to repel the American assault on Canada, Governor Guy Carleton turned to Indian warriors to bolster his defenses.[5] Even though Charles Langlade's war party arrived too late to help in 1776, Carleton ordered him to bring a force of "200 chosen Indians in the Spring." Carleton sent De Peyster two medals and a gorget to give to Indian chiefs, designated by Langlade, as tokens of the King's fidelity.[6] Displeased with Interpreters Joseph Louis Ainsse and Charles Gautier, the Governor hoped De Peyster could induce these two key men to put the Crown's welfare before "their own concerns."

Carleton alerted Lieutenant Governor Hamilton at Detroit to have Indians ready to march in the spring.[7] "Keeping the Indians firm to the King's interest ought to be your first and great object when the troubles are composed" Carleton urged.[8]

Carleton anticipated the decision made by Secretary of State for the Colonies Lord George Germain on March 26. Responding to Hamilton's request for permission to send Indian warriors to raid rebel settlements, Germain ordered "that the most Vigorous efforts" be made to crush the rebellion. Hamilton was directed to assemble war parties from the Ottawa, Chippewa, Huron, Shawnee, Seneca, Delaware, Cherokee, and Potawatomi nations. He was to place "proper Persons at their Head," and "employ them in making a Diversion and exciting an alarm upon the frontiers of Virginia and Pennsylvania." Germain instructed that loyalists and "inoffensive Inhabitants" be spared. To compensate the warriors, the Crown sent presents and military supplies.[9]

De Peyster and the British were not the only ones seeking to secure the loyalty of the western nations. Don Francisco Cruzat, Lieutenant Governor of Upper Louisiana, residing in St. Louis, sought their allegiance to Spain. The Spanish, having received Louisiana from France in the 1760's as a result of the Seven Years War, hoped to use the colony as a buffer between Mexico and the British advancing from the east.

St. Louis, located near the confluence of the Missouri and Mississippi Rivers, was the seat of local government and the center of a growing Missouri and Upper Mississippi Valley fur trade. Spanish traders penetrated both sides of the Mississippi, competing directly with the British. For many years the French settlements of Cahokia, across the river from St. Louis; Kaskaskia, some fifty miles downstream; and Vincennes on the Wabash River, 180 miles east of Kaskaskia, all had served as centers of the French trade. When the Illinois country was ceded to Great Britain in 1763, many French moved west across the Mississippi to St. Louis, preferring to live under the Spanish flag. Spain encouraged this migration as a means of populating its new possession.[10] British influence east of the Mississippi was further reduced when they abandoned Fort de Chartres in 1772. Only a few British troops remained at Kaskaskia, and they departed in 1776. Thereafter the regular troops nearest to the Illinois were stationed at Michilimackinac and Detroit.

MISSOURI HISTORICAL SOCIETY

Francisco Cruzat, Lieutenant Governor of Upper Louisiana

Furs brought to St. Louis were easily shipped down the Mississippi to the port of New Orleans. There trade goods were purchased and poled upstream to the St. Louis merchants. Pelts procured by Spanish, French, and even some British traders passed through St. Louis and New Orleans. The British feared that gunpowder and other goods might be imported from New Orleans by the rebels in Kentucky because the Spanish were eager to make trouble for their British competitors.

A Naudowessie (Sioux) family drawn during the 1760's for Jonathan Carver's travel account.

Despite Spanish attempts to keep foreign traders out of their territory, daring Michilimackinac merchants such as Jean Marie Du Charme were drawn to the riches of the Missouri. One night in late fall of 1772, Du Charme spirited two canoe loads of merchandise across the Mississippi and slipped quietly up the Missouri. Trade with the Little Osage was brisk until Spanish troops appeared. Du Charme escaped in a hail of musket balls, but his crew and possessions were captured.[11] He did not forget this humiliation. Later he returned to La Baye and Prairie du Chien, both beyond Spanish control, but in the back of his mind lurked thoughts of revenge and of profits to be made along the Missouri.[12]

To expand their influence among the western tribes, Spanish officials circulated wampum belts telling of their King's good wishes. In 1777 informants gave Cruzat a report of the size of each nation:

Sioux — undertermined number of warriors
Menominee — 200 warriors
Fox — 300-350 warriors
Sac — 400 warriors
Winnebago — 150 warriors
Mascouten — 200 warriors
Kickapoo — 300 warriors
Potawatomi — 150 warriors
Ottawa — 3,000 warriors
Chippewa — 3,000 warriors
Peoria and Kaskaskia — 100 warriors

These figures were by no means precise. Other records indicate that the Ottawa were fewer and the Potawatomi and the Chippewa may have been more numerous than the Spanish believed.

If De Peyster had seen Spanish accounts, he would have been alarmed at their assessments of tribal loyalties. The Spanish surmised Sac and Fox to be particularly trustworthy even though the Sac received "more liberal presents" from the English. The Ottawa and Chippewa were considered somewhat dissatisfied with the British and could have "affection" for Spain. "Little confidence" was placed in the Winnebago and the Potawatomi, for both tribes occasionally robbed Spanish traders. Favorable reports were made of the Menominee, Mascouten, Kickapoo, Peoria, and Kaskaskia although the latter two were almost eliminated through wars with neighboring tribes.[13] In addition to pro-Spanish attitudes among some nations, there was a lingering allegiance to the departed French.

Carver's 1769 map shows the location of Indian tribes in the western Great Lakes.

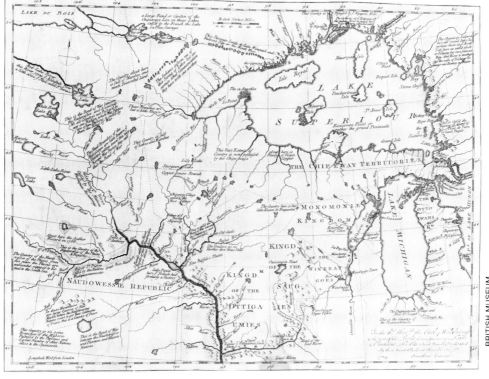

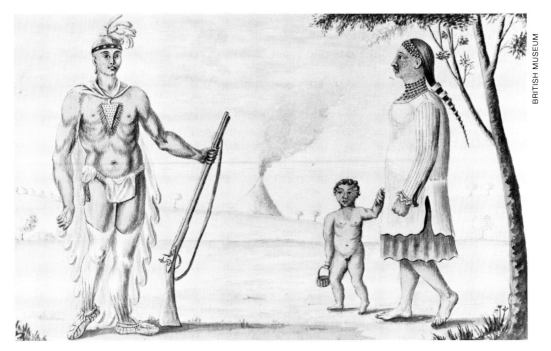

An Outtigaumie (Fox) family in the 1760's.

During the winter De Peyster prepared to send a war party to Canada the following summer. In February when some of the Indians wintering near Michilimackinac contracted the dreaded smallpox, De Peyster reasoned that only those who had had the disease should accompany the mission.[14] On April 12 the Commandant dispatched several canoes of provisions, through floating cakes of ice, to La Baye to outfit Menominee warriors raised by Charles Langlade.[15] Eight weeks later, on June 4, Langlade led sixty auxiliaries to Michilimackinac. To De Peyster's dismay many returned home before the Ottawa and Chippewa joined Langlade's party.[16] The next day Langlade's expedition left to join General John Burgoyne near Lake Champlain. Burgoyne had brought British reinforcements to Canada to form a base from which to reconquer the rebelling colonies.

On June 6, De Peyster received intelligence from Laurent Du Charme, a trader at Milwaukee, stating that Spanish agents had given a wampum belt to the Potawatomi Chief, Black Bird.[17] Du Charme reported that Cruzat wanted Black Bird to entice the nations between La Baye and the Mississippi to join hands with Spain. The Spanish hoped to gain a greater share of the fur trade while the British were involved with the rebellion.[18]

One week later Charles Gautier appeared out of the northwest with a group of Sac and Fox warriors. Despite Carleton's previous displeasure with him, Langlade had commissioned his nephew to raise these braves. Gautier knew their language, and they respected him. He, too, brought De Peyster news of Spanish intrigue among the Indians. De Peyster was confident no other man could have blunted the efforts of the rebels and Spanish and delivered this band of still loyal warriors. Furthermore, Gautier had sold his goods, some at a loss, to devote all his energies to the King's service. De Peyster had no doubt about the reliability of Charles Gautier. Only hours after they reached Michilimackinac, De Peyster dispatched Gautier and his warriors to Canada.

The Commandant expected the imminent arrival of a band of Potawatomi from St. Joseph, but only fifteen men actually appeared with the elderly Louis Chevallier. Chevallier had traded and lived in St. Joseph for over thirty years and exerted great influence over the Potawatomi surrounding that post. Although British officials at Detroit distrusted him, De Peyster felt the Frenchman could be useful. Since the Potawatomi did not use bark canoes, De Peyster hired a trading canoe that was scheduled to return to Montreal to transport them.[19] Thus within two weeks auxiliaires from six nations had been dispatched from Michilimackinac to assist British forces in Canada.

In mid-July Langlade's force joined Burgoyne's army which was moving down Lake Champlain to cut the colonies in two by gaining control of the Hudson River. Burgoyne instructed the Michilimackinac Indians to follow the British officers' commands. Except in battle, no one was to be killed, and warriors were to take scalps only from men killed "in fair opposition." Burgoyne emphasized that many Americans were loyal to the King, and they should be protected.[20]

Undisciplined pillage by either British regulars or native warriors increased the resolve of the rebels. When an Indian killed the loyalist Jane McCrae, the colonial propagandists trumpeted it to the world. In the face of a growing colonial force and British frustration with the Indians' failure to obey orders, Langlade and his party left Burgoyne on August 19.[21] When Burgoyne's army was entrapped and forced to surrender on October 13, 1777 at Saratoga, the British northern offensive collapsed.

Meanwhile at Detroit, Henry Hamilton held a large council on June 17, and he ordered officers and interpreters from the Indian Department and militia to lead raids on the Virginia and Pennsylvania frontiers. During the next month alone fifteen parties from Detroit created a reign of terror. Angered by the death of many men, women, and children, the frontiersmen accused Hamilton of brutally killing defenseless people. Hamilton denied these charges, but his Indian war parties stiffened the resistance of the western rebels.[22]

Scalping was a common practice by both Indians and whites on the frontier.

A potential problem for De Peyster and Hamilton was American sympathizers who might be stirring up Indians. Governor Carleton ordered his officers "to seize all suspected persons passing upon or near the lakes, and all persons attempting to sow sedition or to stir up insurrections among the people in that part of the country." Dubious visitors were to be sent to Quebec for trial. The commanders were to pay particular attention to unprincipled traders.[23]

When Thomas Bentley arrived at Michilimackinac from Kaskaskia, he soon found himself in trouble. An English merchant, who had operated a store at Manchac in West Florida, Bentley had been active in the Illinois country from about 1770. However, he had fallen into disfavor with Philip Rocheblave, the British agent at Kaskaskia, who accused him of furnishing supplies to an American boat which transported munitions from New Orleans up into the Ohio River. Rocheblave also claimed that Bentley had corresponded with rebels in other colonies and spread propaganda among the Illinois population. In response to these charges, Henry Hamilton had ordered Bentley's arrest.

Shortly after Bentley landed at Michilimackinac on July 21, De Peyster, accompanied by the sergeant of the guard and two privates, confronted him. The Commandant examined the passport given him by Rocheblave, took him into custody, and seized his property. Bentley steadfastly proclaimed his innocence, charging Rocheblave with malicious intent. A few days later he wrote his friend Daniel Murray in Kaskaskia asking him to care for his wife during his absence and confinement. After several weeks, De Peyster placed Bentley on a vessel bound for Detroit. From there Bentley went to Quebec.[24]

MERSEYSIDE COUNTY MUSEUM

This rare view of Fort Erie and Fort Niagara was drawn in 1773 by Henry De Berniere of the 10th Regiment. It also shows two Great Lakes sailing vessels.

F ear of rebel incursions and intrigue caused Carleton to restrict navigation on the Great Lakes. On May 22 he issued a circular permitting only vessels "armed and manned by the Crown" to navigate the open waters. Traders who sent arms and gunpowder through Lake Erie were required to put them on board the King's ships; under no circumstances were any munitions to be transported in an open batteau. Private trade goods would be shipped on royal vessels if room permitted, but the King's provisions assumed first priority.[25] Moreover, no one was permitted to build a vessel larger than a "common boat" except for use by the King.

Although His Majesty owned only a few vessels on the upper lakes, British officials managed to control private shipping. Commanders and crews got their orders from Captain Alexander Grant, Naval Commander of the Upper Lakes, at Detroit. When at Michilimackinac, they reported to De Peyster for further instructions. The Crown had not conscripted all vessels, including John Askin's *Welcome*, but the sloop was armed and subject to royal disposition.

By 1777 eleven sailing vessels and one row galley navigated the upper lakes. The Naval Department at Detroit detailed their armaments and crew size:[26]

Schooner *Gage* (His Majesty's Ship) — mounting 16 carriage guns & 6 swivels — requires 48 men, officers included a commander, 1 Lt, 1 mate, 1-Boatswain, 1-gunner, 1-carpenter

Schooner *Dunmore* — (His Majesty's Ship) — mounting 12 guns & 4 swivels — requires 36 men

Schooner *Ottawa* (His Majesty's Ship) — mounting 12 carriage guns, [?] four pounders, six swivel-blunderbuses — requires 36 men

Schooner *Hope* — taken into King's employ 25 Aug, 1775; mounting 4-4 prs — 18 men

Schooner *Faith* — 4 swivels — 10 men — including a Master to command, a Boatswain, & a Gunner

Sloop *Wyandott* — 4 guns, 2 pounders to be sent up and 6 Swivel blunderbusses, Ten men, a master, a mate, Boatswain & Gunner

Sloop *Angelica* — 6 swivels — 12 men including officers

Sloop *Felicity* — 4 swivels — 8 men — including a Master to command, a Boatswain & a Gunner

Sloop *Welcome* — 2 swivels, -2 blunderbusses -8 men including a Master to command one Boatswain & Gunner

Sloop *Adventure* — 6 men and one man as Boatswain & Gunner

Sloop *Archange* — 6 men and one man as Boatswain & Gunner

Row Galley — 21 men exclusive of Lieut, one Mate, one Boatswain, & one Gunner, to row with 16 Oars and to mount a 12-pounder in the Bow & two 6-pounders in the Stern, also 10 swivel blunderbusses.

All these vessels had been built at Detroit except the *Welcome* which Askin constructed in 1775 at Michilimackinac. The *Gage* could transport 450 barrels while the *Adventure* could carry only one hundred. Fully loaded the *Gage* carried eighty troops; with only 160 barrels, 120 soldiers could be taken on board.[27] The *Welcome*, which regularly sailed to and from Michilimackinac, was rated at forty-five tons and measured fifty-five feet long and had a sixteen-foot beam. Her capacity was sixty-seven persons, many of whom must have been crammed into every corner.

Sailing ships were a British innovation on the upper lakes. Though the French had constructed the ill-fated *Griffon* in 1679 and had a small vessel on Lake Superior during the eighteenth century, they relied on frail birchbark canoes and wooden batteaux. As soon as the British captured Canada, they began to build a navy. Lakes Erie, Huron, and Michigan are interconnected and, except for the shallow six-foot bar at the mouth of the St. Clair River, vessels could travel easily for hundreds of miles. Both the military and private traders relied heavily on

*Detroit waterfront
in the 1790's.*

schooners and sloops to maintain communication between scattered
western posts along the lakes.

Pay for naval officers and men compared favorably to that received
by soldiers. A seaman's monthly wage of £2/5 was more than twice
that of a private, while a commander and army captain received 10s
per day. Lieutenants and mates received £5 per month; boatswains
and gunners, £4 monthly. Allowance was made for two servants for
each commander and one for a lieutenant.[28]

Steep transportation costs and inflation drove prices high, consequently this wage did not allow many to prosper. In Detroit a pair of
shoes cost 12s, and coarse stockings, 6s per pair in October, 1777.
Checked linen cloth sold for 3s 6d per yard, while soap went for 2s 4d
per pound.[29] At Michilimackinac, where prices were even higher,
rum brought as much as 20s per gallon.[30] Since the market fluctuated
greatly, the monetary value of goods changed quickly.

Despite the maritime restrictions, Montreal merchants brought
huge quantities of goods to Michilimackinac in 1777 via the northern
route. There were no Americans to contend with in Montreal this year,
and the canoes left on time. At least 120 arrived throughout the season.
Nearly one thousand men were employed to transport the year's
supply of necessities. Additional commodities were shipped through
Detroit. In addition to John Askin's ten batteaux, Thomas Smith,
William Taylor, and Edward Ridley licensed sixteen more for Detroit
and Michilimackinac. Business appeared to be better than normal.[31]

Having lived at Michilimackinac for three years, Captain De Peyster longed for a change. The isolation and harsh climate wore down his spirit, and the constant tensions took their toll. Keeping Indians and traders at peace was difficult enough, but now the rebellion had strained their cooperation and devotion to the Crown. The treachery of some Indians, French, Spanish, and even English traders agonized De Peyster. He requested leave of his duties.

Governor Carleton, in Quebec, had no intention of granting De Peyster's wish. Instead, on July 14 Carleton notified him that he had been promoted to Major. Praising De Peyster for "the prudence and discretion with which you have conducted yourself in the command of your post," Carleton told him it would be "with considerable inconvenience to the King's service" to transfer him at this time.[32] The Major and Rebecca would remain at Michilimackinac.

During the summer De Peyster had a strange encounter. An Indian, sleeping on Beaver Island, had a frightening vision of an evil spirit in the form of a white beaver. The spirit ordered him to go to Michilimackinac where he was to kill De Peyster. Complying with this command, the Indian positioned himself in front of the King's storehouse across the street from De Peyster's home, but he could not bring himself to kill the Major. Joseph Louis Ainsse, the Interpreter, noticing this lonely man questioned his peculiar behavior. The Indian poured out his story, and Ainsse led his troubled companion into the commanding officer's house. Here the Major learned of the threat to his life. In a stern but dignified manner, the Major ordered the Indian to return to Beaver Island next winter, trap the white beaver, and return with its pelt. Only in this way could he rid himself of the burden of his vision.[33]

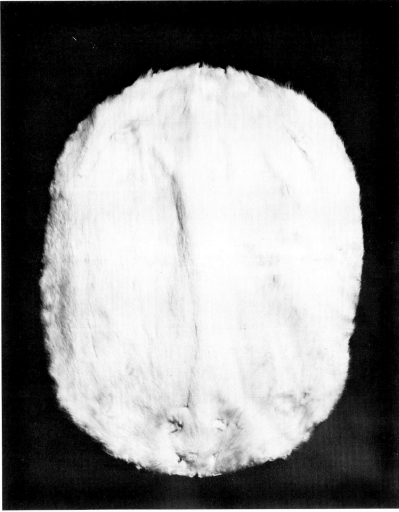

The next spring the Indian brought De Peyster this white beaver pelt. It became one of his treasured souvenirs of Michilimackinac.

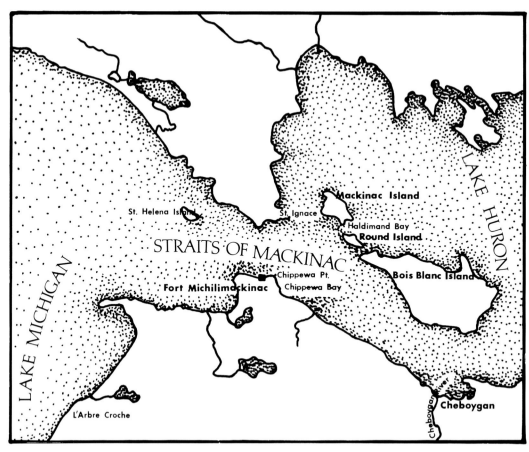

Ste. Anne's Church

VI.

Trade Flourishes

A s winter closed in, Rebecca De Peyster longed to return to a
settlement offering more refinement and comfort. Disappointed
that Governor Carleton had refused her husband's transfer, she worried about his health. The constant strain of duty had eroded his
stamina; he tired easily and at times displayed an impatience and
anger seldom seen by her. It hurt to see the man she loved torn apart by
a seemingly impossible job. She hoped he would get some rest this
winter to rejuvenate both his body and his spirit.

Rebecca kept busy assisting Archange Askin plan the wedding of
her step-daughter Catherine to Samuel Robertson. Although she was
only fifteen years old, John thought "Kitty" was already an old maid.
He enthusiastically concurred with Kitty's intention to marry the
Welcome's Captain, an "Industrious, Sober, Honest man." Samuel had
come to Michilimackinac in 1774 in the employment of the Albany
firm of Phyn & Ellice to command one of Askin's vessels. The young
bride had recently returned from Montreal, where she had studied for
several years at a nunnery.[1] Because no priest resided at Michilimackinac, the ceremony was to be a civil one.

The wedding was cause for celebration. John and Archange proudly
treated their friends to refreshments and a dance, and the guests had
more than the usual "dish of Tea & Grogg" served at the weekly
dances.[2] To Askin's dismay, the new fiddle which he had ordered
from England had not arrived, but his friend Sampson Fleming at
Detroit had sent a "Country Dance Book," which provided a variety of
music.[3] As the musicians played, the groom and his father-in-law
guided their ladies, gowned in their finest garments, across the dance
floor.[4] Joining the merriment, the De Peysters were uplifted as they
shared the Robertsons' and Askins' happiness.

De Peyster honored the couple with a poem written especially for the occasion:[5]

Dancing helped to pass the long Michilimackinac winters. Drawing by George Heriot.

> "Go, happy pair, enjoy the bliss in store,
>> Reserved for those whom Hymen's bans unite;
> Go, steer the course, so often sailed before,
>> By those who've found deep soundings of delight.
> No hidden rocks, or shoals, or boisterous gales,
>> Shall e'er bark annoy, while fraught with love;
> Nor need you ever shift your helm or sails'
>> Your voyage through life, one constant trade-wind
>>> prove."

Gala events only increased the longing for spring when contact with the outside world would be resumed. Desiring the fineries and embellishments of London society, Archange ordered silk with appropriate trimmings and several new dresses.[6] Though it arrived too late for the wedding, John had ordered a fine light blue satin dress of French fashion for Kitty's wedding gown.[7]

The Askins longed for the war's end for they had hoped to move to Detroit, Archange's home. John felt he could better manage his business from the larger community, but the uncertainty of present affairs made it "hard to undertake anything."[8] As a result, he decided to remain at Michilimackinac until hostilities ceased, and he planned to build a two-story house in the suburbs.

By April 27, 1778 the ice was out of the straits, and Askin soon expected a vessel from Detroit. Anticipating the beginning of a new trading season, Askin wrote to John Hay, Deputy Indian Agent, in Detroit, expressing his ignorance of recent events in the east. He believed traders and canoes from Montreal would reach Michilimackinac before any got to Detroit; hence, he promised to inform Hay of any news.[9]

At Montreal the trading firms were busy outfitting canoes destined for Michilimackinac. David McCrae, John Kay, Peter Barthe, and Charles Gratiot, operating a partnership known as David McCrae & Co. of Michilimackinac, signed a three year agreement with William and John Kay on April 6. The Kay's promised to supply McCrae & Co. goods and merchandise needed in the Indian trade, to buy canoes and provisions, to hire voyageurs and guides, and to dispatch the loaded canoes by May 10 unless the war or unforeseen calamities made this impossible.

McCrae & Co. were to settle their accounts by September 1, except for 1778 when their debt was due on December 1. They also agreed to six per-cent annual interest on all cash paid out by the Kays and on any accounts past due. This included payments for liquor, advances on engagés wages, canoes, provisions, lodging for canoeists, and for storing furs and fire insurance on pelts received at Montreal. During September McCrae & Co. had to put in their order for next year's needs.

All furs acquired by McCrae and Co. were to be consigned to William and John Kay. They in turn took them to James McGill and John Porteous in Montreal for appraisal. The Kays could sell the pelts for this amount or try to get a higher price. Hopefully the value of the year's fur harvest would be high enough to pay off all debts and leave a profit. [10]

As John Askin filled his customers' orders, he was painfully aware of increasing impediments to his enterprises. To supply individual traders and the Northwest Company at Grand Portage, Askin bought much of his rum and grain at Detroit. However, Lieutenant Governor Hamilton's refusal to allow liquor or provisions to leave there created a severe shortage at Michilimackinac. By May 18 no liquor had come from Montreal, and less than twenty bags of flour or corn had arrived from Detroit. [11]

Of grave concern was the limited space available for private merchandise on the sailing vessels. Naval commanders had a difficult time satisfying private shippers since holds were crammed with the King's property. They also were pestered by merchants, traders, and clerks not employed by the Crown who sought passage to the western posts. Frustrated ship commanders petitioned Haldimand for regulations determining priorities for non-government cargo and passengers. [12] Askin estimated that he needed two full vessels to transport his provisions, and other traders had similar demands. [13] To make matters worse, on May 8 Major De Peyster took the *Welcome* into the King's service, dispatching it to Detroit two days later. [14]

De Peyster fully understood the traders' difficulties and tried to assist them. He urged Hamilton to lift his embargo so the northern trade could continue. [15] Moreover, he requested General Carleton to allow an armed vessel, preferably the *Welcome*, to be stationed at Michilimackinac year around to carry supplies and to awe visiting Indians who might contemplate attacking the fort. [16]

Askin worked hard to secure his supplies. He urged Alexander Grant in Detroit to convince Hamilton that as many as one-third of the

Askin kept careful record of his business transactions. In 1776 and 1778 he inventoried everything that he owned.

back country people would perish if sufficient corn and flour were not sent up. Askin alone needed one thousand bushels of corn and thirty thousand pounds of flour. The previous year four loaded vessels brought barely sufficient provisions for the trade; this year the demand was even greater.[17]

In late April Askin informed the Northwest Company partners James McGill, Benjamin Frobisher, Charles Patterson, and others at Montreal of his efforts to fill their orders. He had directed his partner Jean Baptiste Barthe at Sault Ste. Marie to dispatch to the Grand Portage eighty eight-gallon kegs of West Indies rum and one hundred bushels of hulled corn. Another 150 bushels awaited pick-up from Indians at Milwaukee; hopefully when the *Archange* got there, more could be procured from them. Added to the two hundred bushels he had on hand, this at least provided a beginning. Askin assured his Montreal clients that they should not be "uneasy" regarding reports of scarcity. He would secure whatever was necessary.[18]

A good business sense and confidence in himself enabled Askin to present an optimistic outlook, but he worried about shortages. Even the garrison troops faced a lack of food. Spoiled flour, pork, and butter were kept in case supply ships did not come.[19] On May 8 Askin authorized James Sterling at Detroit to sell four hundred bushels of hulled corn to Major De Peyster; he wanted this and the remainder of his supplies shipped to Michilimackinac on the next vessel. But Askin was not sure even this maneuver would gain him space on the King's vessel.[20]

Askin employed Sterling to keep his goods safe in Detroit after arrival from Montreal. He sent Sterling copies of his requisitions and authorized him to hire a person to supervise unloading even "if such a person was to cost three Dollars a Day for that time it would be better than have my effects embezeled."[21] Delays in transportation were a costly and unavoidable expense in these turbulent times.

On May 18, Askin arose before sunrise and wrote some letters to be sent on the *Mackinac,* which was preparing to sail for Sault Ste. Marie. He expected the independent trader Charles Chaboillez, who wintered in the northwest, to be at the small picketed outpost. Askin explained to Chaboillez that he would be able to send only half of his order, but hoped to supply the rest long before he needed it. Also, he substituted twenty barrels of whiskey for rum, which could be exchanged later. The first Montreal canoes had come and soon would be heading to Lake Superior. Only yesterday Chaboillez's brothers, Augustin and Hypolitte, had arrived at Michilimackinac with their wives.[22]

Charles Jean-Baptiste Chaboillez.

Askin placed his employee, "The Indian," in command of the *Mackinac*. Joining him were McDonald and Pompey. "The Indian" and McDonald received a daily ration of one quarter pint of rum, but Pompey got only one-eighth pint. All were given their provisions and wages through June 1, but after that Barthe was to pay them and furnish their victuals from the cargo. McDonald's salary was 1170 livres per year, "The Indian's," nine hundred.[23]

Askin wrote in French asking Barthe not to transfer "The Indian" to the *De Peyster*, which was above the falls, nor to use McDonald in loading that boat. Provisions at the Sault were to be forwarded to Grand Portage, but only half of each order was to go on the *De Peyster*. One hundred minots of corn were to be marked "F O" for Forrest Oakes, one hundred minots "N W" for the Northwest Company, fifty minots "C C H" for Charles Chaboillez, and sixty barrels of rum "N W." Pompey and a man yet to be hired were to sail the *De Peyster* across Lake Superior; upon return, Pompey was to come back to Michilimackinac. If the *Mackinac* could not be tugged up the rapids, she was to come back to Michilimackinac for more cargo.[24]

Six days later Askin learned that Hamilton had lifted his embargo. All the rum and corn necessary for the northwest trade could now be shipped, but flour was limited to fifteen thousand pounds, considerably less than what was needed. If De Peyster concurred, Askin planned to send the *Archange* to Detroit upon its return from Milwaukee. When the *Mackinac* got back from the Sault, Askin's men loaded her with corn, but he instructed Barthe to "have it made into lye hominy yourself for I expect only hulled corn from Detroit." Although several traders brought some rum from Detroit, they were bound by oath to use it only in the northern trade. Consequently, the critical shortage of rum persisted at Michilimackinac with only a few barrels on hand.[25]

While endeavoring to supply the traders, Askin procured merchandise for the military officers. Lieutenants Bennett and Clowes ordered coffee, Madeira wine, and common rum. Dr. Mitchell wanted rum and "a Barrell of Sugar, filled up with Barly." Lieutenant Robert Brooke had his heart set on a tierce of Bristol beer and a cheshire cheese. Askin urged Todd & McGill, a large trading firm at Montreal, "Tho these orders are but trifling, yett as they may be an Introduction to more I make no doubt you'll not neglect sending them."[26] The shrewd trader always sensed potential business.

Despite the war, the government intended to encourage expansion of the fur trade. Major De Peyster received orders from Governor Carleton to send an officer and twelve men to the Grand Portage in 1778.[27] The northwest merchants had convinced Carleton to protect their growing business. During 1777 furs worth nearly £40,000 Sterling had been brought from the wilderness beyond Lake Superior. A small contingent of troops could construct a fort and maintain peace between the visiting Indians and nearly five hundred employees of the trade.[28]

In late May De Peyster sent Lieutenant Thomas Bennett, Sergeant Amos Langdown, five privates from the King's Eighth, and seven Canadians employed by the traders to the Portage. Askin furnished his man, "Big Charlie," to serve as their guide.[29] John Pattison, bombardier in charge of the Engineers' stores, issued Langdown thirty-eight pounds of twenty-four-penny nails and forty-four pounds of ten-penny nails to erect a small fort.[30]

The party's voyage was interrupted when their canoes ran aground on rocks in Lake Superior, and they lost their provisions and ammunition. De Peyster, to ensure the success of the mission, replenished their losses with one hundred gallons of rum, two bales of dry goods, a bale of tobacco, and some flour and pork.[31] Bennett was to dispense the commodities as presents to visiting Indians. Two barrels of gunpowder were shipped for the two small swivel guns — their loud roar impressed the natives. De Peyster expected Bennett to obtain any additional provisions from traders.[32]

Upon reaching Grand Portage, Lieutenant Bennett, assisted by traders, constructed a small fortification. Askin had previously ordered Joseph Beausoleil, his agent, to erect a house with a chimney for the soldiers to use until they built their own. The Northwest Company furnished two hundred fourteen-foot pickets.[33] Bennett paid £306/13/4 to Pierre La Oaseur and L'Chandonet to cut, saw, and square 950 thick planks, 950 deals [pine boards], and four hundred timbers.[34] During the summer's brief stay, Bennett's men completed about half of the fort's buildings and furnishings.[35]

At the end of each day the fragile bark canoes had to be patched with pitch.

Shortly after Bennett's departure for Grand Portage, conflicting reports from the east troubled Michilimackinac. One account was that General Clinton had won a great victory and had killed General Gates and seven thousand men near Albany. The news that Canada had been spared from another invasion cheered sagging spirits.[36] Within a few days, however, word of General Burgoyne's defeat at Saratoga the previous October caused grave concern.[37]

De Peyster wondered what the Continental Congress might be planning next. He had good cause to worry. On May 19 the Board of War wrote General Washington about plans to attack Detroit or the Indian country. Three weeks later Congress resolved, "That an expedition be immediately undertaken, whose object shall be, to reduce, if practicable, the garrison of Detroit, and to compel to terms of peace such of the Indian nations now in arms against these states as lie on, or contiguous to, the route betwixt Fort Pitt and Detroit." Congress' wrath was directed particularly against Henry Hamilton, whom they accused of prosecuting a cruel war "with unrelenting perserverance."[38] Congress' designs threatened Michilimackinac.

Throughout June and July, John Askin struggled to fulfill his contractual obligations. On June 2 he dispatched to Grand Portage most of Charles Chaboillez's goods, lacking only rum and flour.[39] Several days later Askin received a requisition from Madam Chaboillez in Montreal asking that an additional twelve bags of corn and twelve barrels of rum be sent to her husband.[40] When Askin's vessel came from Detroit on June 30, he ordered it to the Sault with all Chaboillez's rum and flour on board except that recently requested by his wife.[41]

Askin, with "positive contracts" for over twenty thousand pounds, was not the only trader in dire need of flour. Major De Peyster realized the problem and again wrote to Hamilton pointing out the critical shortage at Michilimackinac and requested that more than fifteen thousand pounds be sent. Because much of the King's flour was already spoiled, Deputy Commissary Askin had baked two thousand pounds of his own into bread for the use of his household and the officers. Hopefully a good grain crop in Canada would provide sufficient amounts. If not, hunger was certain.[42]

During the third week in June large freight canoes from Montreal finally appeared on the northeastern horizon. Askin reported to Todd & McGill that most articles arrived in good shape with a few exceptions. He complained that they sent him "the most common sorts of green Tea," which was not what he wanted. Packed in a paper bale, it had been battered into powder. In addition, the stroud was of poor quality.[43] Inferior goods hurt trade.

During the winter the soldiers' uniforms had worn thin, and they needed waistcoats and breeches. Askin ordered six or eight yards of "fine white cloth" with suitable trimmings to be sent as soon as possible. For buttons, he specified "plain double gilt with Eyes if to be had," otherwise ivory, but he preferred the eyes "as they can be taken off when washing."[44]

To expedite movement of goods to Grand Portage, Askin planned to build a storehouse near the mouth of the French River on Lake Huron. He planned to send an Englishman to manage it, but he instructed Todd & McGill to make invoices for each package in both English and French. At this new depot everything was to be examined before shipment further northwest. Because of the shorter trip, Todd & McGill would only have to hire voyageurs to go to Lake Huron; from here Askin's men could do the remaining work.[45]

Askin was frustrated by Hamilton's policies. Though Askin sent his own vessel to Detroit, he received no preference in shipping. When the *Archange* drew up alongside the wharf, the Crown's cargo was loaded first. Askin's captain pointed out to the Lieutenant Governor that the vessel was not in the service and was "not subject to carry for every person." Hamilton disagreed and ordered other traders' bags and barrels put on board. Alarmed by this, Askin notified the Northwest Company: "I nor no other person in these troublesome times can assure you about Provisions, or anything Else . . ."[46]

Askin seriously considered changing his mode of business. Reluctantly he concluded that no more contracts should be made until the war ended because of the risk of non-delivery. New customers would only be taken on a commission basis.[47]

Despite transportation and supply problems, trade expanded in 1778. At least 128 canoes made the thousand mile trip to Michilimackinac with fifty-four going to Grand Portage or points beyond Lake Superior. In addition, nineteen batteaux, sixteen of them Askin's, brought goods to Michilimackinac.[48]

There was one improvement in the management of the trade this year. Askin initiated an ordinance, signed by all the merchants, requiring engagés to live up to their agreements. No one could hire a man who had not received "a proper discharge" from his former employer or a certificate signed by De Peyster explaining why he had none. All the Michilimackinac traders also agreed to refrain from transporting debtors who were not their employees.[49]

Askin had some questions about whether he, a servant of the Crown, could sell his own goods to the government for profit. As Deputy Commissary, he supplied the garrison with provisions. Some of them came out of his warehouse, but was this ethical? Writing to Sampson Fleming, his counterpart at Detroit, Askin argued that there was no reason why he should not make money from his sales. Since the pay he and Fleming received as Commissaries was inadequate to support their families, any profit made without neglecting their duty was proper. As long as they provided merchandise at the same rate as other merchants, Major De Peyster agreed with this policy.

Askin was responsible for overseeing large quantities of military provisions. In 1778 alone the Michilimackinac garrison received 82,848 pounds of flour, 46,700 pounds of pork, 4,288 pounds of butter, 5,745 pounds of oatmeal, 544 bushels of peas, and 150 gallons of vinegar. Packed in barrels, these supplies were shipped in batteaux from La Chine and by ship on the lakes.[50]

John Askin not only traded merchandise and furs, but he also bought and sold black and Indian slaves. During June, 1778 his transactions resulted in new homes and owners for at least three people. He arranged for the mulatto woman belonging to Philip Dejean at Detroit to work in William Monforton's house.[51] On June 8 Askin sold Barthe's Indian slave to Mr. Lavoine for 750 livres, describing him as "too stupid to make a sailor or to be any good whatever."[52] When an unfortunate Indian boy, rumored to be the son of Charles Patterson residing in Montreal, was sold to the Ottawa, Askin got the lad by promising to give the Ottawa an "Indian Woman Slave in his Stead." Not knowing Patterson's designs for the boy, Askin offered to care for him until he could "earn his own Bread without Assistance."[53] Earlier Askin had asked Joseph Beausoleil at Grand Portage to purchase for him "two pretty panis girls of from 9 to 16 years of age."[54]

Askin relied on his two black slaves, Jupiter Wendell and Pompey, to whom he had acquired full title in 1775.[55] Both these men had grown up near Albany, New York before Askin brought them west. During the winter months Jupiter, a skilled cooper, fashioned many of the wooden barrels used by Askin. Both men were competent sailors and regularly manned the *Mackinac* and the *De Peyster*. Askin entrusted them with many responsible tasks on his farm, in construction, and in his trading activities. They were his most trusted and dependable hands.

Cast iron kettle.

A Chippewa family travelling with all their possessions. Drawn by Peter Rindisbacher

Indian affairs occupied much of Major De Peyster's time. On May 29 he dispatched 110 warriors to Montreal and within a few days he planned to send a party of Ottawa. He expected Charles Langlade and Charles Gautier to bring several hundred warriors from Wisconsin.[56] All traders were ordered to carry two or three Indians in each canoe if Langlade or Gautier so requested.[57] But the Menominee near La Baye had lost two chiefs in battle with the Chippewa and were in no mind to follow Langlade.[58] This not only frustrated Langlade, but impeded the trade at La Baye.

During the third week of June, De Peyster welcomed Langlade and Gautier and their force of several hundred western warriors. Gautier, after much hard work, had enlisted 210 braves from the Sioux, Sac, Fox, and Winnebago tribes. A number of Menominee also joined them. These Indians camped along the beach where De Peyster fed them and distributed presents and munitions. Preparing for their mission, warriors, painted in a wide variety of designs, danced around their campfires and sang their war songs long into the night. With relief, the Major saw them off on Wednesday, June 24. Nearly 550 men had gone from Michilimackinac to fight in Canada in less than a month.[59]

Ironically, British officials in Canada did not know how to deploy this large force. After extending courtesies and expressions of gratitude, they sent most of the Indians home.[60] This expedition brought Britain no military advantage, but its cost was high.

The increasing expense of recruiting Indian auxiliaries, paying them, and providing for their families troubled De Peyster. On July 6 he drew on Todd & McGill for £4,486/5/4½ New York Currency to cover the expenses of Langlade and Gautier. Total drafts for the Indian Department through early July totalled £18,879/13/9 New York Currency,[61] including Langlade's 10s per day salary and the 5s per day given to Gautier.[62]

On June 29 De Peyster begged Carleton "for leave of absence for me, my health being so much impaired by the constant attendance I am obliged to give the Indians that at times I suffer the greatest torture . . . ." Particularly troublesome at this time was the bitter hostility between the Menominee and the Chippewa. Even though he knew better, De Peyster claimed that a person who had "any degree of patience" could learn to please the Indians "without any very extraordinary expence to the Government." Because of illness, he was unable to give as much attention to the Indians as he believed necessary.[63] De Peyster drove himself to exhaustion to keep the peace, and as Rebecca had feared, his body was not as strong as his devotion to duty.

It was now almost three years since Father Gibault had visited Michilimackinac. Lack of spiritual ministry was evident and "profaneness and impiety" ran rampant throughout the settlement. Seventy-two concerned citizens petitioned General Carleton to send a priest, and each pledged financial support for the missionary. John Askin made the largest contribution of three hundred livres while John Macnamara donated one hundred, Etienne Campion fifty, Laurent Du Charme eighteen, and Jean Baptiste Datien six livres, respectively. Dr. David Mitchell agreed "to furnish the necessary attention & remedies gratis," and even Ezekiel Solomon, though a Jew, subscribed fifty livres.[64]

De Peyster endorsed the idea, but had one reservation which he asked Carleton to keep confidential. Since the Church of Ste. Anne was located inside the fort, "Many Ignorant Canoesmen and Savages" would have free access to it. He proposed the church be moved into the suburbs because in the event of a "French War," these potentially hostile people could endanger the garrison's security.[65]

VII.

Fire in Illinois

MERSEYSIDE COUNTY MUSEUM

A traveler passing through Michilimackinac in mid-August brought John Askin a letter from Richard McCarty, a trader in the Illinois country. Askin read the alarming news of rebel advances in Illinois. "Was there a few Troops here to encourage the Good, put heart in the weak and intimedate the bad, this Country might be preserved . . ." mourned McCarty. The rebels were active on the Ohio and Mississippi Rivers, stealing furs and slaves from English subjects, and collaborating with the Spanish.[1] Immediately Askin showed the message to the Commandant.

Deeply concerned, Major De Peyster forwarded this intelligence to the new Governor of Canada, 60-year-old, Swiss-born General Frederick Haldimand. De Peyster pointed out that others from Illinois had verified the increased rebel activities. Their reports were even more frightening. It was widely rumored that the French were about to seize control of Kaskaskia and Cahokia. Since no British troops were stationed there, the Virginians could come unopposed. If that happened, the Americans would "poison the minds of the Indians" making it dangerous for English traders.[2]

Unknown to De Peyster, these prophesies had already been fulfilled. In late June the Virginian Colonel George Rogers Clark left Kentucky with a force of about 175 men intent on capturing the Illinois towns. On July 4 his army entered Kaskaskia without a struggle and made Philip Rocheblave a prisoner. Clark then directed his attention

George Rogers Clark

to Cahokia and Vincennes. Captain Joseph Bowman and sixty men marched to Cahokia and encountered no resistance. Pleased to discover that Father Pierre Gibault favored the American cause, Clark sent the priest, Dr. Jean B. Laffont, and others to convince the citizens of Vincennes to swear allegiance to Virginia. This mission, too, was accomplished without violence, and Captain Leonard Helm remained to command the settlement. Before the end of July, Illinois was in American hands.

Clark's conquest was made easier because of the alliance France signed in February, 1778 with the rebelling colonies. Clark capitalized on French loyalties in Illinois. Perhaps he could win the support of all the French speaking people in the Great Lakes region and rekindle Indian allegiance to the French.

To maintain control of Illinois, Clark had to persuade the Indians living from the Wabash and Illinois Rivers northward to Lake Michigan to abandon their support of the British and remain neutral. Having few or no presents to give, he chided warriors who fought for hire. Now that the French had joined the American cause, Clark urged the Indians to follow their old friends and allies. In council the Virginian exaggerated the rebels' power, to impress upon the natives that the English were doomed. Chief Black Bird of the Potawatomi living along southwestern Lake Michigan was most receptive to Clark's appeal. Black Bird believed that the English feared the Indians and gave lavish presents only to keep them on their side.

Clark boasted, "The British interest daily lost ground." Soon the nations living as far north as the St. Joseph River and the southern rim of Lake Michigan took heed of Clark's exhortations. British influence had suffered a serious setback.[3]

Monday, August 31, began as an ordinary day at Michilimackinac. Despite the early morning chill the rising sun illuminated the sleepy community as it stirred. A few Indians and voyageurs on the beach kindled their fires, and the smell of cooking fish filled the air. The musicians beat reveille summoning the troops, who stumbled from their bunks onto the parade ground. Major De Peyster received the morning roll call and issued his orders for the day. He returned to his quarters for a meal of bread, whitefish, fresh squash, and coffee. As he entered the room, Rebecca greeted him and quietly they sat down to eat. Now that most of the pressing Indian diplomacy was over for another season, the Major felt a little better and his appetite improved accordingly. Still, unsettling reports from Illinois were on his mind, and he was unable to concentrate on his wife's conversation.

Following breakfast he planned to meet with John Askin to get a first-hand account of the garrison's provisions. As he strode across the Rue Dauphine toward the King's storehouse, a courier dashed up to him with an urgent message from Louis Chevallier at St. Joseph. "The rebels are in possession of all the Illinois," De Peyster read, "The Traders in that Country and many from this Post are plundered and the whole country in the greatest confusion being at a loss to know which route the rebels will take next."[4]

Momentarily numbed, De Peyster summoned Askin from the storehouse to tell him the news. Then he returned to his quarters to compose a letter to General Haldimand in Quebec informing him of this disaster. Haldimand, however, had already learned of Clark's mischief.[5] Even though Haldimand knew little about the inhabitants in Illinois or the country itself, he had already authorized Henry Hamilton at Detroit to take whatever steps he deemed necessary to "clear all the Illinois of these Invaders."[6]

Hamilton lost no time making preparations to re-establish British rule. Traders heading for the Mississippi were recalled.[7] Then he organized an expedition of thirty-three British regulars, two officers, two milita companies, ten Indian Department officers, three artillerymen, and seventy Indians. They planned to leave Detroit in late

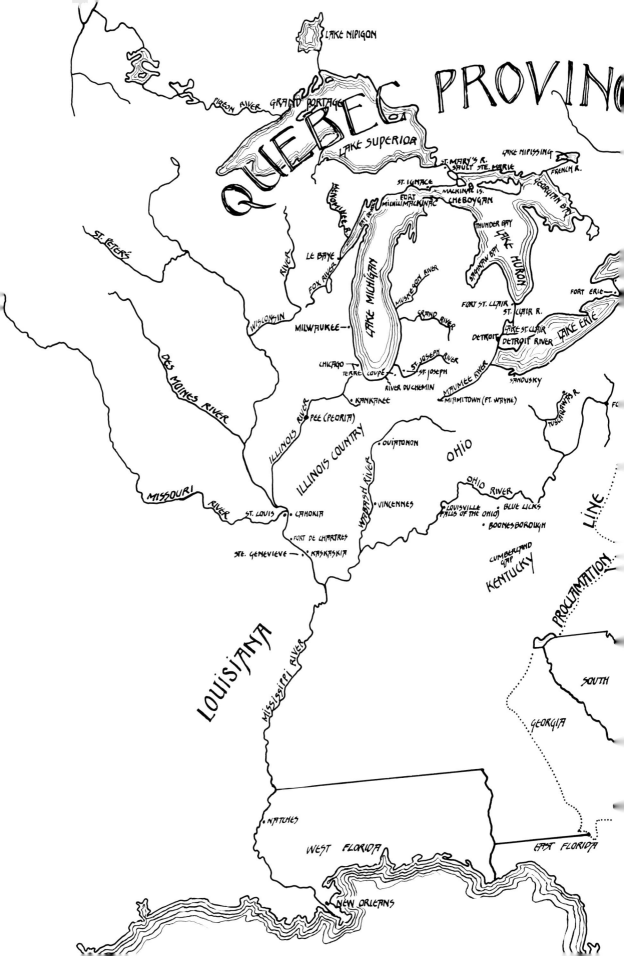

General Frederick Haldimand, Governor of Canada

September for the Maumee River, traverse the portage leading to the Wabash River, and head down to Vincennes. Before he departed, Hamilton asked De Peyster for Indians to assist by way of the Illinois River. Hamilton also requested Louis Chevallier at St. Joseph to encourage the Potawatomi to cooperate.[8]

But Hamilton did not have "the least confidence" in Chevallier, and he suspected him of allowing some Potawatomi to go to Illinois to meet rebels and Spaniards.[9] In reality Chevallier had actually used his influence to block this meeting in late July before word of Clark's victories was received.[10] Despite his reservations, Hamilton recognized one important fact — if he wanted anything from the St. Joseph Potawatomi, he had to work through Louis Chevallier.

After Clark's conquest of Illinois, Hamilton became suspicious of nearly everyone — and with good cause. He believed that not one in twenty French inhabitants at Detroit were loyal to Britain and that most so-called English traders were "rebels in their hearts."[11] Since Clark had designs on Detroit, the dependability of the local French population was critical.[12] In September, 1778 it seemed clear that Clark must be defeated if Detroit and Michilimackinac were to remain under the Red Ensign.

Clark's successes forced De Peyster to use every means at his disposal to keep the Indians in line. It was imperative that warriors be sufficiently rewarded to insure their assistance in the struggle against the Virginians. De Peyster's first concern was to satisfy La Fourche's Ottawa, who were returning from their summer expedition to Montreal.[13]

When they arrived, La Fourche and his men were in rags, and their canoes battered. Pointing to his men, the Chief pleaded with De Peyster for new clothes, blankets, rum, tobacco, and ammunition. They had given over three months of service and now demanded compensation. At least half their muskets required repair at the blacksmith's shop or needed replacement. De Peyster agreed and doled out a large quantity of merchandise.[14]

Before La Fourche had time to count the blankets, De Peyster spoke firmly. The Major warned that while the rebels might have a "shew of presents" now, they could not provide all his village's needs. Only his British father had the wealth and the means to produce and deliver sufficient goods. If La Fourche joined the rebels, the Major warned that he would stop the canoes next spring at the French River and order their packs and kegs back to Montreal.[15] Collaboration with the enemy would bring harsh penalties. Failure to fight for the King would deprive the Ottawa of the munitions and trade goods so essential for their survival.

An Ottawa warrior and his family

COURTAULD INSTITUTE OF ART

An uneasy awareness of his vulnerability, hundreds of miles from reinforcements, motivated De Peyster to present a hard line. Clark's presence in Illinois suddenly brought the war close to home. Traders from Michilimackinac regularly went to Kaskaskia, so the route was familiar. Chevallier's warning, "The Rebels intend to go to your fort for breakfast in the Spring,"[16] sent a chill down the Major's spine. He must do all in his power to prevent Clark's advance.

In mid-September De Peyster sent a messenger, bearing a large wampum belt, to the Illinois nations. He told the Indians, with all the force of a large belt, that the King would drive his foes out of their lands. He also reminded them of his previous efforts in negotiating a peace with their dreaded enemy, the Ottawa, and hoped that they would abandon their present affection for the Virginians.[17]

De Peyster next tried to enlist direct support for Hamilton's expedition to Vincennes. La Fourche and the Indians near Michilimackinac were preparing to go to their winter grounds, and they were reluctant to leave their families during their hunting season.[18] Nevertheless, De Peyster ordered Charles Langlade to visit the Ottawa and Chippewa winter lodges from the Grand River to St. Joseph. Charles Gautier and Joseph Louis Ainsse accompanied him to St. Joseph to enlist Chevallier's assistance in raising some Potawatomi braves to join Langlade's Indians. They hoped to take the shortest route to Illinois to second Hamilton's operations.

De Peyster's plan came to naught. Most of the Ottawa refused Langlade's appeal, citing "want of previous notice," but declared they would join an operation in the spring. Remarkably, eighty warriors did take up the hatchet. Bad weather prevented Langlade, Gautier, and Ainsse from reaching St. Joseph until December 2. There they learned from Chevallier that Hamilton's army had passed more than a hundred miles to the south. Langlade's Indians refused to go any further and the expedition dissolved.[19] Disappointed, the three men returned to Michilimackinac enroute to their winter posts.

Musket and tomahawk were the primary weapons in frontier warfare.

A war chief returns from a successful raid carrying a scalp.

VIII.

Fearful Times

Cufflinks

The wedding of Charles Gautier and Magdeleine Chevallier, daughter of the late Pascal Chevallier and Magdeleine Larcheveque, welcomed in the New Year, 1779. At the Chevallier's house, before friends and family Charles and Magdeleine exchanged their vows without benefit of clergy. Notary Monsieur Carignon ratified both the ceremony and the formal agreement between the bride and groom, which would be confirmed when a priest returned.[1]

In their marriage contract the couple carefully spelled out the disposition of their possessions. Magdeleine's inheritance was to become common property to be enjoyed by both. To prove his "great affection" for her, Charles endowed his bride with one thousand ecus. Pledging to live in harmony until death, they specified "that their Property be possessed with full and entire enjoyment by the survivor after the demise of either of them, and by these presents they set aside all claims and pretensions that may be set up by their own children, . . ." if they should be so blessed. If the surviving partner remarried, he or she was to provide proper inheritance for the children. If they were childless, the survivor was free to administer the estate "without being molested by the relatives of either family."[2] Apparently unaffected by this document were Gautier's three previous children by his Winnebago wife.[3]

Only a few days after the wedding Gautier slid his canoe into the freezing lake and paddled westward towards the Mississippi country. The necessities of war permitted only a brief honeymoon. Gautier had to organize the Sac, Fox, and Winnebago to be ready to fight in the spring.[4]

Far to the south Louis Chevallier at St. Joseph used his persuasive powers to entice the Potawatomi to join the British forces. Despite his best efforts he found it virtually impossible "to keep this nation in dependence." The Potawatomi lived in six villages scattered fifteen or twenty miles apart, and each local chief influenced his braves according to his own ideas. This winter they listened to rebel speeches and were deaf to the King's words.[5]

PUBLIC ARCHIVES OF CANADA

Indian encampment drawn by George Heriot

In late March De Peyster received an express from Captain Richard Lernoult, Commandant at Detroit, informing him that an American attack on Detroit appeared likely. De Peyster urged the Ottawa wintering at the Grand River to go directly to Detroit. He also dispatched Chief Matchekewis and his band of Chippewa from Thunder Bay to Detroit to encourage the tribes there and to defend the settlement if necessary. With danger so imminent, De Peyster felt it wiser to keep these warriors nearby rather than send them to assist Hamilton at Vincennes.[6]

On April 24 De Peyster learned that Hamilton and his men had been captured by the Virginians.[7] Hamilton had seized Vincennes from the rebels on December 17 and had decided to winter there, leaving the conquest of Kaskaskia and Cahokia till spring. Undeterred by winter, George Rogers Clark decided to surprise Hamilton and retake this vital post. Leading his force of 170 men from Kaskaskia across ice, snow, mud, and swollen streams, Clark took Vincennes on February 25. Hamilton and his seventy-nine man garrison were taken prisoner. Hamilton was sent to Williamsburg, Virginia, where he languished in jail for nearly sixteen months. Upon the success or failure of such small bands of dedicated men the fate of the Upper Great Lakes depended.

At Detroit shortages were severe and inflation rampant. Large numbers of cattle had been supplied to Hamilton and many more had been fed to Indians and soldiers during the winter. Cows and pigs were slaughtered because of the lack of beef and salt pork. A pair of oxen was selling for at least a thousand livres and one hundred pounds of flour for sixty livres.[8]

Of great concern was the pro-rebel attitude of the French residents. Hamilton's earlier opinion was shared by Lernoult who felt the Canadians were all rebels, and that due to British reversals they would not assist in Detroit's defense.[9]

Because of Hamilton's disaster, it was likely that no trade canoes would be allowed out of Montreal this year. James Bannerman in Montreal noted on April 22 that Haldimand probably would not grant licenses at least until favorable intelligence was received from Detroit.[10] Since traders to Grand Portage normally began leaving in late April, the outlook for 1779 was bleak. Furthermore, Haldimand planned to deal severely with anyone who went without permission.

Joseph Howard was usually one of the first traders to head for Lake Superior. Unable to secure a license, he left Montreal on May 6 without one. Angered by this blatant disregard for governmental rules, Haldimand ordered De Peyster to seize Howard's goods and canoes when

INDIANA HISTORICAL SOCIETY LIBRARY

Lieutenant Governor Henry Hamilton surrenders to George Rogers Clark

he showed up at Michilimackinac. If Detroit was safe at the time, De Peyster was directed to send Howard's goods there, where commissioners of peace could dispose of them. Any other traders arriving at Michilimackinac without a pass were to be similarly treated.[11]

To insure that De Peyster had sufficient Indian presents, Haldimand ordered Lieutenant Colonel John Campbell, Superintendent of Indian Affairs for Quebec, to send an adequate supply to Michilimackinac. In mid-May canoes left Montreal, and their cargo included sufficient deerskins to make moccasins for the Indians employed in the King's service.[12] Ships from England were expected shortly; then more Indian presents would be forwarded. In addition, a large quantity of rum was to be shipped via Detroit. De Peyster was not to make purchases from local merchants because they charged exhorbitant prices. But the Governor did not want Indian diplomacy interrupted by this economy.[13]

While De Peyster awaited these presents, he had to face the tribes, who were aware of Hamilton's humiliating defeat. Rumors troubled all the people at Michilimackinac — British, French, and Indian. On May 2 some Indian women reported that the Virginians were constructing boats at Milwaukee and had sent wampum belts to the Chippewa and Ottawa at Grand River asking them to remain neutral until Michilimackinac was captured. These two tribes were reported to have accepted this request, and Chief Black Bird was said to have left Milwaukee with the first division of attackers.[14] Several days later the Chippewa who summered on Mackinac Island came in from the Grand River and charged that all these rumors were "the invention of some evil minded Indians." De Peyster was relieved that the Chippewa and Ottawa remained loyal.[15]

During the middle of May De Peyster learned that his Indian allies were wavering under the impact of Hamilton's defeat. Langlade had organized a party of La Baye warriors to assist Hamilton. But when they reached Milwaukee and heard of rebel successes, they became discouraged and went no further. Likewise, Gautier raised 280 Winnebago, Menominee, Sac, Fox, and Chippewa braves to descend the Mississippi. When they were a few days from Cahokia, they learned of Hamilton's capture and refused to continue. The Sac and Fox insolently laughed at De Peyster's threat to stop the trade canoes from Montreal. "The cunning of those Indians now appears to be such that they want to lay both sides under contributions," reasoned the Major, "Nothing can be expected from the Indians without a strong body of Troops to lead them."[16] Fortunately, despite the defection of the Sac and Fox, the Winnebago and Menominee still pledged their fidelity.[17]

De Peyster dreaded the arrival of the Chippewa and Ottawa for he could barely tolerate their incessant demands. His temper grew short as he was "pulled to pieces by the Indians." Compounding his agony was lack of word from Detroit. He needed to know what was going on there.[18]

De Peyster pled with Haldimand to station armed ships at Michilimackinac. Although the Governor had authorized a vessel the previous winter, none had come yet.[19] If he had sailing vessels, De Peyster wanted to send them along Lake Michigan's coast to "awe the

A warrior on the warpath

Indians" and destroy any rebel boat building. There was a small sloop at Michilimackinac, but she had no crew. Having less than half the soldiers necessary to defend the fort, De Peyster did not dare detach any of them to man the sloop.

De Peyster vowed to protect Michilimackinac with all the vigor his two undermanned companies could muster.[20] He was confident the Indians would "prove stauch" as would the French. He hoped the Canadians' economic ties to Montreal were stronger than any appeal that Clark might make.[21] If Clark came, De Peyster would resist stoutly.

Toward the end of May Charles Gautier returned to Michilimackinac with the Winnebago and Menominee warriors who remained from his Mississippi expedition. Major De Peyster tried to keep them at Michilimackinac, but they feared that the Sac and Chippewa of the Plains might raid their villages during their absence. De Peyster could not hold them. They left promising to go to Kaskaskia and bring back prisoners. To prevent unnecessary bloodshed, De Peyster forbade them to take any scalps.

One of De Peyster's most vexing problems was to gain the simultaneous support of the Sioux and the Chippewa, who had a long tradition of hatred and war. The son of the great Sioux Chief Wabasha, along with Joseph Rocque, an Interpreter, and some young warriors came to council with De Peyster. They reported that Wabasha had led a war party to join Hamilton, however, at Prairie du Chien when they learned of his misfortune they turned back. The Sioux leader now asked if he should punish the Sac and Fox for listening to the rebels and aborting Gautier's mission. Wabasha was ready to strike any enemies of the King. But inter-tribal warfare was the last thing De Peyster wanted. Even now he feared that several hundred Chippewa were about to attack Wabasha's Sioux in retaliation for the deaths of some Chippewa by Sioux hands.

As tokens of his appreciation for the Sioux's fidelity, De Peyster gave them gunpowder and clothing and provided ample presents for the Winnebago and Menominee. These alliances were essential, for if these nations remained loyal, the British could count on them to resist rebel propaganda and incursions. De Peyster ordered Rocque to accompany the Sioux on their return. He also sent Jean Marie Calvé to the Sac and Fox, believing that because he had married a Fox woman, he could have a positive influence on these fickle tribes.

Not having enough presents, munitions, and provisions to supply all these Indians, De Peyster was forced to purchase many items locally. The canoes from Montreal had not yet arrived, and he urgently needed to pacify and impress the Indians before the rebels did. The escalating cost of Indian diplomacy bothered him, but what could he do?

Langlade and Gautier stayed for a time at Michilimackinac. Both were impatient to be out with an expeditionary force, but De Peyster felt raiding parties unaccompanied by regular troops were of no value. Unable to spare any men, he kept his two top Indian officers with him. Living on their government pay, they were appalled by expenses at Michilimackinac. They complained to De Peyster that they could not "live at this Extravagent place upon their allowance having a constant run of Indians who snatch the bread out of their mouths."[22]

Indian encampment on Lake Huron drawn by Paul Kane.

Michilimackinac from the air.

De Peyster was hampered by the uncertainty of communications between Michilimackinac and Detroit and Quebec. Haldimand, equally concerned, ordered Lieutenant Colonel Mason Bolton, Regimental Commander of the Eighth at Niagara, to send the Lake Erie vessels up Lake Huron to forge a link with Michilimackinac.[23] Any news regarding enemy motives, Indian inclinations, material needs, or public affairs were to be promptly relayed to other upper posts.[24] Yet communication remained slow. The fastest express took fifteen days to get from Michilimackinac to Montreal, and a loaded canoe took almost a month. Letters from the wilderness took weeks or longer unless sent by special courier. As a result, De Peyster was forced to make decisions based on old and frequently inaccurate information.

On June 14 De Peyster was relieved to learn from his wilderness informants that the rebels would not launch an attack on Michilimackinac. Clark had instead gone to Natchez in an effort to relieve his convoys which had been intercepted.[25] Two weeks later visitors from Illinois confirmed this intelligence. De Peyster was also pleased that rebel leaders, lacking presents, were trying to intimidate the Indians in their councils.[26]

When Joseph Howard's two canoes arrived from Montreal on June 9, De Peyster sent a guard to summon Howard to his office to present his pass. Howard could produce none, and the Major ordered his soldiers to confiscate Howard's arms, munitions, and liquor. After drying out his wet packs, he surrendered them to the Commandant who locked them in the King's storehouse. Howard, a wily trader, had not brought all his canoes. Two had been sent directly to Grand Portage and De Peyster was unable to stop them.

Howard himself was sent back to Montreal. William Grant, John Kay, and David McCrae posted a bond guaranteeing his appearance there on June 30. When the case finally came to trial the following March, Howard was found guilty and fined £50.[27]

De Peyster worried about the lack of edible food for the soldiers. He hardly dared issue their ration of salt pork, which appeared so "rusty" that half of it had to be thrown away.[28] The troops ate the best of the lot while the worst was "reserved" for Indians. De Peyster personally supervised the dispensing of food to Indians to ensure that nothing was wasted.[29]

If the men were to be fed properly, adequate provisions had to be sent up from Detroit. Though some fish were caught to supplement the diet, most of the catch was fed to Indians. One rarely saw wild game around the fort, and Indians seldom brought in any animals to trade. The previous year they traded less than five carcasses. De Peyster complained that after the war started, the natives became "very idle, even in the hunting season." As a result, all the Indians who lived within fifty or sixty miles of the fort came to him for food. Starvation was averted only by tons of maple sugar produced each spring.[30]

Throughout the summer the government officials in Quebec strove to procure adequate stores. Their goal was to have at least two years supply on hand at Michilimackinac. It was frustrating work; this year's flour had been damaged by being "put up warm." Consequently, it had to be spread over a large room, dried for two or three days, and then repacked before shipment.[31]

Due to the increased tempo of military activity, the provisions shipped for 1779 were increased nearly fifty percent. Six hundred Canadian casks of flour weighing approximately 210 pounds each totalled 123,161 pounds, three hundred barrels of pork totalled 62,608 pounds. Michilimackinac also received 5,704 pounds of butter packed in ninety-two firkins and 162 tierces of peas containing 732 bushels. Only the quantity of vinegar remained about the same — 142 gallons in two barrels. To add to this De Peyster purchased all the Indian corn he could find in case some was needed at Detroit or even at Niagara. He hoped all this food was useable and would end the shortages.[32] As usual, the rum supply was inadequate.[33]

"The Welcome"

De Peyster's demand for an armed ship finally resulted in permission to purchase a sailing vessel to be stationed at Michilimackinac. Long covetous of John Askin's sloop *Welcome,* the Major offered Askin a fair price for her. On June 27 the two friends drew up the papers transferring ownership to the government for £900.[34] Askin hated to give up his sloop, but since she was already sailing under government direction, he had not really controlled her for the last year.

The "Welcome" under sail drawn recently by David Morehardt.

Having his own vessel at his beck and call made De Peyster feel a little more secure. All the other ships were being kept busy on Lake Erie, and as late as July 21 only the *Welcome* had dropped anchor in front of Michilimackinac. De Peyster worried about danger from Lake Michigan, and now the *Welcome* could scout the situation there. He also could send her to Detroit to exchange correspondence, quell rumors, and keep his allies informed. In managing Indians De Peyster knew it was necessary "to hear often."[35]

Restless Indians wandering about Michilimackinac made De Peyster nervous, and he strictly forbade any Indian woman spending the night in the fort. Trader John Long, wanting "to introduce a great chief's daughter and her sister" inside the stockade, devised an ingenious plan to slip them past the sentry. He bored some holes in a large wine barrel; the girls crawled inside, then he replaced the lid. Two soldiers were persuaded to roll the cask towards the land gate from Chippewa Point, several hundred yards away. As they neared the entrance, they encountered Major De Peyster. When questioned, the soldiers told their Commandant they had "bottled porter for a trader." Just then one of the privates stubbed his toe, and the barrel rolled free. Suddenly the top popped off. The Indian girls tumbled out and dashed towards the woods.

Surprised, De Peyster chortled, "Pretty bottled porter indeed." Returning to his quarters he summoned Long, who was living with an Indian family at the Point. Sternly the Major scolded Long and threatened to put him in irons and send him to Montreal. Fully aware of his impropriety, Long admitted his guilt and apologized, begging for a pardon. De Peyster released the frightened trader after admonishing him to never commit such chicanery again. As the door slammed behind Long, De Peyster flashed a wide grin. Though Long had flagrantly violated his orders, the Commandant respected his imagination.[36]

Indian women were often very alluring to lonely soldiers and traders.

By June 20 De Peyster concluded the rebels were not coming to Michilimackinac by way of Chicago. Rather the chief threat was a possible Indian attack. Consequently he strengthened his defenses. He purchased two houses built close outside the fort walls, tore them down so that they could not shelter attackers, and salvaged the lumber. The troops cut logs over twenty feet long to replace the rotten pickets in the palisade. As an added precaution, De Peyster erected a stockade around the barracks. The soldiers also built a banquette which enabled them to fire from an elevated position through the loopholes in the fort stockade. For days twelve men calloused their hands as they leveled sand dunes which had blown in close to the fort. To their dismay, strong winds often undid their work by blowing the sand into new hills.[37]

Despite the flurry of construction, De Peyster realized the inadequacy of his small garrison. To protect the vast region of the Upper Great Lakes and to man the fourteen hundred feet of fort walls during an attack, De Peyster had only eighty men, including himself. His post return for July 1 showed: [38]

Majors — 1	Rank and file fit for duty — 62
Lieutenants — 3	Sick in quarters — 3
Adjutant — 1	Sick in hospital — 1
Mate — 1	Recruits not yet joined — 1
Sergeants — 4	Total rank and file — 67
Drummers — 1	
Royal Artillery — 2 (1 bombardier and 1 matross)	

Short of men, De Peyster decided not to send a detachment to Grand Portage this year.[39]

IX.

De Peyster Takes
the Offensive

In late June De Peyster learned that the Americans were on the move. It was reported that Godefroy de Linctot, a trader, had enlisted a force at Cahokia to advance to the Pee [Peoria] and on to Ouiatonon. There Linctot was to join an army of fifteen hundred men coming from Vincennes and strike at Detroit. Other intelligence indicated that some Indians had surprised the Virginians at Vincennes and had captured their munitions and provisions.[1] Despite conflicting stories, De Peyster was certain that George Rogers Clark was headed for Detroit. Something must be done to stop him.

De Peyster was glad that he had kept his most trusted Indian agents at Michilimackinac. On June 28 he sent Charles Gautier and a few Indians to burn the small fort at the Pee and if possible capture Linctot. This would show the enemy that the Indians remained loyal to the British and were ready to go on the warpath.[2] Four days later the Major summoned Charles Langlade to recruit warriors from L'Arbre Croche and nations living along the western shore of Lake Michigan. He was to lead his men south to Chicago and join the troops De Peyster would send down the eastern shore of Lake Michigan under Lieutenant Thomas Bennett on a march into Illinois.[3]

Before Langlade and Bennett could get underway, De Peyster received new intelligence. Supposedly seven hundred rebels from Illinois were coming up the Wabash and Miami Rivers to attack Detroit. They were to join Linctot, who was leading two hundred cavalrymen by way of St. Joseph. Believing this report had merit, De Peyster detached Lieutenant Bennett with twenty soldiers, two hundred Indians, and about sixty traders and militiamen to St. Joseph to intercept Linctot. The *Welcome* followed them, carrying their provisions.[4]

By deploying almost one-third of his garrison De Peyster seriously weakened his defenses, but he knew that if Detroit fell, so would Michilimackinac. He realized that his information might be false, but even so he thought this show of force would encourage unreliable Indians, particularly the Potawatomi, to remain faithful to the Crown. In addition, this expedition would encourage Detroit.[5]

Detroit needed encouragement. In June at a large Indian council the Ottawa, Chippewa, and Potawatomi declared themselves ready to accommodate the Virginians.[6] Fearful of Clark, Captain Lernoult had constructed a new and stronger fort during the winter. But even this did not guarantee security.

De Peyster used his own prestige to enlist Indian support when he convened a great council of the western tribes at L'Arbre Croche on July 4. Around the council fire the solemn chiefs made an impressive appearance dressed in laced scarlet coats, feather plumed hats, with numerous silver gorgets hanging around their necks. Behind the chiefs stood the warriors each painted in his own individual design.

Standing, De Peyster spoke with animated gestures. Beside him
Joseph Louis Ainsse, the Interpreter, translated:[7]

MERSEYSIDE COUNTY MUSEUM

> "Great Chiefs, convened at my desire
> To kindle up this council fire,
> Which, with ascending smoke, shall burn
> Till you from war once more return,
> To lay the axe in earth so deep,
> That nothing shall disturb its sleep"

Continuing, De Peyster discounted rebel arguments:

> "The French, my sons, are not your friends,
> They only mean to serve their ends!
> In this alliance lately made,
> Their aim is our tobacco trade.
> I heard *Gebau* [Gibault] say, 'tis no sin
> to sell each pound, one otter-skin:
> This priest cares not how dear he sells,
> To those he styles poor infidels;
> The French, I say by this convention,
> To all this country wave pretension!
> See, here, I hold it in my hand,
> While Clark would have you understand,
> He only seeks to mount this bench —
> To counsel for his friends — the French;
> Who're still in hopes, ere long, to check,
> The British arms, — to storm Quebec,
> And seize the key of that great door,
> Through which all merchandize must pour;
> For, while Britannia rules the main,
> No goods can come from France or Spain.
> Be sure this part you well explain."

Wampum belt
(detail)

Then he called upon the nations to defeat Linctot at St. Joseph. He
reminded them of their willingness three years earlier to drive the
enemy from Montreal and their assistance to General Burgoyne in
1777. Telling them of rewards upon their return, De Peyster promised:

> "I saw each separate chief's provisions
> Divided, to prevent divisions
> Twixt the Ottowa and Chipp'wa nations,
> Long used to filch each other rations; —
> And now agree to the same thing,
> If you, my sons, will serve the king;"

Pleading with them to be their "father's faithful friends," De Peyster warned them not to take scalps. Prisoners could be taken and
brought to him, but their lives must be spared. After the council, some
Indians took up the hatchet and departed for St. Joseph.

Major De Peyster returned from the L'Arbre Croche council on July 6 just as the great Sioux Chief Wabasha arrived. As Wabasha's flotilla approached from the west, De Peyster ordered the artillerymen to fire the cannon. They did not shoot blanks as was the normal custom. Through the smoke young warriors could be seen waving their paddles at the bursting balls and shells flying over their canoes. On the beach local Ottawa and Chippewa and a few visiting Choctaw and Chickasaw shouted greetings. De Peyster in a loud voice proclaimed:[8]

"Hail to the chief! who his buffalo's back straddles,
When in his own country, far, far from this fort;
Whose brave young canoe-men, *here*, hold up their
    paddles,
In hopes that the whizzing balls may give them sport.
    Hail to great Wabashaw!
    Cannonier — fire away,
Hoist the fort-standard, and beat all the drums;
    Ottawa and Chippawa,
    Whoop! for great Wabashaw!
He comes — beat drums — the Scioux chief comes.

They now strain their nerves till the canoe runs bounding,
As swift as the Solen goose skims o'er the wave;
While, on the lake's border, a guard is surrounding
A space, where to land the great Scioux so brave.
    Hail to great Wabashaw!
    Soldiers your triggers draw,
Guard — wave the colours, and give him the drum!
    Chocktaw and Chickosaw
    Whoop! for great Wabashaw!
Raise the port-cullis! — the King's friend is come."

Stepping out of his canoe, Wabasha returned the salute. Standing near the Commandant, he fired his pistols. His ears still ringing, De Peyster led his faithful friend into the fort to council with him. Of all the Indians who called at Michilimackinac, De Peyster held Wabasha and his Sioux in the highest regard, and he was rewarded in turn with unwavering loyalty.

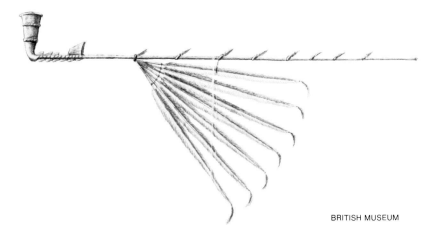

BRITISH MUSEUM

Chippewa Canoe drawn by Peter Rindisbacher

Threatening rebel advances put the fur trade in serious jeopardy, just as James Bannerman had predicted. In late May Haldimand allowed twenty canoes to leave Montreal destined for Lake Superior. He felt compelled to let the northwest traders take enough provisions and clothing to the wilderness to keep their employees alive and to prevent the trade from coming to a complete halt. Finally in July the Governor granted passes for forty-four more canoes.[9] As a precaution he directed De Peyster to stop the canoes at Michilimackinac if he felt it was in the King's interest that they go no further.[10]

To slow intense competition for limited trade goods, De Peyster proposed that traders pool their resources. On July 1 twenty-six merchants agreed to form a general store to function until July 31, 1780. The articles of agreement called for the partners to pool their merchandise and to abide by the company's decisions in conducting the Indian trade.[11] Those trading northwest of Lake Superior also joined together to share their trade goods and provisions.[12]

Throughout August De Peyster worried about the fate of the expedition to St. Joseph. He had good reason for concern. Lieutenant Bennett held a council on July 28 at St. Joseph with the Potawatomi and offered them the war hatchet. At first he pled with them, but this made little impression. Taking a stronger line, Bennett warned them that British officials would deal harshly with those who turned against their King, and threatened: "If I had not feared to show myself to you, do you fear what I will do to you?"[13]

Within days, however, all hope for enlisting the Potawatomi vanished. Petit Bled, Chief of the Nipicon Potawatomi, claimed he desired peace, but he "held sacred, the hatchet of his former father the French King & would never quit it, . . ." He also returned "the detested hatchet and Pipe, which were brought here only to render their Villages miserable, . . ."

The French-American alliance was having ominous effects upon the Great Lakes nations. Even the Ottawa Chief Quieouigoushkam (Kewigushum) from L'Arbre Croche, a long time ally of the English, began to waver. Intimidated by the Potawatomi, he explained to them that his people had been forced to accompany Bennett's mission. He remained in St. Joseph only to drink Bennett's rum. Nibeingushkam and "the old Grey headed Chippewa" left St. Joseph with their warriors complaining that De Peyster had "sent them naked from Michilimackinac."[14]

Meanwhile De Peyster received later reports of Clark's intentions. Still unaware of Bennett's difficulties, the Major confidently reported to Haldimand on August 9 that five hundred Indians had been recruited to stop the rebels headed for Detroit. To assist Bennett he sent the *Welcome* down Lake Michigan carrying Lieutenant Clowes, Matchekewis and ten warriors, and additional provisions.[15]

Bennett sent a letter to Captain Lernoult in Detroit informing him of his presence at St. Joseph. When Bennett received no word from Lernoult, he sent another messenger on August 15 with the report that the expedition would soon return to Michilimackinac. Supplies were running low, and there was no sign of the enemy. Bennett was upset with the Indians' behavior, but pleased that both the Canadian and English militiamen were in good spirits.[16]

Two days earlier Langlade had arrived at St. Joseph with twenty-one Canadians and sixty Indians. Originally his force included two hundred Indians, but word of the "French war" and the hostile Potawatomi caused most to leave. Only a few Chippewa remained and they had no muskets. When they demanded guns, rum, and provisions, Bennett, infuriated by their "haughty" manner, refused.[17]

As he waited at St. Joseph, Bennett sent Corporal Gascon and a few men to the River Du Chemin on the southern shore of Lake Michigan to arrest the pro-rebel, black trader Jean Baptiste Point du Sable. Gascon took Du Sable and seized his packs of trade goods and furs, but he did not burn Du Sable's house. Among his holdings was a supply of goods left by the trader Pierre Durand.[18] De Peyster would be pleased with the capture of this able man, whom he described as "A handsome negro, well educated (and settled at Eschecagou*); but much in the French interest."[19] Du Sable informed Bennett that Linctot and thirty Canadians had departed Peoria to join Clark.

In mid-August Bennett headed back toward Michilimackinac without receiving a message from Lernoult. Langlade remained at St. Joseph one day longer, then rejoined Bennett at the mouth of the St. Joseph River. Still there was no news from Detroit, so Bennett and his men proceeded up the coast by canoe.

Stone pipe carved in the shape of an Indian.
Excavated at Michilimackinac.

*Chicago

PUBLIC ARCHIVES OF CANADA

A North West canoe

Unexpectedly Bennett spotted the *Welcome* out in the lake sailing southward. Emanuel Hesse, a trader, paddled out to intercept her and learned from Lieutenant Clowes that sufficient provisions were on board for their party. Bennett's canoes turned around and headed back to the St. Joseph River to meet the *Welcome*. But when they arrived, they discovered the *Welcome* had already sailed. Disappointed, Bennett set up camp and ordered Langlade up river to St. Joseph to see if anything new had developed. Langlade returned with no news. After waiting 2½ days without sighting the *Welcome*, Bennett set out again for Michilimackinac.[20]

Major De Peyster and the garrison enthusiastically greeted Lieutenant Bennett and his tired men on September 1. Cannon boomed and a noisy crowd at the waterfront shouted and waved as the canoeists splashed up on the beach. Bennett reported to his Commander that both the Canadians and soldiers had displayed great zeal for the King's service. He then turned over Du Sable to the Major, who ordered him confined to the fort. De Peyster thanked the men for their devotion to duty, then he and Bennett entered the Commandant's quarters for a long talk.

De Peyster was disturbed by the behavior of the Potawatomi and the other nations. Particularly alarming was the wavering of the Ottawa from L'Arbre Croche, upon whom he had lavished so much time and so many presents. The faulty communication between Clowes and Bennett which prevented further operations was also upsetting. De Peyster felt that French influence among the Indians must be challenged whenever possible; it was a serious obstacle to British policy. Although Bennett's mission appeared to have been a failure, the Major believed that any show of strength by the British was beneficial. It was some consolation that the rebel sympathizer Du Sable would no longer be working among the Indians living along southern Lake Michigan.

Meanwhile George Rogers Clark, prevented by his lack of men to attack Detroit in 1779,[21] was amused by the futile expedition sent out from Michilimackinac. He believed American movements had so confused De Peyster that he sent Bennett to St. Joseph to chase away a foe that would never appear. Even more humiliating to the English was the refusal of the Indians to join their expedition. Clark boasted that this caused Bennett's retreat to Michilimackinac.[22] Though there was much truth in Clark's observations, Clark, himself, had little success with his own plans. Later in the fall when he proposed sending a detachment to capture Fort St. Joseph, he was unable to raise and to equip an adequate force.[23] Neither side had the strength nor the resources to defeat the other.

111

Sir John Caldwell dressed in a chief's finery

De Peyster received a welcome letter from Quebec in early August. After breaking the wax seal, he glanced at Governor Haldimand's words and excitedly summoned his wife. Rebecca's heart throbbed as she read that her husband would be transferred. Because there was great need for competent officers at the upper posts, he probably would go to Detroit, not New York as he wished. But at least they would be allowed to leave Michilimackinac. The new Commandant would be Lieutenant Governor Patrick Sinclair.[24]

The Indians were saddened by De Peyster's impending departure. Despite their sometimes ambivalent behavior, the Indians trusted and respected him. Before going to their wintering grounds, the Ottawa and Chippewa gathered at Michilimackinac. Around the council fire two Ottawa chiefs poured out their affections and repented of their erroneous deeds:[25]

Wax letter seal found at Michilimackinac

Chief Jinquis Tawanong rose and spoke solemnly through an interpreter:

"Father, — I rise to bid you farewell in the name of the Ottawa nation. I am likewise, to speak for the many strangers assembled at this council-fire — our old men, our wives and children, have hired me to speak for them likewise. It is with *my* tongue they bid you farewell, but it is with their own eyes they will weep your loss. They will stand upon the lakeside and strain their eyes until they can see your bark no more."

The Chief's aides brought De Peyster a present of 150 bags of maize and some packs of skins and furs.

"Father, — You must not look upon this trifling gift as a peace offering. It is a poor mark of our esteem and friendship for you. Every woman and child threw a dishfull, [A wooden vessel holding about a quart] that, in case you might still remain among us, it will help to feed your fowls and cattle. These robes [Blankets of soft dressed buffaloe, beaver, and martin skins] will clothe you and our mother from the chilling frost. These skins you will make into the shoes of our country-fashion — 'tis all your bare headed children have to offer except their tears."

Then Quieouigoushkam rose and spoke:

"Father, — I rise to speak in behalf of the Ottawas, and other nations present.

"Father, we cannot see you leave in anger, — that you have some cause I shall not pretend to deny; but we hope you will, after some days reflection, think us not altogether so much to blame as was at first reported of our conduct.

"When we returned from St. Joseph's, who dared to speak to you? You gave such killing looks, your eyes flashed fire.

"No one has seen you smile since. The father who used to meet *us* his children with open arms and with a smiling countenance has lately shunned us, or, if by accident any of us met him, gave us nothing but reproachful looks.

"At our first council we dared not look up to him, but silently took a reprimand. When we left this fort we were like wounded deer, — we lay about on the sand in the bushes, without speaking to each other for some days; after which, instead of doing wrong, we assembled, acknowledged the justness of your anger, and determined to take instruction from the past. Yes, father! we are pleased that you took the Frenchman's belts from us in full council and burnt them. And we hope you will do us the justice to say that no one, except *Mandamen,* murmured. It was not, however, his speech at St. Joseph's, that stopped us, — nor was it the loss of Daguaganee at Maskegong, by an accident, which would have stopped us upon any other occasion, as is the custom of Indians. We wish not for a French father, we rather have reason to wish for a continuation of the English father who supplies us with all our wants.

"The reason of our returning was because the enemy did not advance, and finding the country quite exhausted of provisions, our old men began to file off, and our young men followed them. You, father, have since pointed out how we might have been supplied, but you are wise and we are fools. Belts are now sliding through all the Indian country for a general rendezvous in the Illenois country, — when, independent of your further assistance, we are determined to drive off the Big Knives out of the Indian country, where they only spoil our lands.

"Farewell, father! we lose you; but the vile Kitchikomokamans [Americans] shall pay for it. They shall carry water [Become slaves to the English] at this fort of Mitchilimackinac."

John Askin, after attending the council, consulted with the other traders who determined to present De Peyster with a token of their gratitude to him. They appreciated his devotion to their enterprise and his skill in maintaining the peace. On September 20 they ordered from Todd & McGill in Montreal a silver punch bowl and ladle to give their leader and friend.[26]

That same morning Askin, Benjamin Lyon, Louis Chaboillez, Henry Bostwick, and Laurent Du Charme approached De Peyster on the parade ground. At his side stood Rebecca clutching her bonnet as the brisk wind blew sand about the fort's interior. Askin solemnly read the trader's letter which told the departing Commandant of their admiration and respect.

Silver punch bowl commissioned by the Merchants of Michilimackinac to be presented to De Peyster in appreciation for his years of service. The turtle recalls the name "Michilimackinac" which means "big turtle".

Struck by this display of affection, De Peyster replied:

"Your approbation of my conduct, during long command, in the critical situation of affairs, cannot be otherwise less flattering to me . . . . I have ever made it my study to promote the trade of this Post and its Dependencies. Happy! could I have succeeded more to my wishes; but, I am now in hopes, from the assurances of the Indians, that trade will take a more favorable turn soon . . . . I cannot take my leave, without expressing the highest sense of gratitude for your attention to Mrs. DePeyster; she is sensible of your politeness, and desires me to acknowledge it in her behalf."[27]

Despite his best efforts for the past five years, De Peyster left many problems unsolved. Rebel control of Illinois still endangered Detroit and Michilimackinac. Although he had kept the Indians of the upper lakes nominally loyal, they were unpredictable, and the cost of maintaining their support kept growing. The Commandant was caught in an increasingly difficult situation. The British government frowned upon purchasing Indian presents locally, yet it was frequently unable to deliver adequate supplies. At the same time the Crown expected De Peyster to maintain the Indians' allegiance. Fortunately for Arent Schuyler De Peyster he could now turn over his problems at Michilimackinac to his successor. On October 4 he welcomed Lieutenant Governor Patrick Sinclair.

*Silhouette of
Patrick Sinclair as
an old man.*

X.

Patrick Sinclair Assumes Command

Patrick Sinclair, a 43-year-old bachelor, was no stranger to Michilimackinac and the Great Lakes. From 1762 until 1769 he captained a vessel for the Naval Department, first on Lake Ontario and later on the upper lakes. He got to know the Indians and traders, who came to respect his judgment. In 1764 Sinclair built Fort Sinclair, a fortified house, near the St. Clair River. There on September 27, 1767 the Detroit merchants presented him with a silver bowl as a symbol of their gratitude.[1] The following year two Chippewa Chiefs named Maskeash [Massigiash] and Ottawa gave Sinclair as a gift the property on which the fort stood.[2]

Sinclair was born in 1736 in Lybster, Caithness, in northern Scotland. At age 22 he obtained an ensigncy in the Forty-Second Royal Highland Regiment, known as the Black Watch. During the Seven Years' War he saw action at Guadeloupe in the West Indies and in the Colony of New York before being assigned to the Naval Department. In 1769 he returned to Great Britain, but he longed for America. Often he thought of his property along the St. Clair River, and he tried unsuccessfully to exchange it with the British government for a house in Detroit.

After considerable effort Patrick Sinclair on April 7, 1775 received the King's commission as Lieutenant Governor and Superintendent of Michilimackinac under the provisions of the Quebec Act.[3] Almost immediately Sinclair sailed for America, docking at Baltimore on July 26. Proceeding overland to New York, he planned to travel north up the Hudson River, then on to Quebec and finally to Michilimackinac.

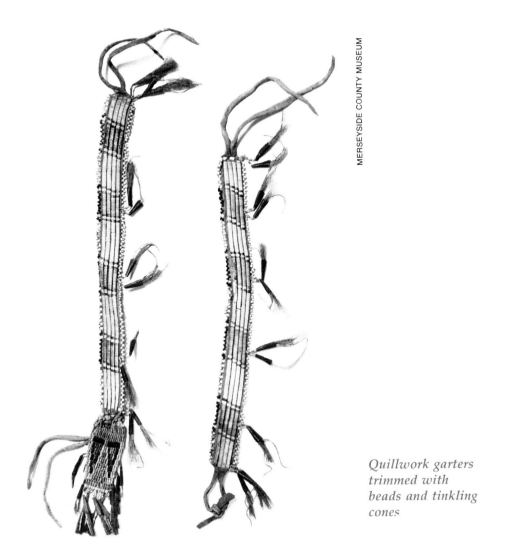

Quillwork garters trimmed with beads and tinkling cones

Unfortunately hostilities had begun, and the Continental Congress knew of Sinclair's reputation and influence among the western nations. Fearing he would enlist the Indians' support on the Crown's side, Congress on August 3 ordered Sinclair's arrest. Not until the following March was he able to return to Britain. In 1777 Sinclair again sailed to America, landing at British-held Philadelphia late in the year. After wintering there, he accompanied the evacuating British fleet to Halifax. Bad luck struck again when the French fleet blockaded Nova Scotia and forced him to winter there. At long last in June, 1779 Sinclair finally reached Quebec.

Shortly after Sinclair's arrival General Frederick Haldimand gave him his instructions. He was to be responsible for Indian affairs and the civil business of the post. This included regulating the fur traders, establishing local ordinances, and settling minor legal disputes. Whenever Sinclair received intelligence, he was to relay it to headquarters. Likewise he was to regularly correspond with Niagara and Detroit.[4]

The new Lieutenant Governor fumed when he learned he was not to command the garrison troops. Haldimand would allow him to purchase a captaincy and maintain his earlier military rank, but Sinclair would have to yield command to a senior officer. If Sinclair desired to use any soldiers, the commandant must first approve. This seemed intolerable to Sinclair.

Sinclair became so agitated that he asked permission to return to England. Although Haldimand agreed that the civil and military powers were "unhappily blended," he felt Sinclair would have to live with them. The Governor believed the King's servants were capable of setting aside petty disputes and working in harmony. He denied Sinclair's request and ordered him to Michilimackinac at once.[5]

At Michilimackinac Patrick Sinclair plunged into his long anticipated work. On his first day he learned from Major De Peyster that the situation at the straits was ominous.[6] The fort was dangerously exposed and virtually defenseless. There were only 403 six-pound iron balls for the fort's cannon and 129 empty shells for the 4-2/5 inch brass coehorn mortar. The additional ammunition was unserviceable. As they inspected the fort, other serious shortages were pointed out. The subterranean powder magazine near the southeast bastion contained only 16½ barrels of powder belonging to the Crown. Little iron and steel and very few entrenching tools were to be found in the Engineer's storehouse. Also lacking were skilled artisans such as a blacksmith and a ship's carpenter.[7] Hay and wood could only be procured from distant locations. Furthermore, sailing vessels anchored offshore had no protection from either man or nature. Sinclair, quick to size up the problems, believed he had a solution to these difficulties.

Brass barrel hoop fragments, stamped with the King's Broad Arrow, excavated at Michilimackinac.

appearance from Isle bois blanc Dist.^e one mile & a quarter

Sinclair's 1779 sketch of Mackinac Island as it appeared from Bois Blanc Island.

Even before he docked at Michilimackinac, Sinclair had stopped briefly at Mackinac Island. Carefully scrutinizing the forest-covered hump of the "great turtle," he concluded that the bluff facing south above the water would be an ideal place for a fort. On the day after his arrival he sailed the straits to revisit the island, accompanied by a mason, a carpenter, a brickmaker, and a farmer.

Sugar Loaf Rock

Arch Rock

Climbing the steep hill, they enjoyed the majestic view from the plateau 150 feet above the lake. Below them was a fine natural harbor, and Round Island only a half mile distant protected the harbor from the southeast. Turning northward Sinclair and his men tramped through the tall woods and noted adequate beech, maple, oak, elm, and cedar for construction and firewood. Several times they stopped and gazed in awe at dramatic limestone formations. Arch Rock, Sugar Loaf, Devil's Kitchen, and others had religious significance for the local Indians. Sinclair, more interested in the practical value of the rock, reckoned that the abundance of limestone on the island was ideal for building a fortification. Good clay for making bricks was found, and there was even some land suitable for farming on the 2100-acre island. Leaving his mechanics to explore for another day, Sinclair returned to the mainland.

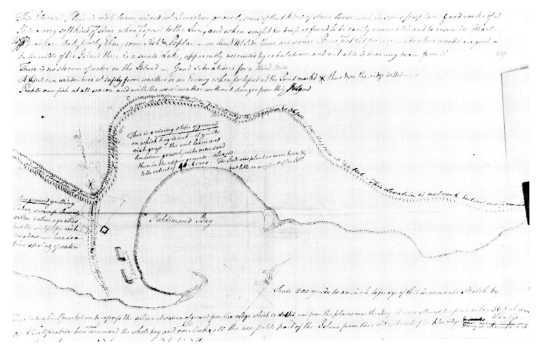

Sinclair's sketch of the harbor on Mackinac Island. The site of his proposed fort is also indicated.

Within just three days the Lieutenant Governor had formulated grandiose plans. He sent a sketch of his proposal for a new fort to Captain Dietrich Brehm, General Haldimand's aide-de-camp. Presuming Haldimand's approval, Sinclair cautioned, "For God's sake be careful in the choice of An Engineer & don't send up one of your paper Engineers fond of fine regular Polygons."[8]

Sinclair also designed his Indian strategy. Observing some natives returning from Montreal laden with arms and clothing, he pled with Brehm to stop passing out goods so liberally. Indian trade goods were cheaper at Montreal than at Michilimackinac, but the Indians could never understand why. Sinclair felt it imperative that the natives in the Michilimackinac district remain dependent upon him alone for their presents. Sinclair would remind them that Great Britain desired to preserve their hunting grounds from rebel advancements, but that support for the Americans would contribute to further encroachment and settlement on Indians lands.

Learning from De Peyster of the Indians recent vacillation at St. Joseph, Sinclair decided that it was best to keep them busy. He hoped to use them against the rebels in Illinois. Since he could not spare his own troops, any offensive actions would have to be undertaken by Indian warriors.[9]

C louds and gusty winds greeted Lieutenant Alexander Harrow as he stepped out into the cold morning air on Friday, October 15. Hopefully the weather would soon clear for today Major and Mrs. De Peyster were to board his vessel *Welcome* for Detroit. The squalls quieted in the early afternoon and Harrow ordered his crew to load the ship.

Around four o'clock the Major, Rebecca, and Sinclair emerged from the commanding officer's house and walked before the troops assembled in ranks on the parade ground. After briefly addressing the men, De Peyster and his wife turned and walked through the water gate to the wharf. As they passed the soldiers and inhabitants, they thought of the five difficult years they had spent here. They were eager for the more civilized life at Detroit or possibly New York. Yet they were leaving behind many friends. Since coming to Michilimackinac, their world had changed dramatically; peace had been displaced by a horrible revolution which threatened to separate the colonies from England. Though living at the outer fringe of the British Empire, their lives had been profoundly affected by distant events.

For the inhabitants, too, this was a time of reflection. They would miss their beloved leader. Lieutenant Governor Sinclair seemed impulsive and at times arrogant and abrasive. He appeared to lack De Peyster's wisdom, patience, and understanding, but perhaps he would learn.

Slowly the Major and Rebecca, accompanied by Sinclair, were rowed out to the bobbing *Welcome*. His passengers on board, Harrow ordered the sails set and the anchor weighed. On shore arms waved and a six-pounder roared six times as the *Welcome* shrank into the distance. An hour later she anchored in the harbor of Mackinac Island for the night.

Early the next morning De Peyster and Sinclair went ashore, and the Lieutenant Governor explained his plans.[10] The Major took one last look at what was to become the location of a new settlement in the straits. About eight o'clock De Peyster wished Sinclair success during his command and bid him farewell. De Peyster reboarded the *Welcome* and sailed to his new command at Detroit. Patrick Sinclair hardly noticed the *Welcome* as she slipped by Bois Blanc Island; he had more important thoughts — he was going to build a new fort.

I n late October Sinclair, wanting to impress "wavering" Indians living along Lake Michigan, ordered Samuel Robertson to sail the *Felicity* around the lake and confiscate corn stored along the rivers. Sinclair instructed Robertson to buy on the merchant's credit. If any refused to sell, he was to seize it and give a receipt. Robertson was to destroy any grain that could not be brought back in the *Felicity*. Sinclair dispatched several other small vessels into Lake Huron on similar missions.[11]

The "Felicity"
painted by
Homer Lynn

Catching a warm southerly breeze, the *Felicity* sailed westward on October 21. On board with Captain Robertson were Charles Gautier, Interpreter, and two Canadians familiar with the rivers flowing into Lake Michigan. The weather soon turned nasty, and strong winds, driving rain, snow, and sleet pelted them mercilessly. After ten days of pounding, the mouth of the Muskegon River was a welcome sight.

About one-half mile offshore Robertson dropped anchor. Gautier and the two Frenchmen climbed into a small boat "to fetch the negro on Board." Black Piter, accompanied by three Indians, including a chief from L'Arbre Croche, greeted the visitors and rowed out with them to the *Felicity*. They presented Robertson with some venison and received in return two bottles of rum, a piece of tobacco, bread, and some pork. Standing on deck Gautier gave Black Piter several strings of wampum, two gallons of rum, and a carrot of tobacco which he promised to deliver to the Grand Sable, one of the Chippewa chiefs from Mackinac Island. When Gautier inquired about a small vessel manned by a black crew, he was informed that it had passed fifteen or twenty days earlier enroute to Michilimackinac with Pierre Durand on board.

Black Piter informed Gautier that two traders had 150 to two hundred bags of corn cached along the Grand River. Since the Indians had already left for their winter wigwams, he presumed it remained in storage. Wanting this corn, Robertson sailed to the Grand's mouth and sent Gautier up the river with three men to acquire canoes to transport the prize. True to Black Piter's report, the village was deserted. "Some distemper" had killed many and driven the survivors away. Unable to find the corn and having learned nothing about the rebels, the frustrated Robertson sailed on. After several unsuccessful attempts to make further contacts on the eastern shore, Robertson set course for Milwaukee, which he reached at midnight, Wednesday, November 3.

Gautier went ashore and brought back to the ship St. Pierre, a Canadian trader, his nephew Marong, Chief Lodegard, and two other Indians. Gautier presented three bottles of rum and half a carrot of tobacco and then recited Sinclair's message. He directed St. Pierre to give wampum, rum, and tobacco to chiefs of the several tribes living at Milwaukee. Gautier made a special point to tell him to present Chief Chambolee with a gift of wampum and tobacco to encourage him to capture the pro-rebel Chief Black Bird "either by fair or forc'd method." When Black Bird was delivered to Sinclair, Chambolee would be well rewarded. Black Bird had taken a rebel belt and tried to get his neighbors to proclaim neutrality. Chambolee, who planned to make peace with the British at Michilimackinac, resisted Black Bird's pleas. Gautier now hoped to exploit this division for the King's benefit.

The Indians had bad news; the corn crop had been poor. Thinking that no traders were going to be allowed among them this winter, they hid their corn. However, they might be able to trade two to three hundred bags at Michilimackinac next spring. Gautier acquired fifteen bags from St. Pierre in exchange for a keg of rum. It was clear that no trade goods meant no corn. Before the visitors disembarked, Robertson gave them some peas and pork. The *Felicity* headed home. Her sails caught a stiff southwest breeze, and she made Michilimackinac in only two days.[12]

Sinclair lost little time in establishing his civil authority. He issued proclamations banning horse races in the streets and requiring all inhabitants to have water buckets handy to combat fire. All chimneys were to be swept weekly and kept in good repair, and no fires were to be built in houses without chimneys or in the streets. In the suburbs citizens were forbidden to throw "sweepings, feathers, or nastiness" in the thoroughfares. When disputes arose, Sinclair appointed three arbitrators to settle them. The Lieutenant Governor also decreed that no person was to hire or harbor panis or Negro slaves without their owner's consent.

Sinclair appointed Christian Burgy to serve as master of the police and notary public. He was to advertise the Lieutenant Governor's instructions, and everyone was expected to obey them. Violators summoned before Sinclair, a Justice of the Peace, paid fines to the Crown if found guilty. Sinclair required citizens to have all bonds, leases, and contracts notarized. Should a merchant or trader fail to do this, Sinclair vowed to pay them no heed if a dispute arose over the terms of a legal transaction.[13] Sinclair also insisted that all civilians take an oath affirming their allegiance to George III.[14]

On October 29 Pierre Durand's vessel arrived at Michilimackinac. Durand brought 120 packs of furs and another hundred were expected in the spring. He had spent four years in the Illinois country, and rumors circulated that Durand had made "Lampoons upon the King, which were sung" at Kaskaskia.[15] Suspicious, Sinclair thoroughly scrutinized Durand's papers and at first found none requing immediate action. He did find, however, several bills drawn by "Colonel Clark" in account with a Jean Baptist and Jean Baptiste LaCroix. Consequently Sinclair required Durand to bond himself for £1000 Sterling and ordered him not to sell or give away any of his property before May 1.

Fort Michilimackinac

Questioned about this damaging evidence, Durand explained that he feared Captain Fernando de Leyba, the Spanish Lieutenant Governor at St. Louis, would confiscate his property unless he subjected himself "to His Catholic Majesty." Therefore he accepted rebel money for his merchandise. Next spring, Sinclair planned to send Durand to Quebec where he could answer to Haldimand.[16]

Without waiting for General Haldimand's approval, Sinclair made preparations for moving the fort and town to Mackinac Island. To pacify the Chippewa living in a village on the island, he sent Charles Gautier to present a wampum string to their chief before he left for his wintering grounds. The chief agreed to permit Sinclair "to cut down some brush this winter."

With this formality out of the way, Sinclair detached a corporal and four privates of the King's Eighth, a carpenter, and some traders' servants to the island. They were to clear the upper ground, cut timber, construct a wharf, and build a blockhouse.[17]

Crews were also busy sawing logs on the mainland southeast of Michilimackinac. The workmen rafted the freshly cut timber over to the fort. On November 3 a northwest breeze churned up a swell, forcing two black lumbermen riding a raft into a bay off the south side of Bois Blanc Island. Fortunately the *Welcome* was heading for Mackinac Island, and Captain Harrow spotted the distressed woodsmen. He took them on board, fed them, and warmed their cold bodies with rum.[18]

On November 5 Harrow's crew loaded parts of a dismantled house onto the *Welcome*. Two days later Harrow transported it to the island and then sailed for Detroit.[19] The first building at the new settlement was a transplant from the mainland. While navigation was still possible, the *Felicity* ferried back and forth across the straits carrying engineer's stores, timbers, and provisions.

Previously, vessels wintering at Michilimackinac had moored in the safety of the Cheboygan River, sixteen miles southeast of the fort. However, Sinclair believed that the Ottawa Chief "Manetewabe" possessed a rebel commission and that the mainland harbor was no longer safe. This was not a serious problem though since the *Felicity* could tie up at the new wharf being built in Haldimand Bay on Mackinac Island.[20]

The Smoker's Companion is a small tongs used to take a coal from the fire to light a pipe.

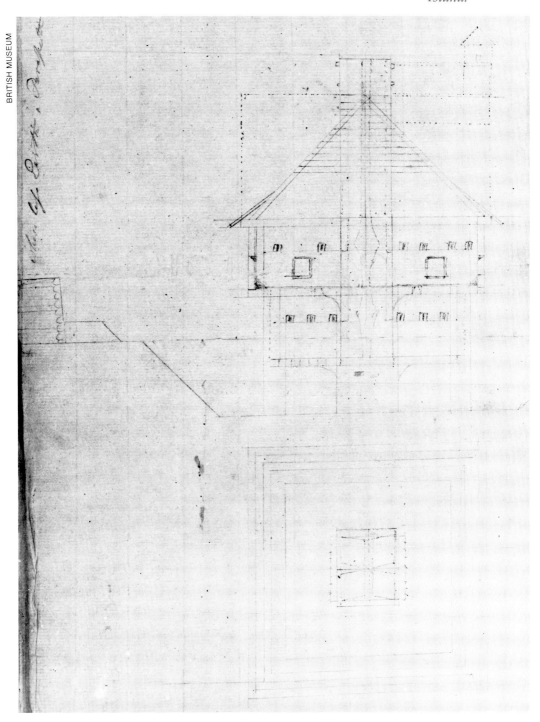

Sinclair's sketch of a blockhouse to be built on Mackinac Island.

XI.

Target: St. Louis

Medio real coin.

For several months Patrick Sinclair thought about how to drive the Americans and their allies out of the Illinois country. As a first step, he sent Charles Gautier to tell the Indians that Matchekewis and the Ottawa Chief Nimable and their warriors would join a force of Sioux, Sac, and Fox to attack the rebels. Braves were encouraged to enlist in this expedition, which was to be "directed against Bodies of armed Men and against Forts."[1]

Now by Tuesday, February 15, 1780, Sinclair had most of the details worked out. He sat before a blazing fire in his quarters, lost in thought, totally unaware of the cold, gusty winds howling through the cracks. With his quill pen he wrote to headquarters that he would send as many Indians as possible to strike the Spanish settlements far down the Mississippi River.[2]

Earlier in the month Sinclair had received from Detroit General Haldimand's circular containing Lord George Germain's orders directing the western governors to attack these Spanish posts. This had been prompted by Spain's declaration of war against England on May 8, 1779. Hopefully De Peyster and Sinclair would be able to cooperate with Brigadier General John Campbell, who was expected to take New Orleans from Spain and advance up the river to Natchez.[3] Sinclair would capture St. Louis, the closest Spanish town to Michilimackinac.

Wearing a heavy blanket coat and carrying snowshoes, this habitant is ready for a winter trek.

Sinclair had already dispatched over the ice and snow to the Sioux country a war party recruited along the southern shore of Lake Superior by Jean Baptiste Cadot of Sault Ste. Marie.[4] The English Interpreter, Alexander Kay, accompanied them, and Rocque, the Interpreter for the Sioux, was to meet them west of the Mississippi.[5] Here they would join Wabasha, who could easily raise two hundred men.[6] They were to advance as far south as Natchez. Sinclair promised to send out other Indian parties as soon as he could safely make known the purpose of their mission. With luck General Campbell would have already taken the lower Mississippi.[7] But unknown to Sinclair, the Spanish had already thwarted Campbell.

To assemble an adequate force, Sinclair enticed some Indians to winter at Michilimackinac instead of going out hunting. Although this was costly, the Lieutenant Governor wanted to have a large group of warriors ready for action. Having numerous Indians living around the fort caused some problems and prompted Sinclair in January to forbid any Indian "to lodge in town without permission."[8]

On Thursday, February 17 Sinclair sent the trader Emanuel Hesse, formerly of the Sixtieth Regiment, and a friendly chief to gather Menominee, Winnebago, Sac, and Fox warriors. A number of traders and their employees, serving in the militia, accompanied Hesse. He was to assemble his party at the carrying place between the Fox and Wisconsin Rivers. There he was to collect canoes and corn for his men and the nations who would join him at Prairie du Chien. Sinclair ordered Hesse to remain at the portage until Sergeant James Phillips of the King's Eighth and Matchekewis and his band came from Michilimackinac in late March.[9]

Sinclair's preparations were carefully watched by Pierre Prevost, a trader in the Sac and Fox country, who had a British license in 1778. He wrote George Rogers Clark at Kaskaskia on February 20 that Sinclair's emissaries in the wilderness including Jean Marie Calvé were having success. Potawatomi warriors from Detroit had brought two American scalps and the message that the Sac and Fox must attack Clark, or the British and their Indian allies would declare war upon them. Prevost warned Clark that Sinclair's agents at the Des Moines River told the Indians to pillage anyone who came from Illinois and said that Clark was the "meanest of wretches."[10]

A rare peek inside an Indian tent.

Some of Sinclair's warriors at Michilimackinac were eager to join war parties in order to escape the arduous task of sawing timber. By mid-February they had "produced 16000 feet of Plank and Boards" in the fort's sawpits. On the island other workmen fashioned three thousand cedar pickets and thirty thousand shingles and quarried limestone. Hoping to encourage the French inhabitants to move to the island, Sinclair ordered the church dismantled. The traders and their employees prodded cattle which pulled the logs over the frozen straits. Within six weeks the carpenters expected to have the church rebuilt in the middle of the new village below the fort.[11]

Samuel Robertson, whom Sinclair had placed in charge of the island construction crew, had already built on the lower ground a two-story blockhouse with a large central chimney. On the second floor carpenters had cut cannon ports through the cedar logs. In front, the newly erected wharf extended 150 feet into the harbor. Tied to it were the *Felicity* and several other small vessels frozen solid in the ice.[12] Sinclair hoped to use the "excellent oak, Cedar, & Mast Timber," to build additional ships.[13]

On the mainland at Michilimackinac the soldiers labored to strengthen its flimsy defenses. Lieutenant Mercer directed a detail which cleared away brush growing near the fort. With Robertson's help, he built a blockhouse outside the land gate "to overlook & command hollow ground behind a Sand Hill which the Troops could not reduce." Without this protection, Sinclair reasoned, "The Oxford Blues might have come within 50 yards of our Picketts unseen."[14] This square structure, sixteen feet on a side, had large portholes on three sides allowing cannoneers to ward off attackers up to six hundred yards away. The land gate could now be opened in relative safety.[15]

Every day great quantities of food were needed to feed the busy community. Sinclair detached a sergeant and six privates to fish. Despite the dangers of shifting ice, they caught enough to feed all the Michilimackinac Indians and had a surplus of about a thousand pounds to ship to Niagara. The cleaned trout were salted down for one night and then smoked with juniper. Sinclair estimated that with proper tackle three expert Canadian fishermen could produce one hundred thousand pounds of fish each winter.[16] While the Indians ate mostly fish and corn, the soldiers and the workmen hired by Sinclair consumed huge quantities of bread, pork, and peas.[17]

On bleak winter days the Island seemed far away.

The windswept ice became a busy highway, though free passage was not allowed to the island. Sinclair required everyone who went to obtain a pass from him. The penalty for violators was confiscation of their sleighs, cattle, and merchandise.[18] Before the ice broke up, Sinclair planned to drive the King's cattle across and pasture them in a thirty-acre field. At the moment some Canadians were splitting rails and cutting posts for the fence.[19]

Though Sinclair planned to launch a major raid employing hundreds of Indians, he questioned the reliability of Charles Langlade and Charles Gautier. The Governor believed that they were eager to serve, but he did not have full confidence in their ability to carry out their assignments successfully.[20] Langlade's wife Charlotte Bourassa complained, "The Commandant, influenced either by his [Langlade's] enemies or by Caprise, has given him much annoyance by making use of his own Pupils instead of him."[21] Sinclair did not yet appreciate the prestige these two men had among the Indians.

Sinclair prepared nine large wampum belts to distribute to the nations. The belts told of the geographical progress of both English and Spanish colonization along the Mississippi. The purple and white beads pictured "two Indian figures with joined hands & raised axes in the Country between this & that River."[22]

Chippewa scalp dance

No Indian was more involved in organizing the raiding party than Chief Matchekewis. As a reward for his services, Sinclair employed Pierre Durand, whose loyalty Sinclair had questioned only four months earlier, to dismantle a log house and move it to the Chippewa village along the Cheboygan River. Durand transported Matchekewis's house over the ice on white wood rollers and re-erected it.[23] At Cheboygan the Chief was a neighbor to John Askin and Jean Baptiste Barthe who owned a couple of dwellings occupied by a Negro and a panis slave.[24] Durand then proceeded up the river to search for red and white pineries and a suitable place to construct a sawmill.[25]

Before Matchekewis could enjoy his new home, he, his warriors, and Sergeant Phillips, who served as Lieutenant, set out on March 10 for the Fox-Wisconsin portage, carrying their canoes over the rotting ice. Sinclair, having only sixty-seven rank and file troops,[26] sent only Phillips and Privates McDonald and Creige who served as Sergeants. He hoped that with their assistance Captain Hesse would be able to maintain discipline among the growing army of Indians and traders.

Jean Marie Du Charme was particularly eager to join the expedition. He vividly remembered his flight from Spanish territory, and he longed for revenge. Sinclair's promise to give trading rights along the Missouri River to the traders who helped wrest it from the Spanish was also attractive to Du Charme.

Meanwhile De Peyster at Detroit planned to send Captain Henry Bird into the Ohio country to "surround" the Indians' Kentucky hunting grounds. His force was to consist of fifty soldiers equipped with small cannon, volunteers, Indian officers, and many Indians. De Peyster flattered himself "that this little movement will favor Lieut Gov. Sinclair's Party down the Mississippi, divert the attention of many from Niagara, and be of some service to Brig. Genl. Campbell in case he had not already taken New Orleans." The Major had also summoned the Wabash Indians to Detroit and received their promises to keep Clark at the falls of the Ohio River.[27]

Even the Potawatomi at St. Joseph appeared to join the British offensive. A party of about sixty warriors set out on March 12 for Vincennes. Two days later some warriors from Terre Coupé, the most unpredictable of these people, left to join their brethren "singing the death song."[28]

To complete this grand design Sinclair planned to dispatch Charles Langlade, Pierre Durand, some Canadians, and a band of Indians to Chicago to "second the attack" on St. Louis by way of the Illinois River.[29] Sinclair was going to send yet another force "to watch the Plains between the Wabash and the Mississippi."[30]

S inclair believed that Deputy Commissary John Askin dispensed the King's stores too loosely, and he stationed a sentry at the entrance to the storehouse. After summoning Askin into his office, Sinclair relieved him of his duties and appointed Dr. David Mitchell in his stead.[31]

Door lock.

Inside the King's Storehouse at Michilimackinac

On April 24 Sinclair threw open the doors of the storehouse and ordered several soldiers to begin counting barrels. When the inventory was completed, Askin and Mitchell drew up a receipt showing discrepancies in supplies:[32]

	Should have been in the store	*Amount that was delivered*
Rum	832 gal. 2 half pts.	804 gal. 4 half pts.
Flour	115,420 lbs.	98,378 lbs.
Pork	53,228 pds. 9 oz.	48,866 pds. 5 oz.
Peas	5,227 gal. 1 pts.	5,619 gal. 10 pts.
Butter	3,676 pds. 13 oz.	2,512 pds. 2 oz.
Oatmeal	3,545 pds. 7 oz.	3,784 pds. 8 oz.

This was not the first time that Askin and Sinclair had clashed. Earlier in the winter Sinclair had ordered Jean Baptiste Cadot to cut down the pickets surrounding Askin's trading post at the Sault.[33]

Several days later on April 27 Sinclair arrested Samuel Robertson, Askin's son-in-law, and confined him to the guardhouse. The Lieutenant Governor accused him of intercepting a letter on Mackinac Island being carried by an Indian courier to Jean Baptiste Cadot at Sault Ste. Marie. It contained a request that Canadian volunteers be sent to Michilimackinac. Robertson and Askin employed many Canadians, and their loss would seriously disrupt business. Robertson allegedly opened the letter and cut out the offensive words. To inform Askin of Sinclair's intentions, he sent the letter back to Michilimackinac in the pocket of John Taylor, a sailor, who had a pass. The bearer tragically died enroute and the letter was found on his body.[34]

Robertson's request for bail was met with "very extraordinary terms." The next morning Christian Burgy set the bail at £2000 Halifax Currency, requiring Robertson to leave for Quebec as soon as navigation on the Grand River resumed. There, he would appear before General Haldimand. Unable to post bond, Robertson was returned to his cold, damp cell.

Upon learning the charges against him, Robertson requested that twelve men be chosen to hear the evidence and decide his guilt or innocence. Following an inquest Sinclair agreed, and a jury composed of six men chosen by Robertson and six by Lieutenant Clowes met in a council room to hear witnesses and excerpts of letters written by Robertson. The jury cleared Robertson of all serious accusations. Furious, Sinclair rejected their opinions, saying that he had not intended this to be a trial, but only an opportunity to hear the evidence.[35]

These legal proceedings proved expensive. Coroner Matthew Lassey charged £4/5/4 for administering thirty-two oaths to witnesses and jurymen. The twelve jurors sitting on the inquest panel received 2s each for their day's work while those on the court of inquiry jury also got 2s per day for five days. Lassey paid Christian Burgy £90 for his services. Another pound was spent to purchase a shirt to put on Taylor's body before burial. The total cost to the Crown was £109/17/4.[36]

The guards escorted Robertson back to jail. There he languished, unable to see any civilians, including his wife. His anguish was keen because Kitty had recently given birth to a child and both needed him.[37] Also weighing heavily on his mind was the knowledge that his possessions left on the island were being pillaged. His furniture, provisions, and liquor were being distributed to the soldiers. Sinclair confiscated his flour, boards, planks, house frames, and tools, but gave no receipt in return. Coupled with his losses at Sault Ste. Marie, Robertson was virtually destitute.[38] Despite the warmth of spring, these days seemed the darkest of his life.

Prairie du Chien buzzed with excitement. It was April 27 and Captain Hesse, Matchekewis, Wabasha, Lieutenant Phillips, Jean Marie Du Charme, and a large conclave of warriors and militia were preparing to descend the Mississippi. Phillips pleased the great Sioux Chief by bestowing Haldimand's commission upon him. Impressed by the Sioux warriors, Phillips described them as "nothing inferior to regular Troops in regard to Discipline in their own way, it being their first & principle care to examine their arms in the morning, by drawing & drying Their Powder and always fresh loaded at Sun Sett."[39]

Several detachments patrolled the river, clearing it of rebels and capturing enemy supplies. Alexander Kay and a Menominee party brought in an armed boat, loaded at Cahokia and St. Louis by Charles Gratiot, with its crew of twelve men and cargo. Among those captured was Juan [Jean] Baptiste Cardinal. Another group took seventeen prisoners at the Des Moines lead mines and stopped fifty tons of ore from going down the river. Not wishing to be encumbered by prisoners, Hesse sent Cardinal and some other captives by canoe to Michilimackinac.

War dance of the Sac and Fox.

WEST POINT MUSEUM

On May 2 the army finally was ready to move.[40] Emanuel Hesse looked over his troops numbering about 750. Sioux, Menominee, Winnebago, Sac, Fox, Chippewa, Ottawa, Kickapoo, and Potawatomi warriors painted in a multitude of designs danced around their war post and sang the war song. Conspicuously, Matchekewis, resplendent in his scarlet chief's coat, strode among his braves. Among the militia, only three British soldiers could be seen. It was unfortunate that the King could not spare more regular troops to accompany this vital mission. Yet Hesse, confident he would soon surprise St. Louis, issued his departing orders.

British fortunes among the St. Joseph Potawatomi were less encouraging. A war party, confronted by a Canadian trader outside of Vincennes, listened to his exaggerated claims that a force of four thousand men awaited them at that post. Eager for an excuse and not wanting to offend the French, they turned back, except for a few who proceeded to Vincennes and discovered only twenty-three Virginians.[41] The Potawatomi had again failed the British, but their retreat would not affect Hesse's assault on St. Louis.

While Hesse's canoes glided down the Mississippi, Captain Fernando de Leyba prepared for their visit. Having learned of British intentions at least two months earlier, Leyba frantically fortified his settlement. The seven hundred residents of St. Louis devoted their money and energy to constructing a tower and other defenses. On May 9, learning that Hesse was on his way, Leyba ordered sixty militia sent up from Ste. Genevieve and called in all traders living near town. This added 150 defenders to his army. Across the river at Cahokia, Colonel John Montgomery prepared for the onslaught, and the inhabitants' spirits were raised when George Rogers Clark arrived on May 25.[42]

On Friday, May 26, Hesse attacked. Expecting to easily overrun the village, he was shocked to find the Spanish waiting for him. Gunfire stabbed at the advancing English force from the newly erected fortification. The deep boom of the cannons surprised the Indian warriors who did not like to fight pitched battles in the open. Only Europeans were fool enough to charge an entrenched enemy. The rattle of musketry was punctuated by the cries of women and children and the screams of agony as musket balls tore into men's bodies. Unable to capture the town quickly, the invaders broke ranks and drifted away. Retreating, they shot cattle and destroyed crops as they scattered. People caught in the fields when the battle began were killed or captured. St. Louis and Cahokia had resisted and had beaten back the force from Michilimackinac. Disheartened, Hesse's troops began the long trek home.[43]

Map of St. Louis in 1780

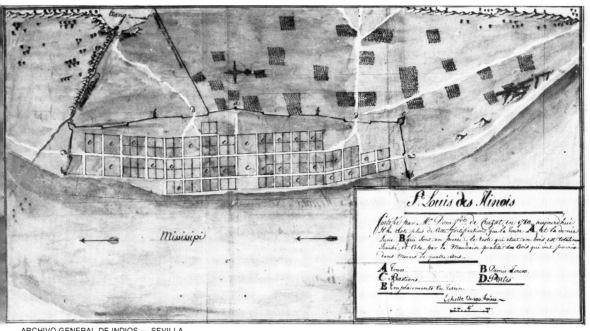

Back at Michilimackinac Sinclair believed the expedition was going as planned. A band of Menominee had brought in the Spanish boat with the prisoners taken on the Mississippi and at the lead mines. Delighted by his captives, Sinclair informed Haldimand on May 29 that he had sent six prisoners to Quebec, employed four on Mackinac Island, and allowed traders to engage six more. Since seven were Spanish subjects, he would feed them out of the King's provisions until he received Haldimand's instructions regarding their future.[44] Sinclair considered Cardinal and a man named La Roche as especially dangerous, and he had them clamped in irons and locked in the guardhouse.[45]

Sinclair ordered Langlade with the *Felicity* and a small private ship to Chicago.[46] Upon arrival, Langlade was to disembark and lead his men toward St. Louis. Then the vessels were to take on board Matchekewis and any prisoners he might bring with him on his return by way of the Illinois River.

Buoyed by apparent success, Sinclair made plans for the territory he expected to capture. The Illinois villages would be required to support garrisons to be established there, and they would send cattle to Michilimackinac. The Winnebago, Menominee, Sac, and Fox would guard the lead mines. While Hesse was securing St. Louis, Wabasha was to go further downstream and take Kaskaskia and Ste. Genevieve.[47]

In early June Sinclair made a treaty with La Fourche and the L'Arbre Croche Ottawa to join about thirty Chippewa warriors from both the island and Saginaw to go to Vincennes. Hopefully some Potawatomi would also go along,[48] but Sinclair believed this unlikely. He suspected that Louis Chevallier was sympathetic to the rebels.[49]

Flintlock musket lock

During normal times canoes from Montreal would soon begin arriving, but this year Haldimand held up the licenses. Both he and Sinclair feared that too many unprincipled traders got passes and carried goods into the interior only to enlist themselves in the rebel interest. Sinclair worried that some northwest traders might send merchandise to the Illinois country from the south shore of Lake Superior.[50]

Fearing huge losses, the northwest traders pleaded with Haldimand to permit them to carry on their business as soon as possible. On May 11 they sent an impassioned petition from Montreal pointing out that their employees in the wilderness would starve or be killed unless supplies were sent. They reminded the General the fur trade was also lucrative for Great Britain.[51]

Sinclair felt that restrictions should be maintained on these untrustworthy characters. He remembered their petition to the Continental Congress in 1776 and believed they would do anything for money. Exercising his authority, he had confiscated John Askin's and Jean Baptiste Barthe's vessels at Sault Ste. Marie. The *Mackinac, De Peyster, Archange,* and the "Great Batoe Pompe" were brought to Michilimackinac and placed under Sinclair's control.[52]

Despite Sinclair's suspicions, Haldimand finally acceded to the merchant's demands and allowed the fur trade to proceed. Before the season ended 103 canoes headed west for Michilimackinac. Of these fifty-three were destined for Lake Superior and points beyond.[53]

The further west the voyageurs carried their cargo, the more valuable it became. Charles Grant, a northwest trader, estimated that a canoe load costing £300 Sterling in England was worth £450 by the time it reached Montreal, £660 at Michilimackinac, and £750 at Grand Portage.[54]

Lieutenant Governor Sinclair had fielded a sizable Indian army, and its cost was staggering. Nevertheless, the reduction of St. Louis and Illinois would be well worth the expense. He reasoned his superiors would see it that way for the King's interests had to be protected.

In Quebec General Haldimand had become alarmed at the size of Major De Peyster's drafts for the Indian Department for 1779. Haldimand demanded that the Major give a full accounting of his Michilimackinac expenses.[55] From Detroit De Peyster replied that large gifts had been necessary to reconcile the Menominee with the Chippewa of Bay de Noc and the Sioux with the Chippewa of the Plains. Moreover, he sent a large present to the Sioux to enable them to awe the Sac and Fox. Langlade and Gautier had incurred additional costs while trying to raise warriors to aid Hamilton. Also, De Peyster had to supply Indians who took part in Lieutenant Bennett's expedition to St. Joseph. Finally, the families of the Indian auxiliaries had to be fed and clothed, canoes had to be furnished, and Indian visitors to Michilimackinac had to be welcomed with gifts.[56]

Now Haldimand wanted Sinclair to reduce the costs. The General reasoned that the problem was caused by Indian Department employees, many of whom used their position to enrich themselves.

English anti-war cartoon ridiculing the British use of Indian allies to fight the Americans.

Allegedly, they encouraged Indians to make excessive demands upon the commanding officer, whom they counciled to submit to Indian requests or run the risk of alienating the nations. In order to satisfy the Indians, the superintendent then had to purchase goods from local traders, who apparently rewarded the devious government agents. Though it would be difficult to reverse this policy, Sinclair was to impress upon the Indians one fundamental fact. They were dependent upon the British for supplies; the enemy could not possibly provide for their needs. Sinclair was to give or withhold presents only on the basis of merit.[57]

Five canoes loaded with Indian presents arrived in mid-June. But even as these packs were being carried into the storehouse, opened, and inventoried, Sinclair knew they would not meet his needs.[58] As much as he tried to avoid the local traders, there would be many times when only they had what he needed. Knowing a profitable deal when they saw one, the general store partners asked Sinclair for permission to furnish the Indian goods that he needed to complement those sent from England.[59]

Since the island was not yet ready to receive the garrison, Sinclair continued to strengthen the old fort. On the vacant ground where the church formerly stood he erected a blockhouse, eleven feet-six inches square, set on a stone foundation.[60] If the enemy overran the post, the

142

troops could make their final stand here. The soldiers worked tirelessly "making the two Land Bastions, Terraces, & giving thickness to one curtain as well as preparing Fascines, oak Plank, &c., to redoubt one-half of it in case of the worst."[61] All this work left little time for drilling, which caused concern among the officers.[62] If an attack came, the defense would be bolstered by the militia, composed of all traders and employees.[63]

While the army dug in at Michilimackinac, Sinclair employed many civilians to build the fort on the island. Voyageurs who brought the Indian presents and government provisions were impressed for a month into sawing timbers and quarrying limestone. The traders' servants put in long days loading their masters' homes and possessions on board the sailing vessels which ferried back and forth to the island.[64] Muscle power did most of the work since there was a shortage of tools and working cattle.

The merchants, including John Macnamara, Benjamin Lyon, and Henry Bostwick, had little choice but to move. On the island their property and lives would be safer from rebel or Indian attacks. The soil was more fertile, and the better fishing would enable them to procure food easier. If Sinclair permitted them to have private vessels, the harbor would provide a convenient refuge. For many their houses were not worth moving; hence, new ones had to be erected. Labor was expensive and their employees ought to be fishing or transporting furs. Despite the cost, the community followed the garrison.[65]

Sinclair ordered that all men having Indian wives meet in the suburbs. He would then choose two representatives to go to the island to locate good summer and winter fishing sites, a garden for each family, and suitable land for raising corn. Persons not engaged in the trade would be placed 120 yards apart, while those employed in the trade would be given lots in the village for their houses.[66]

Responding to Haldimand's demand, Sinclair in late June went to the island to arrange for its purchase. Happily, chiefs from eight nations rejoiced at the change. He explained to the natives that the "whole island" was to be used for corn fields with the fort on the upper ground. The Indian agent's house would be located in the village below.[67] Although all whites who had "connected themselves with Indians" were to be given a lot on the island, they would not hold title to it. The King maintained control over these properties.[68] The Lieutenant Governor also observed that the new fort's location would please the local Chippewa though the Ottawa might "be a little jealous at first." This was because it was being built on Chippewa lands, while the old fort was located on the line dividing Ottawa and Chippewa ground. Sinclair thought this must have been the only good reason for choosing that site.[69]

144

XII.

Turmoil at Michilmackinac

Returning militiamen and warriors astounded Michilimackinac in early June when they brought news of Hesse's defeat at St. Louis. The *Felicity*, carrying Matchekewis and his men, had escaped from Chicago just five days before two hundred rebel cavalrymen arrived there. Sinclair could hardly believe the outcome of this expedition, which he had worked so hard to organize. After questioning Matchekewis and others, he reported the grim tidings to General Haldimand.

Sinclair directed most of the blame toward Jean Marie Calvé and Jean Marie Du Charme. Allegedly, they failed to maintain discipline among the Sac and Fox who fell back from the attack once they were fired upon. This prevented the Winnebago and Sioux from storming the Spanish lines. Without this thrust, even the best efforts of the militia were futile. Sinclair accused Calvé and Du Charme of duplicity because he believed they had profitable commercial ties with Illinois merchants.

Following the battle, Matchekewis lead his force to Chicago via the Illinois River. Along the way they met Langlade and his men who had come, aboard the *Felicity*, to continue the offensive. Instead, he now helped Matchekewis fight off an ambush led by Black Bird near Kankakee; then both Langlade and Matchekewis safely made it to Chicago. The rest of Hesse's army retreated in two divisions. One came over land, and the other led by Calvé retired by way of the Mississippi. This group made up of Sac and Fox warriors allowed their prisoners to fall into rebel hands, much to Sinclair's dismay.

The Winnebago suffered the only casualties among the British force. One chief and three warriors were killed and four wounded. Rebel losses were greater. At Cahokia one officer and three men died, and five prisoners were taken. At St. Louis, the attackers reportedly killed sixty-eight and captured eighteen black and white prisoners. Warriors brought forty-three scalps to Sinclair. In addition, the retreating army slaughtered many cattle.[1]

Sinclair learned that the Spanish had received intelligence of his plans long before the attack. William Brown, a prisoner, identified Mrs. Joseph Howard as one of the informants who alerted the Spanish to British preparations.[2] The element of surprise had been the cornerstone of Sinclair's strategy. But with that gone, the Spanish had time to strengthen their defenses. Hesse had not expected St. Louis to be fortified, and his army was surprised instead.

Despite this debacle, Sinclair wanted to try again. He proposed that another assault be launched next year employing one thousand Sioux under Wabasha's leadership. For the present he hoped to send small parties to harass the rebels until autumn brought an end to the harvest season.

Quill decorated moccasins.

Sinclair learned that his attempt to purchase a captaincy had been successful. Effective April 1 he had command of a company in the Eighty-Fourth or Royal Emigrant Regiment of Foot.[3] A sergeant, corporal, and twelve privates of his new company came to Michilimackinac by canoe. Because all of them were artificers, he employed them on the new works. Sinclair wanted to use the men to construct a sawmill, but Haldimand ordered him to strengthen his defenses first. Since no engineers were available for Michilimackinac, Sinclair designed the new fort himself.[4]

Until Sinclair received his commission, Lieutenant Clowes technically was the commanding officer of the garrison. This responsibility had devolved upon him when Major De Peyster departed. Now Clowes turned over command of the troops to Sinclair.[5] He had finally achieved what he wanted — control of both the military and the civil affairs at the straits.

Private, 84th Foot

During the summer tempers flared. On July 1 Lieutenant Daniel Mercer of the Kings Eighth reprimanded David McCrea for saying he could send some of the King's soldiers to settle a dispute with another trader. McCrea, drunk and insolent, swore at Mercer, who "took him by the nose." Two days later when a bystander complained, Sinclair arrested Mercer and conducted a court of inquiry into the matter. Lieutenant Mercer, who refused to testify, was ordered to remain under arrest pending instructions from headquarters. Sinclair resisted his demand to lay his case before his own regiment's commanding officer.[6]

Mercer's troubles brought renewed suffering to Samuel Robertson. After spending forty days in the guardhouse, he had been released when Mercer promised to take him to Detroit. However, he was not allowed within one hundred yards of the fort or beyond Chippewa Bay, about seven hundred yards southeast. The morning after Mercer's arrest, the sergeant of the guard came to Robertson's house, dragged him out of bed, marched him through the land gate, and threw him back in jail. Mercer could not now be his escort. But when Joseph Frobisher and William Grant posted a £10,000 bond guaranteeing Robertson's appearance before General Haldimand, he was permitted to proceed to Quebec.[7]

Officer, 8th Foot

Gilded officer's button of the King's Eighth

Sinclair sensed that many at Michilimackinac did not completely accept his authority. Under De Peyster's administration, officials had been given considerable discretion in their own areas of responsibility, but Sinclair felt they sometimes put their own interests before the Crown's.

Joseph Louis Ainsse, the Indian Interpreter, had returned in late May from a visit to Montreal. Shortly thereafter, Sinclair ordered him to St. Joseph to bring back Louis Chevallier, Ainsse's uncle, and all the French residents living there.[8] Ainsse took six canoes, outfitted by the general store, to the small outpost, and he succeeded in convincing the forty-eight men, women, and children to leave their homes and accompany him to Michilimackinac.[9] Thus Sinclair removed a potential source of French resistance to British rule.

While Ainsse was at St. Joseph, three Potawatomi war parties, headed to Illinois and Vincennes, returned. They had met opposition from the Miami, who killed four of their warriors, wounded three, and captured five others. The survivors went back to St. Joseph where they met La Fourche with the Ottawa and Chippewa Sinclair had sent to attack Vincennes. Angered by their defeat, the Potawatomi asked La Fourche to help them obtain more assistance from Sinclair to avenge the Miami and take Vincennes. Even though the Potawatomi could assemble three hundred braves including La Fourche's men, they thought they needed a larger force and more munitions.[10]

In early July, several days after his return to Michilimackinac, Ainsse met with a group of La Baye Indians beyond the fort's palisades. The Indians were disgruntled because they had received fewer presents than some other warriors who had performed less service. Ainsse alerted Sinclair, who called a council and angrily rejected their demands for two barrels of gunpowder. He haughtily gestured that he would only give them two handfuls. The chief stalked out followed by his braves.

The next day Charles Gautier informed Ainsse that the Commandant wanted to see him. When Ainsse entered his office, Sinclair shouted: "Sir, I order you to stay in the Fort & I forbid you to leave it."[11] Sinclair was furious because an Interpreter had held talks with Indians without first informing the Commandant.

Sinclair also confined Louis Chevallier to the fort after searching his belongings and confiscating all his official correspondence with commandants at Michilimackinac. Despite the Captain's promise, Chevallier's documents were not returned.[12] This made it difficult for him to prove that his actions at St. Joseph were consistent with past orders.

*Fort
Michilimackinac*

Both Ainsse and Chevallier demanded that they be permitted to travel to Quebec to settle their disputes with Sinclair. Before Sinclair allowed them to depart, he required that they post a bond. Ainsse then hired three canoes to transport himself, Chevallier and his family, and some others from St. Joseph.[13] For the 70-year-old Madame Chevallier and her husband, this voyage was difficult.

The Potawatomi at St. Joseph could not understand why their traders and blacksmith were taken from them. When they questioned De Peyster at Detroit about this, he replied that Sinclair would allow traders to return, but perhaps not the same ones who had just left. De Peyster was puzzled by Sinclair's action at a time when these unpredictable people were finally supporting the King.[14]

Meanwhile Sinclair was perturbed by De Peyster's apparently lax supervision of the traders. The Lieutenant Governor accused the Major of allowing traders to go to Saginaw Bay and the Grand River where rebel belts were known to be present. He also criticized De Peyster's Indian officers for mismanaging their posts.[15] In addition, Sinclair was frustrated because De Peyster had not sent him needed oxen, horses, and artisans from Detroit.

When De Peyster learned of Sinclair's complaints, he became exasperated. Writing to Haldimand he lamented, "My disputes with Capt. Sinclair are all chemerical, the meer produce of his own brain . . . ." If Sinclair thought De Peyster was encroaching on his authority, he would "freely give him up one half of my Command. . . . I have too mean an opinion of my abilities to offer to grasp at Power."[16]

As Lieutenant Alexander Harrow sailed the *Welcome* toward Fort Michilimackinac early on July 29, everything seemed in order. In the hold Harrow had carefully stowed fifty-six tierces of flour, three tierces of peas, forty-two barrels of pork, and twenty-one firkins of butter, all of which he had taken on board at Fort Erie. While at Detroit, his crew had loaded four big boxes, some harnesses, and rye seed for Sinclair. As the anchor chain rattled down the ship's side, the passengers prepared to disembark. Corporal Davidson and a matross of the Royal Artillery, two wives and a child from the men of the Eighty-Fourth, several traders, Chief Maskeash, his wife, and other members of his band were all eager to be reunited with friends or family.[17]

Harrow climbed down into a batteau and was rowed toward the wharf. As he approached the pier, an officer bluntly told him "You are not to Land here Captain Harrow." The baffled Harrow returned to the *Welcome* and ordered his passengers to go ashore. Two hours later Sinclair sent word that Harrow and his crew could now begin unloading and come to the fort.

About six o'clock in the evening the *Felicity* arrived from Mackinac Island. Harrow greeted her Commander Normand McKay who complained that he had been making frequent trips with a virtually empty hold.[18] Bothered by this wasteful use of the King's vessel, Harrow directed McKay to sail the *Felicity* to Detroit and transport goods from Fort Erie to that post. Harrow, however, added that if Sinclair countermanded this command, McKay was to obey the Lieutenant Governor.[19]

Next morning when McKay showed Harrow's order to Sinclair, the Commandant flew into a rage. The *Felicity* had not been making empty trips, Sinclair exclaimed. In fact, McKay had been carrying hay, cut along a river on the mainland north of the straits, to the island to be stored in the church.[20] Sinclair sent Sergeant Phillips, the acting Post Adjutant, to ask Harrow where he received authority to give such orders and informed the Lieutenant that if it ever happened again, Harrow would find himself under arrest. At four o'clock Harrow weighed anchor, but Phillips paddled after the ship in a canoe. When he caught the *Welcome*, Phillips ordered Harrow to wait until Sinclair gave permission to depart.

Within minutes Phillips, another sergeant, and six privates, all carrying loaded brown besses, boarded the sloop and took Harrow at gunpoint to shore. Stripped of his side arms, Harrow was ordered to remain inside the fort until Sinclair received instructions from General Haldimand. If Harrow wanted any of his effects from his cabin, he was to make a list, and Phillips would get them for him.[21]

Sinclair berated Harrow for bringing the Chippewa Chief Maskeash to Michilimackinac. The Captain claimed it was too late in the year for him to be here, but Harrow replied that Major De Peyster had ordered him to take the Chippewa on board the *Welcome*. Maskeash had been a regular passenger from the time his old friend Patrick Sinclair returned to the Great Lakes.

Maskeash asked Sinclair that Jean Baptiste Point du Sable, still detained at Michilimackinac, be sent to manage the pinery near Fort Sinclair and replace Francis Bellecour. Sinclair, perhaps anxious to rid himself of another remembrance of De Peyster, agreed and ordered James Guthrie, the *Welcome's* new Commander, to take Du Sable, along with Maskeash, to the Pine River.[22] Also on board were Archange Askin, her children, servants, and baggage. They were finally moving to Detroit.

Grumbling and conflict surfaced in other areas of the post. In the barracks the men of the Grenadier Company bitterly denounced Lieutenant Clowes because they had not been paid for eleven months. The men pointed out that twice a day they were required to answer roll call dressed in neat, clean uniforms, and at two shillings per pound, they could not afford to purchase flour to keep their hair powdered. Clowes rejected their demands that at least they be issued tobacco and rum as "working money." Lieutenant Brooke, meanwhile, paid the General's company with paper money, but Clowes refused to follow his example.[23]

Several times delegations of soldiers approached Sinclair complaining about inadequate provisions and lack of pay. On one occasion the Lieutenant Governor was heard throughout the fort shouting, "Damn you for a pack of Villians & Scoundrels none of your Majors or Mr. Askin's ways with me — it won't do." With no where else to turn, the men on July 30 petitioned De Peyster in Detroit to help redress their grievances. Realizing that their Commandant would be furious, they decided to "let the consequences be what it will, . . ."[24]

Lieutenant Mercer had more difficulties. Sinclair had ordered him to take Louis and Madame Chevallier into his home. Mercer bitterly complained that there was only one fireplace in his house, and there were "Soldiers in possession of houses unmolested and yet an officer is to be thus abused without the possible means of doing himself Justice."[25] Mercer requested permission to pitch a tent rather than live in such a crowded dwelling, but Sinclair refused to approve a suitable location.[26]

Sinclair accused Mercer of forcing him to draw "money without printed Bills, or destroying the Credit of my Promissory notes issued for the purpose of carrying on the works here." Apparently Mercer had failed to requisition enough of the forms used whenever the Commandant or other officials made local purchases.[27]

Amid all the bickering, the Sac and Fox paid a visit to Michilimackinac. In council Sinclair harshly denounced them for listening to the rebels and acting in their interest. As punishment Sinclair informed the Indians that he would allow no traders to visit them this year.

Castigating them for being "short sighted," he sent them on their way.[28] Despite his threats, Sinclair did allow some merchants to go to Illinois and the Mississippi region later in the year.[29]

Sinclair's contemptuous attitude puzzled Jean Marie Calve. When he returned to Michilimackinac, the Lieutenant Governor severely chastened him for alleged cowardice and disloyal behavior during the campaign against St. Louis. He tried to absolve himself by requesting permission to speak to Sinclair, but was unable to gain an audience. Finally Calvé petitioned Haldimand, claiming that he had taken great "pains and trouble" to keep the Sac and Fox loyal. Woefully he observed that he could not understand the reasons for his plight, unless Sinclair and the interpreters made false reports regarding his conduct.[30]

Among the traders the general store experiment lost its appeal. The Indians could not understand why they had to purchase goods from one store at high prices, when in the past they had been able to bargain with individual traders. Now that more merchandise was available, the merchants decided to dissolve the partnership and sell their own goods.[31]

One benefit of the general store had been that Sinclair selected only trusty people to go to the wintering grounds.[32] The other traders stayed at the fort and conducted limited transactions there. To further stabilize business, Sinclair ordered all government employees to refrain from any "meddling with Commerce."[33]

To his great distress, John Askin, "out of business and living at great expense," was only an observer of the trading activity within the community. After Sinclair refused his application to leave Michilimackinac in late July, Askin wrote to Commissary General Nathaniel Day pleading for permission to go to Quebec to settle his public accounts. Askin complained, "My situation is the most disagreeable I ever was in."[34]

Meanwhile in Detroit Askin's friend, Major De Peyster, wrote to Lieutenant Colonel Mason Bolton that Askin had performed useful service to the government. The Major mentioned that he had permitted Askin to borrow a few barrels of flour from the King's storehouse to feed his family. If Askin "exceeded the bounds of reason," he did so without De Peyster's authority, but he was convinced that Askin never acted dishonestly.[35] Later in the year Askin was able to leave Michilimackinac.

In mid-August De Peyster sent Captain John Mompesson with a sergeant, a corporal, and twenty privates of the King's Eighth Regiment to Michilimackinac to replace the Battalion Company. The new troops disembarked on Mackinac Island and joined the contingent of the Eighty-Fourth working there. Mompesson then went over to Michilimackinac to meet the Lieutenant Governor.[36]

When Mompesson arrived at the fort, he went to Sinclair's office and asked, "You are Building a Fort there?"

"Yes," was the reply.

"When will it be finished?"

Sinclair responded, "I cannot tell perhaps not in ten years."

To which Mompesson said, "What is it good for then?"

Back came the answer, "To put the troops in security as soon as possible which, with your help, I hope to do in a few months."

When he was shown his house, Mompesson did not like it, and he asked Sinclair to store his baggage until he could find more suitable quarters.[37]

The next day Captain Mompesson directed Lieutenant Clowes to read an order informing the troops on the parade ground that he was their new commanding officer. Claiming that he had no authority to do so, Clowes refused. Lieutenant Brooke then carried out Mompesson's order. Angered by Clowes' insubordination, Mompesson threatened to arrest him, but because Lieutenant Mercer, the only other officer in the fort, was under house arrest, Mompesson temporarily overlooked Clowes' action.[38]

Grenadier private, 8th Foot

Mompesson's pretensions infuriated Sinclair. The two officers refused to speak. Sinclair sent Mompesson, who was residing at the disgruntled Mercer's house, a note wanting "to know when he could be ready to go to Detroit as he did not choose to act under authority here." When Mompesson did not reply, Sinclair directed Lieutenant Clowes, the officer of the day, to find out why. Mompesson, through Clowes, informed Sinclair that he would neither receive nor answer correspondence from him.[39]

Mompesson then wrote a blistering letter to Haldimand informing him that he was the senior officer at Michilimackinac, and therefore the commanding officer.[40] Accusing Sinclair of opening and detaining his mail, Mompesson sent a duplicate letter by another vessel in case Sinclair confiscated the original.[41]

Sinclair also pleaded his case to Haldimand. He asked the General to resolve this dispute quickly for it created much confusion and discontent upon the traders and their employees. It was essential that the troops know who really was their commander.[42]

In the midst of this controversy Sinclair received intelligence that the rebels were assembling at Chicago.[43] Rumors flew about that "200 Pirogues with Creoles" were headed to Michilimackinac to avenge the attack on St. Louis. Fortunately, many of the traders and their engagés were still at the fort and could be called upon to repulse an assault.[44]

News of the confrontation between Sinclair and Mompesson spread quickly. On August 22 eighteen traders met at Mr. McGulpin's house and issued a declaration in support of Sinclair. They said Sinclair had not oppressed them; nor had he restrained their business.[45]

Four days after the outbreak of the dispute, Sinclair became sick and was confined to bed.[46] For over a week the Lieutenant Governor languished in his quarters, unable to carry out his duties. He was attended by Mrs. Thomas Shirley, who did his washing and cleaning as well as managing his household.[47]

Ivory medicine syringe

Turlington's Balsam of Life bottle

Sinclair's illness prompted sixty-five traders and merchants on September 6 to petition Mompesson to take charge of Michilimackinac's civil affairs until Sinclair regained his health. Many needed passes to go to their winter posts or to Montreal. Since the season was well advanced, it was essential that they be permitted to leave soon. In addition, a number of Indians were preparing to go to their wintering grounds. Before they departed it was necessary they be given presents, otherwise they would become discontented.[48]

Mompesson was faced with a difficult dilemma. On the other hand, he had no desire to usurp Sinclair's civil responsibilities, particularly after their bitter dispute. On the other hand, the situation required action. Mompesson tried "to make things go on smooth," but his efforts were not always successful.[49]

Mompesson felt compelled to send the prisoners, Juan Cardinal and La Roche, to Montreal. They caused great discomfort to the soldiers on duty in the guardhouse. The captives were "full of Filth and Vermin," and their cooking "Victuals at the Guard House fire, caused altogether an insufferable stench for people in health to be in."[50]

Because winter was approaching, Captain Mompesson was relieved to find enough provisions in the storehouse to provide for one hundred men for 3½ years. In addition, the *Welcome* was expected to deliver one more load, and the *Angelica* was believed on her way, carrying one hundred barrels of rum.[51] Mompesson hoped to purchase a large quantity of Indian corn from L'Arbre Croche and Saginaw.[52]

Fortunately Sinclair's health improved by mid-September, and he was able to meet with Indians and issue passes to traders. Before the snow fell, he had numerous other details to look after. There was a lot of work still to be done on the new fort, which Haldimand ordered named "Fort Makinac," rather than Fort Haldimand as Sinclair first proposed.[53] The rebel prisoners were kept working, though he received permission to send his Spanish captives to Montreal.[54]

The return of John Long's party from Prairie du Chien marked the conclusion of the ill-fated St. Louis expedition. Sinclair had sent Long with nine large canoes, loaded with Indian presents, and thirty-six Fox and Sioux warriors and twenty Canadians to retrieve a large quantity of furs left by the Mississippi traders who had accompanied Emanuel Hesse. After Charles Langlade retreated from the Illinois, he had gone there to guard this prize until it could be taken to Michilimackinac by Long. Five days after Long left Prairie du Chien with three hundred packs, the rebels arrived. They found only the ashes of sixty bundles of furs which Long had been unable to fit into his canoes. When Long applied to Sinclair for his pay, the Lieutenant Governor told him to collect from the traders. Long never received a shilling.[55]

Sinclair wrestled with the perplexing problem of whether or not to accede to the St. Joseph Potawatomi's demands that traders be sent to winter with them. Frequently these Indians rode their horses to Detroit to council with De Peyster, but because they did not use canoes, they seldom came to Michilimackinac.[56] De Peyster recommended to Sinclair that traders should be sent to St. Joseph to keep the

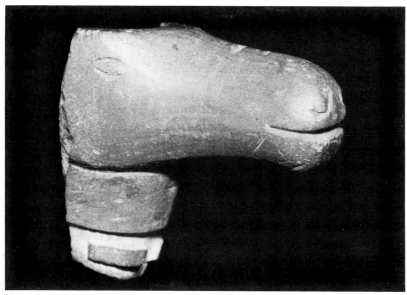

Tobacco pipe carved in the shape of a horse

Potawatomi in the King's interest. Otherwise they would either become estranged or make great demands for presents and provisions at Detroit.[57] For a change, Sinclair followed De Peyster's advice and authorized Benjamin Lyon, Henry Bostwick, Etienne Campion, and Antoine Reilhe to winter with these undependable people.[58]

De Peyster and Sinclair made this friendly gesture despite the Potawatomi's shameful performance at the falls of the Ohio. There a force of two hundred took one scalp, but fled when they heard that the Piankashaws had fallen upon some of their warriors. When Dagneau De Quindre brought them to Detroit, they demanded presents, but De Peyster refused to reward their cowardice.[59]

Even as the King's engagés carried this season's final shipment of Indian goods into the storehouse, Sinclair contemplated his needs for next year. To properly outfit the Indians would require six thousand blankets, four thousand shirts, and one hundred pieces of stroud and moulton with a large quantity of small articles.[60]

Autumn brought additional troubles to Lieutenant Clowes. Acting upon complaints from Captain Mompesson, Major De Peyster ordered Ensign John McDougall to Michilimackinac to relieve Clowes. The Major was so distressed at the Lieutenant's behavior that he took action without waiting for Lieutenant Colonel Bolton to render his judgment.[61]

Gilded officer's button

Meanwhile, the strife between Sinclair and Alexander Harrow continued. Harrow complained to Alexander Grant that letters to Grant at Detroit had been opened by Sinclair and may never have been sent.[62] On September 13 Harrow got his wish to go to Detroit to settle his difficulties. He arrived there on September 19 on board the *Angelica*. One week later, Captain Grant ordered Harrow to resume command of the *Welcome*.[63]

In Quebec Samuel Robertson, Joseph Ainsse, and Louis Chevallier presented themselves to General Haldimand. Robertson had been permitted to return to Montreal to rejoin his family. However, he could not yet stand trial because Haldimand deemed it necessary that Sinclair be there to face the accused.[64] Similarly, Haldimand was unable to proceed against Ainsse and Chevallier, for Sinclair had not furnished enough evidence to support specific charges against them. When both laid large drafts for goods provided the government before Haldimand, he felt legally obligated to honor these unless Sinclair could prove otherwise.[65] Their fate remained undetermined.

News of the muddled state of affairs at Michilimackinac upset Haldimand. Writing to Bolton he complained that De Peyster was "not ignorant of the state of Public affairs at Michilimackinac," and he should not have sent Mompesson there. The General was also perturbed with De Peyster for entertaining the grievances of Lieutenant Clowes' company, which should have been submitted to Bolton, the Regimental Commander.[66] Haldimand then ruled that Sinclair was the senior officer on the basis of his former rank; consequently, he was the commanding officer.[67]

Haldimand authorized Sinclair to keep the *Welcome* and the *Hope* at Michilimackinac. Contrary to Sinclair's wishes, Haldimand wanted all repairs done at Detroit in order to keep the ship carpenters and their tools together. Furthermore, only one vessel was to winter at the straits.[68]

Hoping to clarify the touchy subject of authority over ship's commanders, Haldimand issued guidelines. Sinclair could continue to give orders, but it would be best if he did not interfere with "the interior destinations of the officers." In situations where the King's service would be vitally affected, Sinclair could countermand any previous orders.[69]

The ships' captains were in a potentially explosive situation, having to answer to Captain Alexander Grant at Detroit and the Lieutenant Governor as well. Only discretion by all parties involved could prevent future squabbles among the King's officers similar to the dispute that had arisen between Sinclair and Harrow.

Pewter soldiers' buttons

Detail from De Berniere's 1773 drawing of Fort Erie

Before the ice formed, Sinclair had hoped to welcome a company of the Forty-Seventh Regiment. On October 17 De Peyster ordered forty privates and their non-commissioned officers on board a ship headed to Michilimackinac. Strong winds and driving rain and snow turned the vessel back. Sinclair learned from a courier sent overland by De Peyster that reinforcements would not arrive this winter. Since no evidence of the rumored rebel activity at Chicago had been received, there was no immediate need for more troops.[70]

Nevertheless, Sinclair's garrison was larger than it had ever been. The October return showed:[71]

	King's Regt.	84th
Captains	1	1
Lieutenants	2	
Mate	1	
Sergeants	6	1
Drummers	3	
Rank & File fit for duty	83	22
Sick in quarters	1	
On Furlough	2	
Recruits not joined	1	
Prisoners of war	7	
Prisoners in Canada	1	
Total rank and file		117

In the powder magazine rested nine barrels and forty-seven pounds of gunpowder. The artillery at the fort included two heavy iron six-pounders, two light brass six-pounders, four brass ambuzettes blown in the vent [two were on the *Felicity*], one brass 4-2/5 inch mortar, and two wall pieces. Also in the stores were 5,046 musket flints and 780 carbine flints.[72]

On October 22 tragedy struck the *Welcome* crew. John Donald, age 29, while walking along the island wharf, fell into the icy water and drowned. Within ten or twelve minutes his body was recovered, but it was too late to revive him. Harrow ordered his men to take the corpse to a nearby house and watch over it until a coffin could be built and proper funeral arrangements made.[73] Two weeks after Donald's death, Harrow made William Dennis, a prisoner, a member of his crew.[74]

By early December the season had advanced so far that it was time to lay up the *Welcome* and the *Angelica*. The crews took down the sails and rigging and put the spars on shore.[75] Harrow tied the ships to the wharf and hoped the harbor would afford them safety.

On December 10 a northeast gale blew until five a.m. and then switched to the southwest. Powerful white and gray waves demolished about forty feet of the wharf, and two holes were punched in the *Angelica's* bilge. Her hold quickly filled with water. Harrow ordered the soldiers to man the pumps and bail out the water. Working feverishly in the teeth of the cold storm, they discovered "a large hole under the round of the Bow," which they patched immediately. Having secured the *Angelica,* they "hauled the *Welcome* to the shore — got everything out and hove her Bow up." The next day they did the same to the *Angelica.* Two weeks later she was further damaged by another storm.[76]

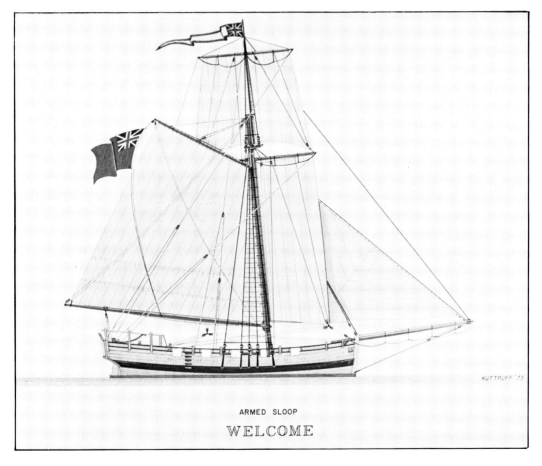

ARMED SLOOP

WELCOME

XIII.

War Costs Rise

Spanish two bit piece

New Year's Day, 1781 provided a well-deserved rest for the community. Despite the bitter cold, Patrick Sinclair had been working his men relentlessly both on Mackinac Island and at Michilimackinac in an effort to have the new fort ready by early summer. To celebrate the holiday he issued each soldier and sailor a half pint of rum and a pound of tobacco.[1] The civilians, too, welcomed the day off and the opportunity to make merry, skate, and relax. The reprieve was short, for the next day banging hammers and rasping saws again punctuated the frosty air. Sinclair lost no time getting back to the business at hand.

On January 27 Etienne Campion and a party of Canadians approached the land gate leading three rebel prisoners.[2] Passing by the sentry, Campion went directly to the commanding officer's house. He brought disturbing news — the rebels were on the move. In October a Frenchman, Augustin de la Balme, who had come to Illinois, raised a contingent of about one hundred Indians and French to attack Detroit. On his way he destroyed an Indian village at Miamitown [Fort Wayne, Indiana] on November 3. Before La Balme could move on, an Indian war party led by Little Turtle attacked his army and killed him.[3]

More alarming, in early December a force of sixteen men led by Jean Baptiste Hamelin from Cahokia attacked St. Joseph and captured a few traders and fifty bales of merchandise. The raiders swiftly departed toward Chicago, hoping to return home by way of the Illinois River. Lieutenant Dagneau de Quindre, stationed near St. Joseph, assembled an Indian party and pursued the rebels. Catching up with them just beyond the River du Chemin, De Quindre attacked Hamelin's force when they refused to surrender. De Quindre killed four, wounded two, and captured seven, while three escaped into the woods.[4] Campion now delivered three of these prisoners to Sinclair; De Quindre took the others to Detroit.

Sinclair worried about these offensive probes, and ordered Campion to travel among the western traders warning them to be on "guard against similar attempts." They should watch their merchandise carefully.[5]

Unknown to Sinclair and Campion, Don Eugenio Pourée and Black Bird, accompanied by Louis Chevallier, Jr., were leading sixty-five Spanish militiamen from St. Louis toward St. Joseph. There on February 12 they surprised the fort for the second time and took it without losing a man. The Spanish flag fluttered from the flagpole during the single day they occupied the post. Most of the captured goods were given to the Indians as rewards for their support. De Quindre arrived the next day, but this time was unable to catch the retreating army.[6]

These Spanish operations were in part an effort to forestall Sinclair from sending Wabasha against them in 1781. Lieutenant Governor Francisco Cruzat, who had succeeded the deceased Leyba, believed that Sinclair himself might lead the expedition and that the English were distributing large quantities of merchandise among the Sioux and neighboring tribes to gain their support. In December Cruzat informed Governor General Bernardo Galvez that he planned to disrupt Sinclair's intentions.[7] Perhaps the successful raid on St. Joseph would place Sinclair on the defensive.

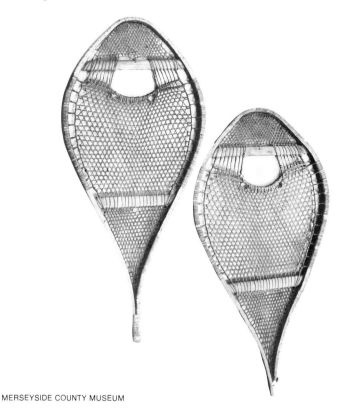

Ein Britischer Soldat auf dem
Posten, in der Canadischen
Winter kleidung. 1766.

kail   F. v Germann

*A British soldier in
Canadian winter
clothing.*

The soldiers at Michilimackinac found their lives seriously disrupted this winter. Those not working on the island were forced
to move into the newly constructed blockhouse on the church
grounds or into traders' houses because carpenters had dismantled
their barracks. Now that the ice bridge was safe, Mompesson's men,
bundled up in their warm great coats, hauled the squared logs and
sections of roof to the island.[8] They also transported the King's
storehouse and the guardhouse to the new fort.

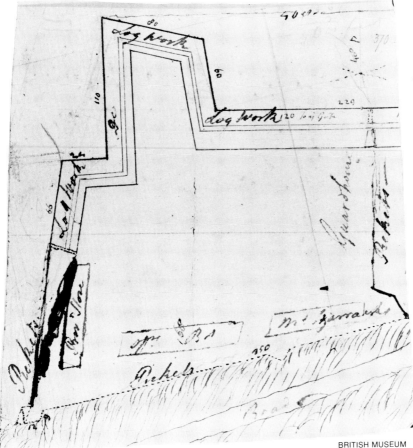

Sinclair's map of partially completed Fort Mackinac

On the island the men clapboarded the blockhouse, built the previous winter, and constructed sleeping berths and partitions inside.[9] A ramp cut into the steep hillside led up the bluff and provided the main access to the fort. Attackers advancing up the path would be subjected to fire from the fort walls and from a projecting gun emplacement which enfiladed the entire approach. The main gate was at right angles to the ramp and was entered by steps which passed through a stone archway. The face of the walls was carefully laid of squared stone, but behind them a jumble of rubble was dumped in as filler. Nearby circular stone kilns glowed as limestone was reduced to finely powdered lime for mortar. Construction with stone was slow, so the landward bastions were first made by filling cribs of horizontal logs with earth. Masonry facings would come later.

Soon buildings would occupy the fort's interior. The guardhouse would stand sentinel beside the main gate. The barracks waited to be reassembled on the landward side of the central parade ground, and the provision storehouse was ready to be re-erected along the west end. Sinclair planned to construct a stone powder magazine and dig a deep well. He also sketched plans for a massive stone building along the harbor side. Solidly built, the one-hundred-foot-long structure would serve both as a blockhouse and as officers' quarters.

Even with the passage of time, Sinclair and Mompesson barely tolerated each other. Mompesson, in accordance with Haldimand's order, had subjugated himself to the Lieutenant Governor's command, but he did not like him. On March 21 Sinclair nailed an advertisement on the church door proclaiming his "authority as Lieutenant Governor & Commandant." This puzzled Mompesson, for their dispute had been resolved nearly six months earlier. In a letter to De Peyster, Mompesson stated that Sinclair was guilty of more inconsistencies than any man he knew, and all the officers and traders at Michilimackinac held the same opinion.[10]

Early in April carpenters finished repairing the *Welcome* and *Angelica* damaged in the December storms. Harrow's crew mended sails, overhauled the blocks, picked oakum, and made spun yarn. The bowsprits were repaired and put back in place. Exposed to strong winds and snow showers, the seamen set the ships' riggings. Meanwhile, two carpenters caulked the seams and covered the vessels with pitch. On April 17 the sailors tied the *Welcome's* sails and hove the ballast stones into the hold; the *Angelica* was ready to sail a few days later. Finally, at five o'clock in the afternoon on April 24, the *Welcome* made her first voyage of the year to the mainland.[11] Two weeks later the *Angelica* departed for Detroit carrying the season's first mail to friends, officials, and associates.[12]

Throughout the upcoming months the *Welcome* made repeated trips between the island and the mainland. She hauled bricks, window frames, doors, planks, and boards from buildings in the old fort.[13] On board she carried the belongings of Benjamin Lyon, Charles Gautier, David McCrae, Henry Bostwick, George McBeath, and David Rankin. Occasionally the crew sailed to Bois Blanc Island, Cheboygan, and the streams of the northern mainland to pick up loads of hay and logs. Occasionally they towed rafts of timbers.[14]

Mackinac Island harbor

The island was a hive of activity. Traders' houses were brought over and re-erected on the flat land along the harbor. The compact settlement lay to the southwest of the fort so that its guns could protect the town walls. A row of palisades enclosed to the landward side of the village and provided some protection from a surprise attack. Two streets ran the length of the town. One paralleled the curvature of the bay, with buildings only on the land side of the street. On the other thoroughfare, one block inland, buildings lined both sides. Henry Bostwick and the other traders grumbled at the expense of the move, but they appreciated the convenience of the deep harbor.

On Saturday, May 12, in the grove of maple trees below the fort, Captain Sinclair, dressed in his scarlet coat and plaid kilt, faced the Chippewa Chiefs Kitchie Negon or Grand Sable, Pouanas, Koupe, and Magousseihigan. Surrounding them were chiefs from other nations, and subalterns, and traders David Rankin, Matthew Lassey, John Macnamara, Benjamin Lyon, Etienne Campion, and Pierre Antoine Tableau. Solemnly Sinclair read the deed transferring ownership of Mackinac Island from the Chippewa to King George III. The interpreter repeated the text in the Chippewa tongue, and the Lieutenant Governor presented a seven-foot wampum belt to be kept in the Chippewa village as a "lasting memorial" of the transaction. Sinclair signed the deed, each chief carefully scrawled his totem on the side of it, and the traders who witnessed the ceremony stood in line to sign the document. Two copies were made. The chiefs were given more than a dozen canoe loads of presents worth £5,000 New York Currency as payment. Now the island legally belonged to the Kingdom of Great Britain.[15]

Under this maple tree Mackinac Island was sold by the Chippewa to Great Britain

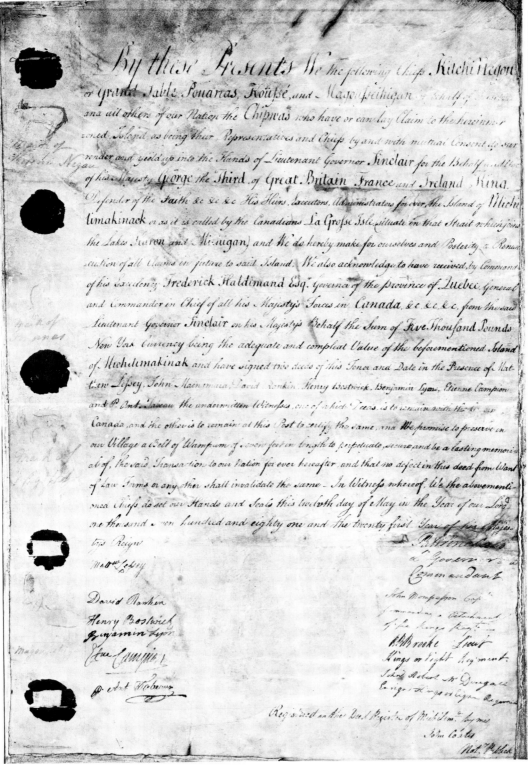

The deed to Mackinac Island signed by both the Chippewa and the British.

Fort Mackinac today

On May 24 the *Welcome* transferred part of the garrison with its belongings.[16] The troops pitched their tents on the parade ground and started work. Their first task was to re-erect the provisions storehouse and attach an addition. When this was completed in June, they began work on the barracks and the powder magazine, but they were slowed by lack of men, tools, and materials. Fortunately the Canadian laborers, who assisted the soldiers, worked tirelessly without complaint,[17] and these buildings were up within a month.[18] By the end of July half of the troops were stationed at Fort Mackinac and the rest were expected by October. The men now began the stone wall of the officers' quarters.[19]

Feeding these workmen was costly. The Canadians depended on the King's provisions, as did visiting Indians, who were more numerous than ever. Sinclair hoped to purchase Indian corn, and he needed enough flour, pork, peas, and butter to feed two hundred men for over a year.[20] Every time the King's canoes arrived the engagés were detained and put to work on the island.[21] This growing labor force drained Sinclair's supplies.

The flurry of construction caused unprecedented disruptions. Some traders were on the island, others on the mainland. Instead of gardening, farming, cutting and transporting wood and hay, and paddling into the interior some inhabitants had to spend their time moving. Yet as much as possible the summer tasks had to be done. Everyone was concerned that the divided community was vulnerable to attack. Fortunately no serious threat arose. Despite antagonisms toward Sinclair and inevitable personal quarrels, the town moved in an orderly fashion.

Sinclair's 1781 sketch of Fort Mackinac.

During 1781 General Haldimand thought it prudent to encourage the northwest trade. While he agreed with Sinclair that unscrupulous traders might possibly smuggle goods to the rebels from Lake Superior's southern shore, he thought it unlikely that any would do so.[22]

The northwest traders' most serious problem was a shortage of Indian corn. Corn, the staff of life for the voyageurs, was absolutely necessary to outfit canoes heading toward Lake Superior. Without it, the merchants would have to abandon that branch of the trade and suffer great losses. In petitioning Haldimand to allow them to buy five hundred bushels at Detroit, they reminded him that Quebec Province could lose over £30,000 Sterling in furs.[23]

As a result of rebel incursions and the questionable loyalty of some nations, the number of canoes was considerably curtailed. Only seventy-eight were licensed for Michilimackinac and beyond, with thirty-eight of these going on to Lake Superior and the northwest.[24] Before the canoes left Michilimackinac, sufficient corn was procured to supply the voyageurs who went into the interior.

Haldimand believed the Spanish raids on St. Joseph clearly illustrated two things. First, it was foolish for traders to send large quantities of unprotected merchandise to remote areas.[25] Secondly, the Potawatomi and other nations must protect the traders; otherwise, he would not permit the traders to go to them. It was the Indians' duty to defend their villages and keep hostile forces away from their wintering grounds.[26] The Indians living in the Mississippi area had been alert and had safeguarded their traders from insults like those at St. Joseph.[27]

Traders were permitted to go to St. Joseph only at their own risk.[28] Those whose goods were looted by the Spanish claimed that because they went there at Sinclair's request to keep the Potawatomi loyal, the Crown should reimburse their losses.[29] Haldimand refused their demand for he had no desire to underwrite their ventures.

One lively branch of the trade was catering to the needs of enlisted men and officers. Sergeant Amos Langdown had an insatiable appetite for cheese, and in July William Macomb at Detroit shipped him twenty-six pounds at 4s and two pounds of green tea at 20s. Earlier Macomb had sent up on board the *Mackinac* sugar, tea, pepper, vinegar, and rum for Ensign John McDougall. McDougall also sought to purchase a panis girl to assist his wife with her work.[30]

F or three years Governor Haldimand had tried to convince his commanders at Niagara, Detroit, and Michilimackinac to reduce their presents to the Indians. Despite his efforts to obtain more supplies from England, each year the superintendents bought larger quantities of goods from local merchants. Exasperated he decided to end this practice. On June 22 he notified the commanding officers of the upper posts that they were "strictly required upon no account whatever after the receipt of this order to purchase from the Traders residing at the said Posts or any others, Rum, Liquors or any articles whatever for the use of Indians in behalf of the Crown . . . ."[31] Only canoes and provisions were excepted.

Haldimand was also disturbed about the presents of furs, corn, and grease that visiting chiefs gave the commanders at Detroit and Michilimackinac. They reciprocated by giving the chiefs gifts from the King's stores while keeping for their personal use the items received from Indians. The larger the Indian's gift, the more he expected in return. Local merchants encouraged this practice, thereby forcing Sinclair or De Peyster to buy additional goods from them. Haldimand thought that considerable savings could be achieved if the presents from the Indians were kept by the government. If the government refused to accept the Indians offerings, however, they would interpret it as a slap in the face. To compensate the commandants for the loss of income, their salaries would have to be raised. Perhaps the numbers of Indians who came to the posts could be limited, but no one at headquarters knew how this could be accomplished.[32]

Haldimand also wanted to decrease the amount of rum given to Indians. Liquor, he believed, destroyed the character of many warriors and reduced hundreds of Indian families to poverty.[33] Less rum would also save money, and the cost of Indian affairs was prominent in the General's mind. He feared the growing expenditures for Indian affairs would attract "the serious observation of the King's Ministers."[34]

Patrick Sinclair was distressed by the change in policy. Haldimand, in Quebec, did not have to face the insistent chiefs who threatened to ally themselves with Clark or become neutral. If they were snubbed or offended, they would become hostile to British traders, as well as to

Otterskin medicine bag decorated with beads, quills and tinkling cones.

the King. The Crown's goods usually arrived late and in insufficient quantities.[35] Banning local purchases might spare Haldimand embarrassment in London, but it would create chaos at Michilimackinac.

While officials in Quebec stewed about the costs, the Indians continued to come to Michilimackinac. By June 6 twenty-three Sioux chiefs, many Menominee, Winnebago, Ottawa, and Chippewa had already called "to give assurance of their steady friendship . . . ."[36] Within two weeks the undependable Sac and Fox came from the Mississippi to inform Sinclair that they no longer planned to pay any heed to the enemy.[37]

Short of supplies, Sinclair went to the local merchants. On June 10 he bought ten canoes and some provisions from George Meldrum. Since canoes were fragile and had to be replaced frequently, local Indians and Canadians manufactured many each year. One canoe was worth £13/6/8.[38]

On July 31 Sinclair violated Haldimand's order and purchased the incredible amount of £49,503 New York Currency worth of merchandise from Macnamara and Co. Sinclair needed these goods because the King's canoes were late, and more Indians than usual had already come.[39] The Lieutenant Governor was headed for trouble with his commander.

Government goods always got to Michilimackinac too late in the year. Thus Sinclair could not adequately supply his interpreters with presents before they went to their wintering grounds or satisfy visiting Indians. Consequently his agents made charges against the Indian Department in the interior to meet Indian demands. If the natives were detained at Michilimackinac to await the arrival of presents, they became uneasy and ate up the limited provisions. Defiantly, Sinclair told Haldimand, "I shall only add that I made no purchases from Traders, when the necessary articles are in Store, . . ."[40]

In late September eight canoes finally arrived from Montreal loaded with presents.[41] When the bales were unpacked, Sinclair was still short of his needs. Between July 31 and September 30 he charged over £89,430 to the Indian Department on account with local merchants.

Even before these drafts reached Haldimand's desk, he admonished Sinclair for his extravagance the previous year, 1780, when he spent over £57,000.[42] Sinclair pleaded that he did not "overstep the bounds of necessity." He fervently claimed that if presents were reduced, the British could lose their Indian allies.[43] Sinclair was caught in a dilemma. If he obeyed his commander, he would lose the loyalty of the western nations; if he defied Haldimand, he could be held personally accountable for the expenses he had incurred.

The Lieutenant Governor also discovered that building a fort was expensive. By September 30, 1781 he had run up expenses of over £41,000 New York Currency on account with the Michilimackinac merchants. Meldrum, Macnamara, McCrae, and others supplied iron, steel, axes, saws, nails, paint, brass locks and coverplates, chisels, and tin needed to construct Fort Mackinac.[44] These costs were high, but at least Sinclair had something tangible to show.

The Officers' Stone Quarters at Fort Mackinac.

On Saturday, August 19, Patrick Sinclair gladly bid farewell to Captain Mompesson and a detachment of the King's Eighth. On the day before, the *Angelica* had brought to the island Captain Thomas Aubrey and about fifty men of the Forty-Seventh Regiment of Foot to replace the unhappy Mompesson.[45] But Aubrey was none too pleased to be here. When he first learned of his assignment, he requested Haldimand for permission to go to England. Aubrey, aware of the difficulties between Sinclair and Mompesson, did not like being put "under the command of a junior officer."[46] Nevertheless, Haldimand wanted a speedy cure to the dissension at Michilimackinac, and he hoped the Eighth's departure would restore tranquility to the garrison.[47]

In September the *Dunmore* docked in the harbor, and Ensign Gustavus Hamilton, with additional soldiers of the Forty-Seventh, disembarked to complete the transfer.[48] Only Sergeant Phillips and Surgeon's Mate David Mitchell of the Eighth stayed behind. Mitchell had wanted to leave the service, but Haldimand refused his request. The General did permit him to remain at Michilimackinac with his Indian wife when his regiment moved on.[49]

Drummer, 47th Foot

172

Several traders still had outstanding claims against the government for last year's expedition down the Mississippi. Joseph Howard demanded payment of £1443/16 New York Currency due for flour, tobacco, salt, pork, tafia, muskets, powder, shot, and corn furnished Hesse's party. Sinclair gave Howard a bill of exchange redeemable by Haldimand within sixty days after he received it.[50]

John Kay and David McCrae presented a more complicated claim. In 1778 they had sent to Michilimackinac eight loaded canoes. Five continued under the charge of Charles Gratiot to the Illinois, where the rebels captured him and his merchandise. Gratiot continued trading under a Spanish pass, and was so doing when his boat was seized by Alexander Kay in May, 1780. Part of Gratiot's furs and provisions were placed in a warehouse at Michilimackinac, where the boat was being used by the government. Kay and McCrae petitioned for these captured goods up to a value of £4,000 Halifax Currency.[51]

Also bearing a tale of woe, Joseph Baptiste Parent sought permission from Haldimand to leave Montreal. For some years he had traded near Prairie du Chien, carrying a Spanish pass. He claimed that he always befriended Michilimackinac traders that passed his way. In April, 1780 when Charles Gautier arrived with a large party headed for Illinois, Parent offered to supply him. Three days later he was surprised when Gautier took him prisoner and confiscated his goods. When a friend told him that Spain and England were at war, Parent laid down his arms. He was then taken to Michilimackinac, where Sinclair sent him on to Montreal. Now he needed to go to either Detroit or Michilimackinac to provide for his destitute family.[52]

Detroit merchants Normand McLeod, Alexander Saunders, and John Martin complained that John Baptiste Barthe was operating the *Mackinac* and the *De Peyster* upon Lake Huron. Since private vessels were prohibited from sailing on the lakes, they charged that Barthe had an unfair advantage.[53]

Sinclair refuted this accusation by noting that he had ordered these vessels down from Lake Superior last year and had used them in the King's service. On other occasions he had issued passes for these ships to sail to Detroit and transport traders' goods.[54] This year the *Mackinac,* about sixteen or seventeen tons burden, made six trips to Detroit carrying merchandise for Barthe, Macomb and Company, the North West Company, George McBeath, Saunders, Edward Ridley, Meldrum and Park, and several others, including Sinclair himself. The *De Peyster*, of about eight or nine tons, made only one trip, and that was for McLeod's partner, John Macnamara.[55] Sinclair argued he had shown preference to no one, particularly since the petitioners owned no boat themselves.[56]

Pewter button, 47th Foot

As 1781 ended, Sinclair was faced with a difficult problem. Haldimand's orders forbidding local purchases put him in a seemingly impossible situation — Indian demands increased while the availability of authorized presents decreased. This year, in contrast to others, the Indians around Michilimackinac had been relatively inactive. Consequently they had more time to come to the fort and the island seeking a handout. In spite of his difficulties with Indian diplomacy, Sinclair took pride in the successful transfer of the garrison to Fort Mackinac. Many of the traders had moved, and the new settlement on Mackinac Island was becoming a viable community.

Excavated remains of the Powder Magazine at Fort Michilimackinac. This structure and others were burned by the departing British garrison.

XIV.

Exit Patrick Sinclair

Brass Royal Artillery button

During the past seven years Michilimackinac had been jolted repeatedly by news of distant disasters. In the spring of 1782, another bolt struck. Word arrived of Lord Charles Cornwallis' surrender to General George Washington at Yorktown, Virginia, the previous October. Initial reports were unconfirmed, but if true the British would be severely weakened.[1] Despite the defeat in the east, Patrick Sinclair still had to deal with the perplexing war problems at Michilimackinac.

Fortunately news from the Mississippi was reassuring. Everything there appeared quiet, and the traders had not encountered any hostility. In late April, Sinclair urged Haldimand to issue the passes early, for he planned to employ the engagés on the King's works. The sooner they got here, the more labor Sinclair could get out of them before they scattered for their wintering places. Construction was progressing well since he had hired private horses and carts to transport timbers.[2]

Sinclair, frustrated and impatient, tried again to convince Haldimand that he had exercised propriety in managing his expenses. Sinclair reckoned that canoes, provisions, arms, and ammunition at Michilimackinac were worth four times as much as at Quebec. If one used this ratio, the cost of the St. Louis expedition, although expensive, was not as great as it appeared.[3] Because he was unable to equip many distant warriors directly out of the King's store, it was necessary for him to ask the traders to do so, thereby increasing costs.

Furthermore, many of the Indians and Canadians who had accompanied Hesse did not come to Michilimackinac for their payments until 1781. They waited several weeks for the King's canoes, but "the supply when arrived was certainly not adequate . . . ."[4] In previous years Sinclair had to equip Indians for war; now as the pace of war lessened, he had to give them provisions to remain at peace.[5]

The General was not impressed with Sinclair's arguments. On May 9 he informed Sinclair that he would refuse to honor his drafts.[6] Sinclair, himself, was liable for these debts. Merchants holding Sinclair's bills would have to sue him to settle their accounts.

Copper trade kettle

In early May the year's first loads of Indian presents departed for Michilimackinac. In his letter accompanying this brigade, Frederick Haldimand seemed to soften his earlier position regarding local purchases. He hoped this supply would be sufficient for Sinclair's demands. Feeling that the merchants' charges were exorbitant, he warned Sinclair "to take as little from them as possible." Yet Sinclair was "not to delay the King's Service in any material point by our economy."[7] Apparently Haldimand concluded there was no way to stop Sinclair from patronizing the traders. Consequently, he authorized George McBeath, a trader, to provide merchandise for the government "at what is considered at Reasonable Profit, . . ."[8]

To feed the influx of Indians Sinclair bought a large quantity of corn. John Coates supplied 513 bags; Charles Gautier, 500 bags; Hypolitte Chaboillez, 50 bags, with another 580 still on order; and John Macnamara and Co. planned to deliver 457 bags and 2,789 pounds of grease.[9]

Before the summer ended he needed all these provisions. By September 10 John Coates, Clerk to the Indian Department, estimated the number of natives who had resorted to the island:[10]

Tribe	Persons
Ottawa from L'Arbre Croche, 400 men with families	1,000
Ottawa from Grand River & Banks of Lake Michigan	1,200
Chippewa from island	100
(The following were chiefs and heads of families who received presents)	
Chippewa from St. Mary's	50
Chippewa from "Lake Huron Mississagi River La Cloche &c"	150
Chippewa from Lake Superior	500
Menominee from La Baye and Lake Huron	250
Indians of the Mississippi	
Winnebago	150
Sac	250
Fox	200
Aswoés	50
Sioux, "Chiefly the Heads of Tribes"	100
Potawatomi	20
	4,020

Chippewa village at Sault Ste. Marie drawn by Paul Kane in the 1840's.

Sinclair could not satisfy both the Indians and his superiors. He informed John Campbell, Indian Superintendent for Quebec Province, on July 16 that Indians leaving Michilimackinac were "but half satisfied" with their presents. In the fall Sinclair sent Campbell a long list of goods needed for next year, and he deemed it essential that the Crown continue to be generous to their allies even though the war was ending.[11]

Other commodities were also in short supply, and it was a welcome sight when the King's vessels delivered the provisions from Detroit and Fort Erie. This year the *Wyandot* made the first voyage to the island.[12] There was a sense of loss for the *Welcome* no longer sailed the straits. Battered in a severe storm last fall, her damage was so extensive that Sinclair condemned her.[13] This beautiful vessel, after serving the community for six years, had been mortally wounded in the line of duty.

On July 19 two rebel prisoners were brought to the island. They told Sinclair of a battle on June 4 near Sandusky [Ohio] where a force of rangers and Indians commanded by Captain William Caldwell defeated a rebel army of about five hundred men. The captured American Colonel William Crawford was burned at the stake. The Ohio frontier witnessed numerous atrocities, including earlier in the spring the massacre by Pennsylvania and Virginia militia of nearly one hundred peaceful Christian Delaware Indians living along the Tuscarawas River.

The Ottawa at L'Arbre Croche were still willing to follow the British to war.[14] When Sinclair, after receiving De Peyster's plea for help, summoned them, La Fourche and Quieouigoushkam led their warriors to Detroit to serve under their old friend.[15] They joined the Indian agent Alexander McKee and Captain Caldwell on a raid deep into Ohio and Kentucky. There they attacked Bryan's Station and in mid-August at Blue Licks they severely defeated Daniel Boone and a force of Kentucky militia.[16]

While the Ottawa were in Kentucky, it was rumored in Detroit that the Sac had attacked their wives and children. Fortunately a vessel from Michilimackinac brought word that all was well in the Ottawa villages. De Peyster relayed this message to McKee and sent a belt of friendship given him by La Fourche and Quieouigoushkam while he was still at Michilimackinac. The wampum convinced the chiefs that De Peyster spoke the truth and discounted the reports of danger to their families.[17]

When La Fourche's expedition returned to Michilimackinac, they claimed payment for services rendered hundreds of miles away. This raid into Kentucky had to be paid for by Sinclair at Michilimackinac.[18]

The local merchants and residents still longed for a priest. It had been seven years since Father Gibault last visited Michilimackinac. The dying did not have access to clergy; nor could men who traveled from Canada or the interior make confession or partake of other sacraments. In July Jean Baptiste Barthe, Alexis and Etienne Campion, and several other prominent traders petitioned Haldimand to allow a missionary to come and to minister to their spiritual needs.[19]

Others made plans to form a masonic lodge. David Mitchell, George Meldrum, Benjamin Lyon, and John Coates met at various times with Lieutenants Clowes and Brooke and other officers. Many of the prominent traders and officers who came to Michilimackinac were already lodge members. One of the first masons at Mackinac was Robert Rogers. Now the "Brothers" set about to organize the St. John's Lodge on Mackinac Island.[20]

As a result of the relative peace along the Mississippi, the traders' business flourished in 1782. In the trading canoes there were fewer kegs of rum. The ninety canoes licensed for Michilimackinac, with forty of these headed for Lake Superior, carried only about half as much rum as the previous year.[21] Apparently Haldimand's effort to reduce liquor among the Indians was having an effect.

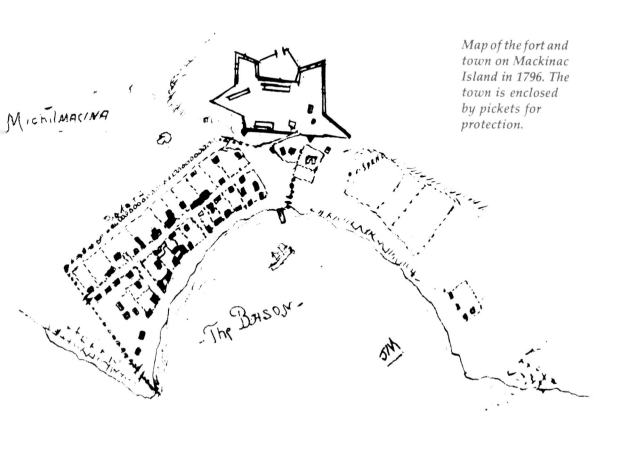

Map of the fort and town on Mackinac Island in 1796. The town is enclosed by pickets for protection.

C ontinued dissatisfaction with the Indian Department prompted
    General Haldimand to send an inspection team to the upper
posts. On August 15 Lieutenant Colonel Henry Hope, the new
Superintendent of Indian Affairs Sir John Johnson, Lieutenant
Richard Hockings, and several others set out by canoe from Quebec
for Fort Mackinac.[22] A month later they arrived. Lieutenant Colonel
Hope immediately puffed up the hill and requested to see Sinclair.
Having exchanged greetings, Hope got right to the point. He bluntly
told his host that he was here to inquire into the "cause of the great
expenses that had been incurred of late at Michilimackinac, and to
apply such temporary remedies to the different abuses that might
appear as were most expedient."[23]

Carefully examining Sinclair's accounts, Hope was appalled by the
large payroll for the Indian Department. Included were Surgeon David
Mitchell; Alexander Kay, James Phillips (Sergeant in the King's Eighth
who had been assigned to the Department), Antoine Ignace and
Charles Langlade, Jr., who were currently with the Ottawa expedition
to Kentucky; and Interpreters Maurice Blondeau, Jean Baptiste
Cadot at St. Marys, and Joseph Rocque in the Sioux country. In
addition, there were two blacksmiths, Augustin Feltcan and Monsieur
Vassuer; Louis Varin, a cooper; and storekeeper John Waters. Each of
these men were paid 8s a day New York Currency. Drawing the same
wages was Thomas Stone, the ferrykeeper on the mainland, and his
two helpers, who earned 4s per day. John Coates received 12s per diem
for his dual role as commissary and clerk.[24]

Hope and Johnson were shocked by the wasteful method of feeding
Indians. There was no prescribed ration, consequently John Coates
never knew how many provisions were actually in the storehouse.
This situation made it possible for food to be improperly dispensed.[25]

Hope saw first hand that frequently shipments of pork and peas
arrived in such poor condition that they were unfit to eat. Even while
he was at Fort Mackinac some pork came in bad casks. Not only did
these spoiled cargoes waste money, but they angered the people who
depended upon the provisions.[26]

Engineer Richard Hockings was unimpressed by Sinclair's creation,
Fort Mackinac. Hockings felt the garrison was too small to defend such
an irregular structure. Since so much of it was still uncompleted, the
fort was vulnerable to attack, and he estimated that it would take one
hundred men a hundred days to finish construction.[27]

It soon became evident to Hope that all was not well at
Michilimackinac, and he was not hesitant about voicing his biting
criticisms and judgments to Sinclair. Only three days after Hope's
arrival, Sinclair, stung by Hope's accusations, asked to be relieved of
his command. He wanted to go to Quebec as soon as possible to clear
up the charges leveled against him.[28]

It had been a little less than three years since the Lieutenant Governor completed his incredible journey to Michilimackinac. Coming
with high hopes, he had encountered turbulence, uncertainty, and
frustration. Now as he left on September 23, his competence and
integrity were in question. The upper lakes had been protected, the
fur trade had prospered, and the community of Michilimackinac —

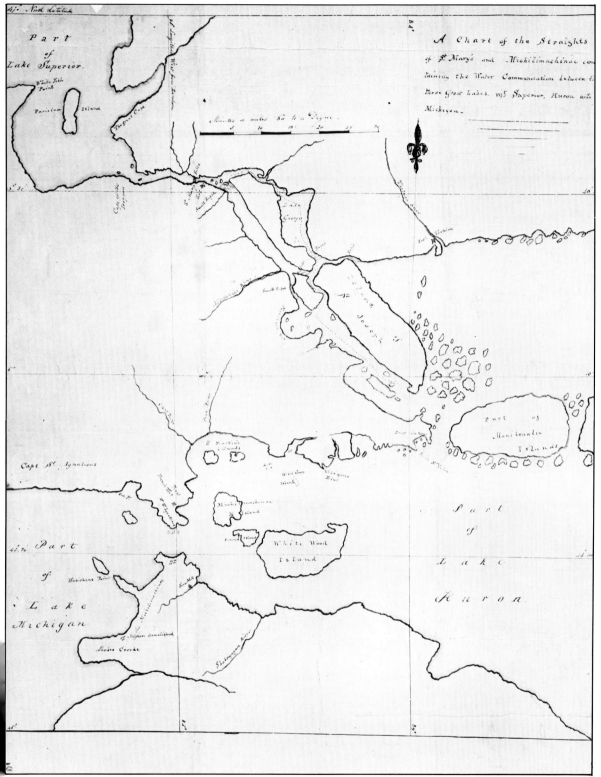

The Straits of Mackinac in the 1780's

181

the hub of the western lakes — had been moved to a safer and more convenient location. Yet his superiors did not seem to understand the problems he had encountered while governing a community whose survival depended upon imported provisions and the good temper of the Indian nations. September 18 was the end of a dream for Patrick Sinclair. At least his battles here were over, but an uncertain future awaited him in Quebec, where General Haldimand would have a multitude of questions.[29]

Captain Daniel Robertson of the Eighty-Fourth Regiment assumed the responsibilities of commanding officer. His government service began in 1754 when he became a surgeon's mate in the army. In April, 1762 he was promoted to Lieutenant, but was dismissed from the service the next year when the British army was reduced in size. He then took up residence in Montreal where he lived until the war broke out and rejoined the army in June, 1775 at his present rank.

Wanting to correct Sinclair's abuses and to reduce expenses, Lieutenant Colonel Hope gave Robertson very specific instructions. Robertson was directed:[30]

1) to abstain from local purchases of Indian presents.

2) to send "Trusty persons" to key points such as Sault Ste. Marie with rum and goods to give to Indians on their way to Michilimackinac, and send them back to their villages.

3) to establish a definite quantity of provisions per ration and a method for dispensing them, thereby creating a check on the store's commissary as to amounts given out and still in supply.

4) to send the contractor for Indian corn to L'Arbre Croche and buy 2,000 bags before any other persons were allowed out, thereby reducing the cost, which was kept high by the traders acting together rather than in competition.

5) to fire all employees of the Indian Department except Blondeau, Cadot, Rocque, Langlade, Jr., Gautier, one blacksmith and the storekeeper, all whose services were considered necessary.

6) to follow the directions of the Engineer left behind "to carry on the works" and dismiss all who presently were supervising construction at the fort and the "Vessel on the stocks." Those employed on the boat were to be fired as the material was used up or the bulk of it finished.

7) to terminate the costly contract with Barthe for the use of the *Mackinac*.

When these directives went into effect, many at Mackinac lost their employment. In the Naval Department, master builder Angus McDonald lost his 16s a day job, as did his two assistants, carpenters Hugh Moore and Joseph Laboise, who were receiving 8s per day.[31] Robertson also dismissed some of the forty-eight civilians presently working as carpenters, masons, axe men, and laborers for wages ranging from 2s 6d to 5s per day.[32]

The men of the Forty-Seventh Regiment were inducted into the Eighth Regiment. Officers of the Eighth returned to Fort Mackinac to replace the Forty-Seventh's officers.[33] Among those who came back was Lieutenant Clowes, who now served as Assistant Engineer. Before he left last fall, Clowes had hired a carpenter and four axe men to build him a new house. To his surprise, he discovered that Sinclair had used his timber to cover the King's bakehouse and had commandeered his window panes, tools, locks, and bolts. Now Clowes demanded the government reimburse his losses.[34]

As the soldiers labored to complete Fort Mackinac, Robertson wondered about his garrison's future. As the war settled into a stalemate on the East Coast, he received orders that all offensive operations were to be stopped.[35] Hopefully the end of the war was near. If so, the new commandant might find it easier to carry out Lieutenant Colonel Hope's directives. When peace returned, perhaps the Indians' insatiable demands would decrease, the fur trade would prosper, and the troops could settle into a regular garrison routine.

Private, Royal Regiment of Artillery

Fort Mackinac in the winter

XV.

The Coming of Peace

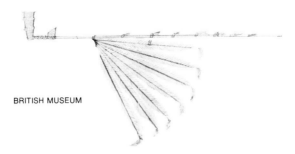

T hroughout the winter of 1782-83 Captain Daniel Robertson and the community anxiously awaited further reports about a peace settlement. Finally on Thursday, May 29, 1783 a canoe hit the beach and a courier carrying an important letter splashed out. Dashing up the hill, past the sentry, through the south gate, and into the fort he found Robertson supervising the construction of the new guardhouse, to replace the one which had burned in April.[1] The Commandant turned to greet the panting Canadian who handed him a sealed document.

Robertson ripped open the seal and unfolded the paper. A smile came over his face as he read that preliminary articles of peace between England and the rebel states had been signed last November. Suddenly his face reddened and contorted in rage. Not only were the Americans to be free of Great Britain, but the boundary line for the new nation passed through the middle of Lakes Ontario, Erie, Huron, and Superior. Mackinac Island was to be in the United States![2] How could this be? With a stroke of a pen the King's ministers undid all the effort and sacrifice of the last eight years to keep Michilimackinac and the upper lakes under British control. All the money, blood, and sweat spent in fighting the war and moving the town and fort were wasted. Government officials in England, convinced that the Imperial cost of protecting the west outweighed the economic benefits of the fur trade, decided to cede the area to the new nation.[3]

The news stunned the entire community. Peace, instead of bringing joy and relief, created confusion. When Robertson recovered from his initial shock and anger, he tried to assure his troops and the questioning citizens that the King would not forget them.

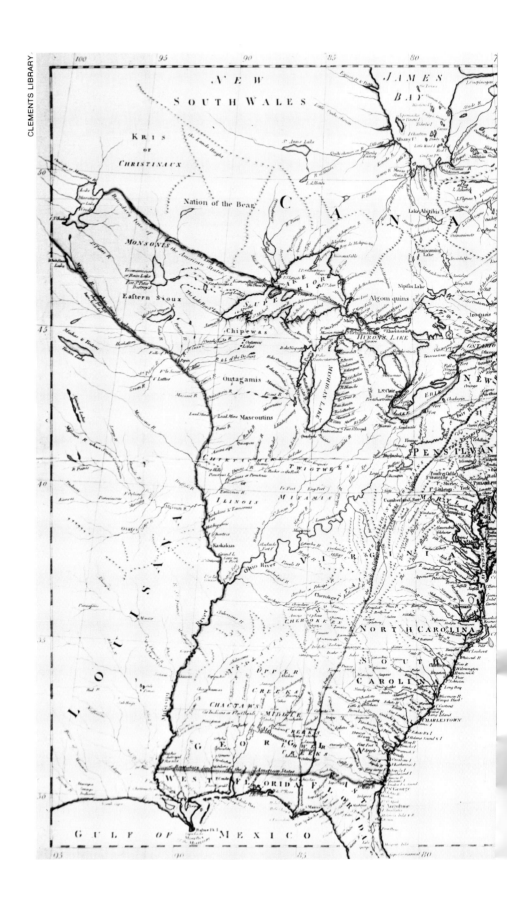

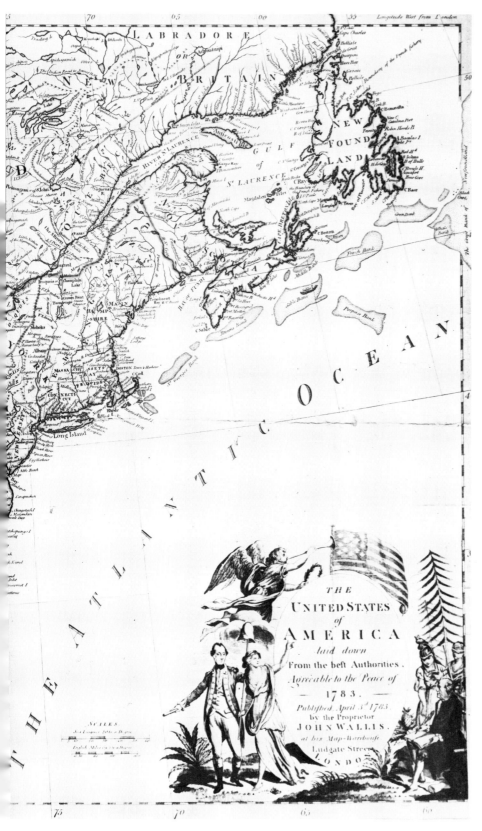

Map showing the boundaries of the United States of America. Michilimackinac was included in the new nation.

The advent of peace did not prevent the Indians from making their usual visits. This summer, however, they came in fewer numbers. Robertson had sent George McBeath and Charles Langlade, Jr., to Prairie du Chien in late April to meet the western nations and give them gifts and rum.[4] McBeath was to try to convince the natives to hunt this summer rather than travel to Michilimackinac.[5] The war was over and warriors were no longer needed. The braves now could provide for themselves; consequently, the King would not dispense as many presents and provisions.[6] McBeath and Langlade, Jr., succeeded in stopping at least one thousand Indians from descending upon Robertson.[7]

Peace stimulated trade. One hundred and one canoes left from Montreal in 1783. Of these only twenty-six were specifically destined for the Lake Superior region, but since some licensees ticketed for Michilimackinac normally went farther to the northwest, they probably headed there again this year.[8]

British officials feared that the Indians, learning that their lands fell under American dominion, might seek revenge against the posts and traders. To prevent this, Haldimand prepared a speech for the Indians of Michilimackinac explaining why the King had permitted the Americans to separate from England. The General sent Jean Marie Calvé, Sinclair's old antagonist, to take this message to the western nations and assure them that the King still considered them as his children. He would continue to protect them and allow the traders to carry on their business.[9]

King George III

Haldimand was vague about exactly how Britain could carry out this pledge once she lost political control over the region. Though he ordered a temporary cessation to the transporting of military stores and provisions to the upper posts, Indian presents were still shipped.

Despite the General's best efforts, Robertson and the English speaking community worried about a possible Indian uprising. Abraham Cuyler, passing through Michilimackinac in June, was mortified that the "good harmony" there might "be too soon disturbed, our allies the natives are alarmed at the sacrifice made of them"[10]

Matchekewis and other chiefs who had supported the British war effort found it difficult to understand the politics of peace. How could their allies surrender lands to their enemy that had not been lost in battle? Certainly one could not trust British promises. This year's presents were less than last; next year's gifts might be even fewer. Guns, powder, lead, blankets, and food were needed to survive, and only the English could provide them. If the British King forsook them, they might have to punish his servants.

The Officers' Stone Quarters at Fort Mackinac

The ramp leading up to Fort Mackinac

R obertson was plagued by a severe shortage of rum. In order to conduct Indian diplomacy he had to "borrow" some from traders. He worried that by the time the government shipment was delivered inflation would force him to give back more barrels than he had "borrowed." Purchasing rum from local merchants violated his orders. When he learned in late June that Haldimand had refused to honor his bills, Robertson was in agony. He lamented to Brigadier General Allen MacLean, "I am sorry & ten times so that I ever came here, to be obliged to cringe & borrow Rum from Traders on account of Government, . . ."[11] Fortunately Haldimand changed his mind and paid Robertson's accounts the next month.[12]

The silencing of the artisans' tools was a sign of peace. All construction on the King's buildings stopped except for limited repairs to the ramp leading up to the fort. A few men were also employed tending the King's cattle.[13]

Since Fort Mackinac was on American soil, Robertson reasoned he needed to find a site for a new post on the British side of the boundary. He thought the best place was Thessalon Bay, seventy-five miles northeast of the island. Situated on the north shore of Lake Huron near the St. Mary's River, it was accessible to both the Indian nations and the Canadian traders. Thessalon could become the new center of the northwest trade. Wanting to be ready when orders came to move, Robertson, without Haldimand's authorization, sent a detachment of soldiers to begin clearing ground and cutting timbers.[14]

When Patrick Sinclair had departed, he had left under Robertson's charge three black prisoners captured in Illinois. Uncertain as to what to do with this old man and woman and young woman, Robertson sought official guidance. Not wishing to return them "to a sett of Spanish Rascalls," he suggested that either he or Sinclair had a "better right to them."[15]

Robertson freed his own black servant, Bonga, who subsequently bought a house in town where he and his wife ran a tavern. Serving tired travelers and thirsty voyageurs, Bonga managed one of the first public accommodations on the island.[16]

A change in government worried Michilimackinac landowners. Fourteen prominent traders begged Robertson to petition to have their property deeds confirmed.[17] If and when a civil authority took control, they hoped to be able to continue business as usual.

The war's end brought Sergeant Phillips a discharge from the army. Having served in the Indian Department since early 1780, he had been relieved of that duty as part of Henry Hope's economy drive in 1782. Now Phillips asked to be released from the military as well. Having served the King for twenty-six years, Phillips was given an honorable discharge from the King's Eighth Regiment.[18]

Others whose lives had suffered dislocation by the war were not as fortunate. Joseph Louis Ainsse, Louis Chevallier, and Samuel Robertson were in Quebec or Montreal still trying to settle their affairs. Ironically, the man who had created their difficulties, Patrick Sinclair, was himself caught in the web of government bureaucracy. Unable to obtain satisfaction in Quebec, he sought permission to return to England and was refused.

On September 3, 1783 Great Britain and the United States signed the final peace treaty in Paris. Though it would be months before the details were known at Mackinac Island, the preliminary agreements had already profoundly affected life. War had disrupted the community, but the end of hostilities did not bring the stability for which all had hoped.

Inter-tribal war in the Indian country was unaffected by peace negotiations in Paris. The Lake Superior Chippewa again warred with the Fox and Sioux. Robertson had sent Matchekewis and Jean Baptiste Cadot to try to quell the uprising.[19]

The community, still not completely settled from moving to the island, now contemplated even further dislocation. Yet no evacuation orders had come from Quebec, nor had any Americans appeared to take possession of the island. For the present the British remained; for how long nobody knew. After eight years of war, it seemed a shame that all the human sacrifice and suffering should go for naught.

Michilimackinac was abandoned and gradually covered by drifting sand. Drawn by Captain Seth Eastman in 1851.

Epilog

E ven though the Peace of Paris in 1783 placed Mackinac Island within the expanded borders of the United States, it was thirteen years before the Americans claimed their prize. Angered by the non-payment of loyalist claims and wanting to exploit the riches of the fur trade, the British government refused to evacuate the northwest posts. The traders of Mackinac maintained their Montreal connections, and the annual ebb and flow of the fur brigades continued their familiar cycle. Construction at Fort Mackinac lapsed due to the uncertainty about the future, but the village continued to grow.

Patrick Sinclair, the founder of the Island community, was harrassed by his creditors and even spent a short time in debtors prison in London. Returning to Lybster, Caithness, Scotland, he married in 1787 and fathered five children. He continued to draw his £200 annual salary as Lieutenant Governor for the rest of his life. He died on January 31, 1820 and was buried in a small plot behind his house.

Fort Michilimackinac reconstructed

ROBERT BURNS HOUSE, DUMFRIES

*Dumfries,
Scotland, where De
Peyster retired and
was buried.*

Arent Schuyler DePeyster served as Commandant at Detroit for nearly five years until 1784. After serving briefly as Commandant at Niagara, DePeyster and his wife accompanied the King's Eighth when they returned to England. Upon the Colonel's retirement from the army they took up residence in Marvis Grove, a country house outside of Rebecca's native Dumfries, Scotland. There he enjoyed the company of Robert Burns, the renowned Scottish poet. DePeyster continued to write poems and in 1813 published a volume entitled *Miscellanies by an Officer*. In 1822 he died and was buried in St. Michael's churchyard, his red sandstone headstone only a few feet away from the tomb of his friend Burns.

*St. Michael's
Churchyard,
Dumfries.
DePeyster's
tombstone is on
the right. The
white mausoleum
is that of
Robert Burns.*

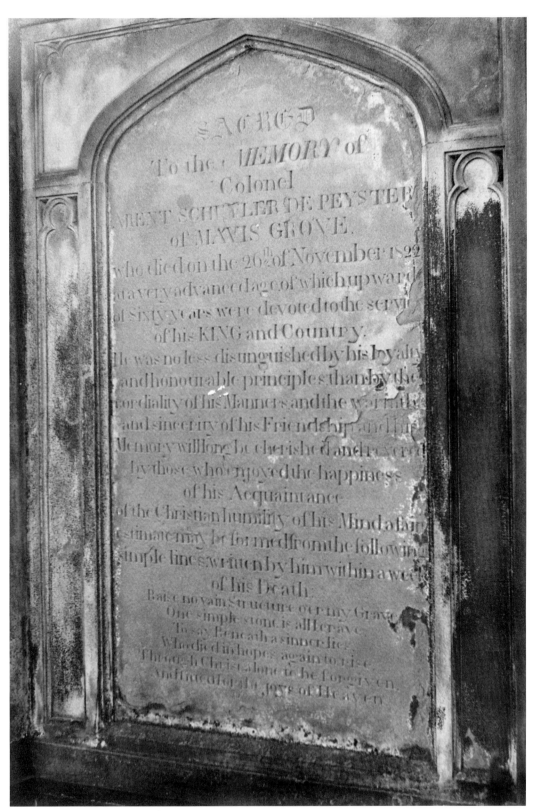

Colonel De Peyster's tombstone.

Matchekewis did not accept the American victory, and he and his men continued to resist them in fierce battles fought in Ohio. However, when the American forces under General Anthony Wayne triumphed at Fallen Timbers, the Chippewa chieftain realized that it was best to make peace with the "Long Knives". Consequently, at the negotiations leading up to the Treaty of Greenville, he made a good-will gesture by giving to the Americans, as a present, the Island of Bois Blanc in the Straits of Mackinac. When the Americans finally occupied Fort Mackinac on September 1, 1796, Matchekewis accepted their presence but followed the British to their new fort on St. Joseph Island in the St. Mary's River. Matchekewis's passed away in about 1805.

John Askin moved to Detroit in 1780. After the Revolution he was saddled with many debts, but the generosity of his friends enabled him to discharge these financial burdens. In 1796 the British left Detroit and moved to the south side of the Detroit River; six years later Askin followed. He remained a loyal British subject until his death in 1815. Archange lived until 1820.

La Fourche in his old age was the most respected chief of the L'Arbre Croche Ottawa. Around the council fire he recounted the events of more than eighty years. Sometime in 1797 the old man spoke no more.

Fort Michilimackinac reconstructed

Fort Mackinac

Wayne's victory in Ohio and John Jay's negotiations in London in 1794 finally brought a reluctant withdrawal of the British from Mackinac Island. Though a number of traders moved to St. Joseph Island, many remained and continued to trade furs.

When in 1812 war broke out again between Great Britain and the United States, the forces from St. Joseph swept down to Mackinac in a swift night attack and captured the Island in the first British victory of the war. The conclusion of the war in 1815 brought a return of the Island to the United States. The fur trade prospered until the 1830's after which the island's economy stagnated.

A growing fishing industry and the influx of tourists in the years after the Civil War restored economic vitality to the community. But the town did not grow much beyond its original borders. Consequently today Mackinac Island still retains much of its eighteenth century character. The street patterns remain the same and while most of the residential buildings have been replaced, the sturdy limestone walls of Fort Mackinac still loom over the bay. The Officer's Stone Quarters, begun by Patrick Sinclair and completed by the Americans, stands as a fitting memorial to the tenacious spirit of the builder and his untiring efforts to keep the Mackinac region loyal to King George III during the American Revolution.

The portage of La Petite Faucille on the French River. At each portage the contents of the canoe had to be unloaded and carried past the rapids. Water color by Thomas Davies c. 1766.

T he workhorse of the fur trade was the birch bark canoe. Though fragile, it carried several tons of goods plus a crew of eight or more men. Printed below is the complete contents of a thirty-five or forty foot Montreal canoe that William and John Kay outfitted and sent David McCrea at Michilimackinac in 1777.

This account is most revealing because it lists the contents of every bale. Each bale contained a variety of merchandise so that when the trader opened it, he had a wide range of goods for his wilderness customers.

The bill of lading reveals the color and type of cloth, tools, utensils, and trinkets exchanged for furs. The names of the crew, their wages, and the supplies provided to outfit them are ennumerated. Although this list is extensive, it does not contain every item that fur traders peddled.

Entries in the first part are in Halifax Currency, while the last section is in French Livres. Both currency systems were in use, and a livre is roughly equivalent to a shilling.

The original of this document is found in the Accounts of David McCrea & Co. of Michilimackinac with William and John Kay, "Quebec Papers," Volume 3, 75, pp. 185-189, Toronto Public Library, Metropolitan Toronto Library Board.

Appendix I

Account of David McCrae & Co. Dr to Goods for one Canoe for Msr. Landoise

W. Kay

	#	Item		£	s	d	£	s	d
D M		1 ps [piece] Blue Strouds	N° 27	3	18	"			
Bale 1		3 pr [pair] 2½ pt [point] Blankets	10/3	1	10	9			
		2 pr 3 pt do [ditto]	12/6	1	5	"			
		1 pr 1 pt do		"	4	6			
		1 pr ½ pt do		"	6	"			
		1 Bunch blue Beeds		"	"	"			
		1 Gro [Gross] Striped Scarlet Gartering		"	11	"			
		6 doz Buck Cutteaux [Knives]		"	11	6			
		1 doz playing Cards		"	3	"			
		3 Mens felt Hatts	20/	"	5	"			
		1 doz large Dutch Look^g Glasses		"	4	6			
		1 Gro awl Blades		"	4	4			
		2 doz red handle Scalping knives		"	4	2			
		20 Bunches blk [black] barley Corn bead	7/2	"	12	6			
		1 quart do Jack		"	1	"	10	1	3
	2	1 ps Blue Strouds		3	16	"			
		3 pr 2½ pt Blankets	10/3	1	10	9			
		3 pr 2 pt do	7/	1	1	"			
		2 pr 1½ pt do	6/	"	12	"			
		2 pr 1 pt do	4/6	"	9	"			
		3 Castor hatts 8	7/6	1	2	6			
		1 Gro Scarlet Gartering		"	11	"			
		6 lb Oznaburg thread	25/	"	12	6			
		1 doz playing Cards		"	3	"			
		½ Gro horn handle folding Knives		"	12	6			
		5 lb Vermillion	4/	1	"	"	11	10	3

No.	Item	Price	£	s	d	£	s	d
3	1 ps Blue Strouds bro [broad] Cord		3	16	''			
	3 pr 2½ pt Blankets	10/3	1	10	9			
	2 pr 3 pt do	12/6	1	5	''			
	1 pr 1 pt do		''	4	6			
	1 pr ½ pt do		''	6	''			
	5 lb Vermillion	4/	1	''	''			
	1 Castor Hatt 5		''	3	''			
	1 do do 5		''	8	''			
	1 Gro Scarlet Gartering		''	11	''			
	1 doz Steel Tobacco Boxes		''	3	8			
	1 doz Small Ducth [sic] Glasses		''	3	8			
	1 quart Jack		''	1	''			
	20 Bunches Mock Garnetts [beads]	7/2	''	12	6			
	14 do Red Barley Corns	7/2	''	8	9			
	2 lb Colour'd Thread	2/3	''	4	6			
	2 doz Box Combs	2/6	''	5	''			
	½ Gro Gun worms	6/6	''	3	3			
	2 doz Red handled knives	25/	''	4	2			
	2 Gro plain Brass rings	3/	''	6	''			
	3 felt Hatts N° 3	1/8	''	5	''			
	2 doz horn Combs	1/2	''	2	4			
	½ doz playing Cards	3/	''	1	6	12	5	7
4	1 ps Blue Strouds Narrow Cord		3	16	''			
	3 pr 3 pt Blankets	12/6	1	17	6			
	3 pr 2 pt do	7/	1	1	''			
	2 pr ½ pt do	6/	''	12	''			
	2 pr 1 pt do	4/6	''	9	''			
	1 Gro Yellow Gartering		''	9	''			
	1 Gro Scarlet Gartering		''	11	''			
	2 doz Box Combs	1/2	''	2	4			
	5 lb Vermillion	4/	1	''	''			
	3 Boys Hatts 2	1/3	''	3	9			
	2 Bunches Beads		''	''	''			
	500 Gun flints	10/	''	5	''	10	6	7
5	1 ps Blue Strouds narr Cord		3	16	''			
	3 pr 2½ pt Blankets	10/3	1	10	9			
	2 pr 3 pt do	12/6	1	5	''			
	1 pr 1 pt do		''	4	6			
	1 pr 1½ pt do		''	6	''			
	2 pr 2 pt do	7/	''	14	''			
	5 Vermillion	4/	1	''	''			
	1 Gro Scarlet gartering		''	11	''			
	3 Hatts N° 2	1/3	''	3	9			
	1 Bunch long blk beads		''	''	''			
	17 Bunches Barley Corn do	7/2	''	10	6			
	6 do do	10/	''	5	''			
	7 do do	7/2	''	4	4½			
	2 doz Scalping Knives	25/	''	4	2			
	1 lb White thre'd N° 14		''	5	8			
	1 doz small Dutch Looking Glasses		''	3	7			
	1 doz pack^g Needles		''	''	6	11	3	9½

Brass trade ring

			£	s	d	£	s	d
6	1 ps Blue Strouds bro^d Cord		3	16	''			
	3 pr 2½ pt Blankets	10/3	1	10	9			
	2 pr 3 pt do	12/6	1	5	''			
	2 pr 2 pt do	7/	''	14	''			
	1 pt 1 pt do		''	4	6			
	1 pt 1½ pt do		''	6	''			
	1 Bunche Small white Beads		''	''	''			
	3 lb Vermillion	4/	''	12	''			
	3 Hatts N° 2	1/3	''	3	9			
	1 Gro flowerd Gartering		''	9	''			
	1/2 doz playing Cards	3/	''	1	6			
	1 doz Small dutch Looking Glasses		''	2	7			
	2 doz Scalping knives red	25/	''	4	2			
	2 doz Box Combs	1/2	''	2	4			
	2 lb White thre'd 60	2/11	''	5	10			
	1 M Needles		''	3	6			
	2 Gro Stone rings	2/6	''	5	''			
	1 ps fine Chinese Ribbon		''	10	6			
	1 ps fine wrought do		''	13	3			
	2 doz figured do	6/6	''	13	''			
	3 doz Tinsell do	5/6	''	16	6			
	1 ps Blk g^d Single		''	9	3			
	3 ps Col^d [colored] do	11/	1	13	''			
	1 ps Crimson do	11/6	''	11	6	15	10	11
	2 doz Woodhandle folding Knives		''	''	''	0	3	8
7	1 ps Blue Strouds bro^d Cord		3	16	''			
	3 pr 2½ pt Blankets	10/3	1	10	9			
	2 pr 3 pt do	12/6	1	5	''			
	2 pr 1 pt do	4/6	''	9	''			
	2 pr 1/2 pt do	6/	''	12	''			
	1 Gro Star Gartering		''	9	''			
	3 Hatts N° 2	1/3	''	3	9			
	4 lb Vermillion	4/	''	16	''			
	2 doz red Scalping knives	23/	''	3	10			
	1 doz large dutch Glasses		''	4	6			
	2 lb Thread N° 60	2/11	''	5	10			
	1 doz playing Cards		''	3	''			
	6 Gro Gun Screws	15/	''	7	6			
	1 Bunch long white Beads		''	''	''			
	1 do Small round do		''	''	''	10	6	2
8	1 ps Blue Strouds		3	16	''			
	3 pr 2½ pt Blankets	10/3	1	10	9			
	3 pr 2 pt do	7/	1	1	''			
	2 pr 3 do	12/6	1	5	''			
	1 Gro Scarlet Gartering		''	11	''			
	1 Gro Star do		''	9	''			
	4 lb Vermillion	4/	''	16	''			
	2 Bunches Beeds		''	''	''			
	500 Gun flints	10/	''	5	''			
	1 lb thread N 20		''	9	6			
	2 doz wood hand folding knives		''	3	8	10	6	11

	Item	Rate	£	s	d		£	s	d
9	1 ps Blue Strouds Narr Cord		3	17	''				
	4 pr 2½ pt Blankets	10/3	2	1	''				
	2 pr 3 pt do	12/6	1	5	''				
	3 pr 2 pt do	7/	1	1	''				
	4 lb Vermillion	4/	''	16	''				
	1 doz playing Cards		''	3	''				
	2 doz Scalping knives	23/	''	3	10				
	1 Bunch small Yellow Beeds		''	''	''				
	2 doz folding wood hand Knives		''	3	8				
	1 lb thread 22		''	10	6				
	1 lb Col'd thread		''	2	2				
	1 Small pack do 1 60		''	2	8		10	5	10
10	1 ps Blue Strouds Narr Cord		3	18	''				
	1 ps Narrow Russia Sheeting		2	3	6				
	4 pr 2½ pt Blankets	10/3	2	1	''				
	2 pr 3 pt do	12/6	1	5	''				
	2 pr 2 pt do	7/	''	14	''		10	1	6
11	1 ps Blue Strouds bro Cord		3	13	6				
	1 ps fine Doulas		3	7	''				
	4 pr 2½ pt Blankets	10/3	2	1	''				
	2 pr 3 pt do	12/6	1	5	''				
	1 pr 2 pt do		''	7	''		10	13	6
12	2 ps red Strouds	80/0	8	''	''				
	3 pr 2½ pt Blankets	10/3	1	10	9				
	2 pr 3 pt do	12/6	1	5	''				
	1 pr 2 pt do		''	6	''				
	3 lb Vermillion	4/	''	12	''		11	13	''
13	1 ps red Strouds		4	''	''				
	1 ps Russia Sheeting		2	6	6				
	3 pr 2½ pt Blankets	10/3	1	10	9				
	2 pr 3 pt do	12/6	1	5	''				
	2 pr 2 pt do	7/	''	14	''				
	2 lb Vermillion	4/	''	8	''		10	4	3
14	1 ps Blue Strouds Narr Cord		3	16	6				
	1 ps Russia Sheeting		2	6	6				
	3 pr 2½ pt Blankets	10/3	1	10	9				
	2 pr 3 pt do	12/6	1	5	''				
	2 pr 2 pt do	7/	''	14	''				
	500 Gun flints	10/	''	5	''		9	17	9
15 VxR	for Joseph Nathar								
	1 ps Blue Strouds		3	16	''				
	2 pr 2½ pt Blanket	10/3	1	''	6				
	1 pr 3 pt do		''	12	6				
	1 ps Blue Romals		''	10	6				
	1 ps Mixed do		''	12	''				
	3 Large pewter Basons	3/4	''	10	''				
	1 ps Check 35½ Ell	9	1	6	7½				
	1 ps do 36½ do	10/4	1	10	5				
	3 Hatts Nº 3	1/3	''	3	9				

202

	Item	Price	£	s	d	£	s	d
	1 M Needles		''	3	6			
	1 Gro Shoemakers awls		''	2	''			
	6 fine Ivory handle Knives	2/6	''	15	''			
	1 doz Buck Cutteaux asesort	2/	''	2	''			
	1 ps White Callico		1	3	6	12	8	3½
16	1 ps Blue Strouds		3	16	''			
	3 pr 2½ pt Blankets	10/3	1	10	9			
	2 Mizilipotam HKFs [Handkerchiefs]	32/	3	4	''			
	4 pss Blue Bernagores	18/	3	12	''			
	1 ps Red Shalloon		1	13	''			
	2 doz Blk Silk HKFs	28/	2	16	''			
	2 doz Scissars	4/6	''	9	''			
	1 doz horn Combs		''	4	''			
	4 Castor Hatts 5	8/	1	12	''			
	3 Hatts 3	1/3	''	3	9			
	1 ps Platillas Royal		1	12	''			
	1 doz playing Cards		''	3	''			
	1 Gro Scarlet Gartering		''	11	''			
	1 lb Brown thread		''	2	1			
	3 pint Basons	8/	0	2	''			
	5 half pss 14^d Sarsnet	16/6	2	1	3			
	1 do Pink do		''	8	6			
	1 pr g^d Crimson		''	12	6			
	1 half ps do	11/6	''	5	9			
	1 ps g^d Single		''	11	''			
	1 doz figured Ribbons		''	6	6			
	1 ps 2 Col^d Callicoe		1	16		27	12	1
17	1 ps Oznaburgs 132 yds		3	6	''			
	2 pr 2½ pt Blankets	10/3	1	''	6			
	3 Quart Jacks		''	3	''			
	3 ½ pint do	6/2	''	1	7½			
	6 lb thread N° 60		''	17	6			
	1 doz Andrews Cards		''	3	''			
	6 Castor Hatts N° 5	8/	2	8	''			
	1 doz women Blk hose		''	16	''			
	1 doz Mens Cotton do		1	10	''			
	1 ps 2 Col'd Callicoe		1	16	''	12	1	7
18	24/4 Yds Embosed Serge	1/4½	1	13	4			
	1 ps Russia Sheeting		2	6	6			
	2 pss Callico 2 Coll^d	36/	3	12	''			
	2 pr 2½ pt Blankets	10/3	1	''	6			
	34 Ells Check	10/4	1	9	1			
	1 ps platillas Royal		1	12	''			
	2 Castor Hatts N° 5	8/	''	16	''			
	3 Felts do 3	1/3	''	3	9			
	1 doz playing Cards		''	3	''			
	1 lb White thread 10		''	4	3			
	1 lb do do 13		''	5	6			
	1 lb Col^d do		''	2	3			
	3 doz & 4 Red Handkerchiefs	26/6	4	8	4			

No.	Description		£	s	d	£	s	d
19	1 ps Russia Sheeting		2	6	6			
	1 ps Lay lock Gro Cotton 13							
	14 yards	2/6	1	15	''			
	1 ps dark Gro^d do 16 14	3/	2	2	''			
	1 ps do do 19 14	3/3	2	5	6			
	1 ps fine light gro^d 20 14	3/5	2	7	10			
	1 ps Cotton Muslin		1	4	''			
	4 ps 2½ pt Blankets	10/3	2	1	''			
	1 ps 2 Col^d Callico		1	16	''			
	1 Large Copper Coffee pot		''	6	6	16	4	4
20	32 Yds 6/4 Cotton	2/2	3	9	4			
	46 Yds Tick	11	2	2	2			
	2 pr 3 pt Blankets	12/6	1	5	''			
	4 pr 2½ pt do	10/3	2	1	''			
	1 ps fine dark gro^d Chints		3	1	6	11	19	''
	1 Fuzil		1	''	6			
	3 pr 2½ pt Blankets for a Mattrass	10/3	1	10	9			
	1 pr 3 pt do do		''	12	6	3	3	9
21 a 35	15 Barrells cont^g 900 lb Gunpowder	85/	38			38	5	''
36	1 Case Cont^g 84 lb Castile Soap	6^d				2	2	''
37	1 do Cont^g 8 NW fuzils	20/6	8	4	''			
	6 Cod Lines	2/		12	''			
	2 pint Jacks	8^d	''	1	4			
	8¼ Brass wire	1/6	''	12	4½			
	24 Cutteaux Croches	6^d	''	12	''			
38 a 42	5 Sacks Ball 3^qts ea is 3^cwt 3^qts O	20/	''	''	''	3	15	''
43	1 Sac cont^g 3^qts 0 Shot B	19/	''	''	''	''	14	3
44 & 45	2 do cont^g 1^cwt 2 O Duck & Pidgeon	18/	''	''	''	1	7	''
46	1 Basket cont^g 2 Nest Copper							
	Cov^d Kettles 92^lb	2/	9	4	''			
	1 Large Kettle for the Canoe 11 lb	2/	1	2	''			
	4 Cod Lines for do	2/	''	8	''			
	11 Ells Sheeting for a Sail	1 yd	''	13	9			
	3 Cod Lines for Bales	2/	''	6	''			
	1½ ps Hessens for do	23/	1	14	6			
	1 Skain Holland twine for do	1/2	''	1	2			
	28 lb Beeds	10^d	1	3	4	14	12	9
						326	15	''
	Advance 50 pct					163	7	6
	Hallifax					490	2	6
VxR	1 Hide Leather 36^lb							
	3/4 for Lardoise	50/	''	''	''	3	15	9¼
	1 Barrell peinture Blanc		''	''	''		14	2¼
						494	12	6
	Equal to Livers					11871	''	''

No.	Item	Price	£	s	d	£	s	d
47	1 Case g 24 half axes	54s	64	16	''			
	24 Tomahawks	40/	48		''			
	3 Large axes	5.10s	16	10	''			
	7 Tranches [cutting knife]	24/	8	8				
	2 Augures	3	6	''	''			
	1 Tille [Slater's hammer]		3	''	''			
	1 Pioche [pick-axe]		2	15	''			
	Case of Cord		3	10	''	152	19	''
48 & 49	2 Barrells Port wine	60	120	''	''	''		
	Barrells & filling ''		11	''		131	''	''
50	1 do Spiritts 8 Gallons	9	72	''	''			
	Barrell		5	10	''	77	10	''
	1 do Brandy							
	8 Gallons for the Men	5	40	''	''			
	1 do do do for Lardoise	5	40	''	''			
	1 Basket for Kettles		3	''	''			
	8 Shot Bags & Making	20/	8	''	''			
	Making a Sail		3	''	''			
	15 Empty Barrells for Gun powder		82	10	''			
	1 fuzil Case		6	10	''			
	1 Case for Soap		3	10	''			
	Packers Account		20	''	''			
	Cartage to & Storage at LaChine		57	''	''			
	28 lb Gum for Canoe	10/	14					
	a Canoe & poles		318	''	''			
	1 Axe for the Canoe	10/	5	10	''			
	Spunge & Canoe Awls		7	''	''	608		
	122 lb Irish pork	12/	73	4	''			
	600 lb Buiscuit	24	144	''	''			
	6 Bags for Buiscuits		15	''	''			
	3 do for Pork		6	''	''	238	4	''
	¼ lb Shot for Lardoise		8	8	''			
	200 lb Buiscuit for do	24	48	''	''			
	2 Baggs for do do		5	''	''	61	8	
	Equiptments & Cash advance the Men Viz't					13140	1	
	Paul Leduc Chemise Couvert & c		28	''				
	1 Ell /2 Indienne		9	''	''	37	''	''
	Paul Gagnier Chemise & c		24	''	''			
	3 Au Indienne		15	''	''	39		

Michel Peltier 1 Shirt	8	"	"			
1 Blanket 3 pt	12	"	"			
1 pr Mittasses [leggings]	4	"	"			
1 Braquet	4	"	"	28	"	"
Alexis Bourgard do do		do		28	"	"
Pierre Gladuc do do	28					
4 lb Tobacco	2	"	"	30	"	"
Ant° Oudit dit Lapoint						
Chemise Couvert Braquet & c	24	"	"			
1 pr Grand Culots	6			30	"	"
Louis Robideaux				28	"	"
Charles Duretour double equipment				56	"	"
JB Menard Guide						
1 Couvert 3 pts	12					
3 Au Cotton	15			27	"	"
Pierre Laberge his Equipment				28	"	"
Advance the Men as follows						
Michel Peltier a Note						
payable this Month	300					
Cash	6			306	"	"
Alexis Bourgard do	"	"	"	12	"	"
Pierre Gladuc Cash	66					
Billet to pay St Mitchel	30					
Cash	2	10	"			
Hankfs & Ribbon	3			101	10	"
Paul Leduc Cash advance	59	6	"			
6 au toille de Russi	18	"	"	77	6	
Anto Oudit dit Lapoint Cash	"	"	"	66	"	
JB Menard Guide Cash & Coffee	51	18	"			
Good as noted on his Engagement	160	10	"	212	8	"
Louis Robideau Cash to Mellish	50	"	"			
Goods advance	99	"	"	149	"	"
Pierre Laberge Cash	12	"	"			
2 Handkfs	9	"	"	21	"	"
Charles Duretour Cash	"	"	"	28	"	"
				14444	5	
Paid Msr Panet for						
Lardoize obligation	"	"	"	9	"	"
Livers				14453	5	
50 lb more Gun powder the Kegs						
having held 950 lb						
fill'd by Lardoise			ℒ	722	13	3
				3	16	6
			ℒ	726	9	9

Appendix II

The John Askin Inventories

The inventories of John Askin, which are the most complete extant lists of objects used at Michilimackinac during the 1770's, provide us with valuable insights into the material culture of the fur trade society. A comparison of the two inventories reveals changes in Askin's material status and demonstrates the effects of the American Revolution as some items increased in value and supply. The fact that Askin was a businessman who bought and sold may account for the many additions and deletions among his personal possessions during the two years. These documents do not indicate all of the household items of Askin's family, since his wife Archange Barthe's personal possessions are not included.

Archaeological excavations several miles from Fort Michilimackinac in 1981-82 revealed a site which is believed to be John Askin's farm. The results of this important find appear in Donald P. Heldman, *Archaeological Investigations at French Farm Lake in Northern Michigan, 1981-82, Archaeological Completion Report Series, Number 6,* (Mackinac Island 1983). This report and several others which appear in the *Completion Report Series,* cast new light on the world of John Askin: Donald P. Heldman and Roger T. Grange, Jr., *Excavations at Fort Michilimackinac: 1978-1979: The Rue de la Babillarde, Number 3* (1981); J. Mark Williams and Gary Shapiro, *A Search for the Eighteenth Century Village at Michilimackinac: A Soil Resistivity Survey, Number 4,* (1982) Elizabeth M. Scott, *French Subsistence at Fort Michilimackinac, 1715-1781: The Clergy and the Traders, Number 9* (1985); and Jill Y. Halchin, *Excavations at Fort Michilimackinac 1983-1985: House C of the Southeast Row House, The Solomon-Levy-Parant House, Number 11* (1986). In all likelihood remains of some objects listed on Askin's inventories have been excavated within the past decade.

The documents printed below, in their entirety, contain the spellings and notations as they appear in the manuscript. The designations "Amounts brought forward," etc. used to carry totals from one page to the next have been eliminated in order to increase the readability of the documents. Each document is in a different hand, and the 1778 inventory is much more difficult to read. Brackets have been used to indicate where the manuscript is illegible or the transcription is uncertain. The 1778 document has notations in the left hand column which might indicate differences in value or quantities of the entry or perhaps the object's location. Also, the notations after the entries for a weighing beam (p. 224), a Bible (p. 227) and a silver spoon (p. 227) are in a different hand. On page 14 of the manuscript are five names which appear to have been entered at a later date, consequently, those names have not been printed.

The 1776 inventory is housed at the Public Archives of Canada in Ottawa (Document No. MG 19, A3), and the 1778 inventory is located at the Archives of Ontario in Toronto among the John Askin Papers. Both documents are printed with the approval or permission of the respective repositories.

Inventery of my Estate Viz:

		N. Y. C.		
1776 Dec.ʳ 31		£	S	D
	Shiping &.c.			
	The Sloop Welcome with everything belonging to her	700	″	″
	The little Schooner Capᵗ: De Peyster	200	″	″
	New York Curr.ʸ £	900	″	″
	Houses Lands &:c:			
	A farm near the Fort of Detroit with the Houses on it and Orchards	300	″	″
	Two farms at the Gros Point at Detroit	120	″	″
	The House I bought of Mʳ Derivien with the Celler and back Houses	110	″	″
	The House formerly the property of Mʳ Bourrisa with the Stables Cow House & Hog House &.c.	130	″	″
	The Bake House with the Brick Oven & all belonging to it	60	″	″
	A House & Lott in the Subarbs I Esteem	80	″	″
	A Large Vault or Cellar out of the Fort	80	″	″
	A House & farm near the Fort, Suppose	80	″	″
	A Smyths Shop worth about	20	″	″
	A House at Chaboyagan River worth about	40	″	″
	Stages for drying Corn worth	8	″	″
	Half a Store House at Fort Erie	20	″	″
	2 Large Kittles in a furnace at Water Side	20	″	″
	N: York Curr.ʸ £	1068	″	″
	Slaves			
	Pompe's Cost is worth I think	100	″	″
	Charles another Negro man the Same	100	″	″
	Derrey a Painis Boy I esteem worth	50	″	″
	Francois a Ditto Ditto I esteem Ditto	50	″	″
	Charlotte a Paunisse Wench worth	50	″	″
	Clariss a Ditto Ditto worth	40	″	″
	N: York Curry:ʸ £	390	″	″

Cattle

	£	s	d
a Bull	16	"	"
a pair of large Oxen worth	50	"	"
A pair of smaller Oxen worth	36	"	"
5 Cowes had Calves @ £ 16	80	"	"
A Large Heifer worth	12	"	"
2 Younger Ditto with Calf @ £ 8	16	"	"
A Young Bull same Age	6	"	"
an other Heifer small not with Calf	4	"	"
2 Last Summers Calves @ 60/	6	"	"
a Mare & young Colt	13	6	8
a Young Horse I esteem	14	"	"
A Young Filley of 2 Years old	8	"	"
A Little Horse Cost	8	"	"
A Large Boar	6	"	"
3 Sows @ £ 5	15	"	"
a Large Hog	6	10	"
4 Young Hogs @ £ 4	16	"	"
2 Young Pigs @ 20/	2	"	"
24 Fowles @ 4/	4	16	"
1 more Young Hog	4	"	"
N: York Curr:^y £	323	12	8

Carriages & Harness

	£	s	d
A Calash worth about	10	"	"
an other with Capt: De Peyster, about	8	"	"
A Large Ox Cart Shodd worth	10	"	"
A Horse Cart worth	5	"	"
A Carriole worth	6	"	"
A Small covered Waggon worth	4	"	"
A new Horse Slay well Shodd	5	"	"
A new Log Slay Ditto	3	10	"
An Ox Log Slay worth	2	"	"
2 pair of spare new Wheels Small @ 50/	5	"	"
A Neat Chair Harness	8	"	"
2 Common Harness worth @ 50/	5	"	"
2 new Spare Collars Cost	2	13	4
A Womans Saddle, Bridle &c.	6	"	"
A Man's Common Ditto Ditto	4	"	"
A fine Saddle, Bridle, Holsters furniture & 2 whips cost at London £ 6„ 11„ 6 Sterling	16	8	9
A Wheel barrow & an Iron Spindle	"	16	"
A pair of Saddle Bags worth	"	16	"
Old Holsters for Pistols	"	8	"
A Cyder Slay worth	1	4	"
N: York Curry £	103	16	1

Tools &:c:			
A new sett of Plow Irons cost	4	"	"
an Old Plow with Irons Say	2	10	"
A Corn Mill partly Used	5	"	"
A New London Corn Mill not yet Arrived cost £ 2„ 4„ 10 Sterling which with usual advance	5	11	1
A large Tool Chest with Locks, Screwes, a Bench Vise and all its Tools, Cost £ 11„ 9„ 6„ Sterling which with the usual Advance is	28	13	9
1 very large weighing Beam £ 3 Sterling with advance is	7	10	"
1 small Ditto £ 1.4 Ditto with Ditto	3	"	"
a pair of double hand Srewes £ 4„ 15„ 6 Ditto with Ditto	11	18	9
A weighing Beam in use cost me	2	8	"
A Machine for cutting Oats cost me	4	"	"
2 Common Scythes I suppose @ 12/	1	4	"
1 Brush Ditto I esteem	1	"	"
12 Large Axes in use @ 16/	9	12	"
A Small Iron for drawing Nails	"	6	"
A Large Auger	"	8	"
2 lesser Ditto @ 4/	"	8	"
a Stone Hammer	"	8	"
2 new hand Saws @ 12/	1	4	"
1 Tenent Ditto	"	16	"
a Large whip Saw	2	8	"
a frame Saw	"	12	"
a Small whip Saw	1	10	"
a Compass Saw	"	6	"
2 Squares	"	4	"
a Large Gouge	"	4	"
1 large pair of Groving Planes	"	12	"
1 pair of smaller groving Planes	"	12	"
1 Large mortizeing Chizle	"	8	"
37 Files different Sizes @ 4/	7	8	"
A Garden Hoe	"	6	"
6 Spades and Shovels @ 12/	3	12	"
a Sett of cast weights for Scales	6	"	"
an English Adze	"	12	"
a narrow Mortizing Chizle	"	3	"
a Mortizing Adze	"	16	"
a Hay fork	"	3	"
a pair of Horsefetters	"	16	"
a Curry Comb	"	4	"
A Watering Pott	"	12	"
An Iron Garden Rake	"	6	"
a Pepper Mill	"	16	"
3 Cow Bells @ 5/	"	15	"
a white wash Brush	"	2	"

On the Road

Item	£	s	d
A Burning marking Iron	"	10	"
A Steel Ditto for marking my Name	"	8	"
a marking Iron for Casks &c	"	8	"
a Proof Bottle	"	4	"
a Turkey whetstone	"	6	"
½ a Diamond for cutting glass Cost	"	18	"
2 Tap Boarers @ 4/	"	8	"
a Sett of Copper measures	4	"	"
A Logg Chain	3	"	"
a pair of Sheep Sheeres	"	6	"
3 Iron Wedges & a maull with Iron Hoopes	1	18	"
at the farm 4 large Augers & a Drawing Knife	1	10	"
2 Hulling Basketts @ 8	"	16	"
Coopers Tools Suppose	3	"	"
In the Smyths Shop an Anvill	10	"	"
a pair of Bellows	4	"	"
an old Vise	2	"	"
A large Sledge	1	10	"
A less Ditto	1	"	"
A large Hand Hammer	"	10	"
a Small Sledge with Cap Robinson	"	16	"
A Bench Vise with Ditto	1	4	"
2 pair of Smyths Tongues	1	"	"
a pair of Pinchers	"	6	"
a Tool for pairing Horses Hoofs	"	6	"
A Small Bench Hammer	"	4	"
2 Carpenters Gages @ 3/	"	6	"
A Half Bushell Measure	"	14	"
A Scuper for Skins	"	3	"
3 Trunnells different Sizes @ 4/	"	12	"
about 12 Brass Cocks in use @ 5/	3	"	"
2 Iron Dogs for Sawyers @ 5/	"	10	"
2 large Square Files Smyths Shop @ 8/	"	16	"
3 flat Files @ 4/	"	12	"
a Screw Plates & Tapes	1	"	"
A Machine for grinding Rasors &c	1	"	"
N: York Curr^y £	168	5	7

My own Necessaries &:c:

Item	£	s	d
A Gold watch	30	"	"
A Sett of Silver & Stone Buckles cost £ 2„ 14			
Ster: with usual Advance is	6	15	"
an English Rifle Gunn	10	"	"
an English Fuzil	7	10	"
A Spanish Barrell Fuzil	6	10	"
A Case of Holster Pistols Cost £ 3„ 18„ 6			
Sterling with usual Advance is	9	3	9
a Leather powder Flask	1	"	"
A tin Ditto Ditto	"	5	"
a Shot Belt with Brass top	"	12	"

Item	£	s	d
a Neat Hanger & Pistol	4	//	//
A Small Knife Bayonett	1	4	//
A pockett compass lent M.^r La Mote	2	//	//
a Spy glass worth	6	//	//
2 Razors with case &c	//	16	//
a pair of best Skeats	1	4	//
a Pistoll Tinder Box	//	8	//
an oil Cloth Umbrella cost	1	7	//
Pinching & Curling Tongues	//	12	//
3 pair of Bullett molds @ 4/	//	12	//
a Stand or Rack for 3 Gunns	1	4	//
2 Gunn Hammers & turn Screwes	//	12	//
Medicines for ab.^t	1	4	//
an old Fiddle Cost	2	//	//
A Worked Pockett Book	1	4	//
New York Curr.^y £	96	2	9

Writing Implements, Books &c.

Item	£	s	d
A Writing Desk cost	6	//	//
A Small Printing Press	6	//	//
A Pewter Ink Stand & 2 lead ones	//	10	//
A Sand and Pounce Boxes	//	6	//
A Square Box with Papers	1	//	//
A Round Box or Trunk with Ditto	1	//	//
A Red Leather case cost	//	12	//
An Ass Skin memor.^{dm} Book	//	16	//
A Slate with Pencills	//	12	//
Mayers Book keeping 1 Vol:	//	12	//
The American Negociator 1 Ditto	//	16	//
Windgates Arithmetic 1 Ditto	//	16	//
The Dictionary of Arts Sciences 2 Ditto	6	//	//
The Ditto of ---------Ditto in 5 Ditto	6	//	//
Ouvers de Grassett 2 Vol:			
Bellisaire . . . . 1 ⎫			
Homme de Qualete 2 ⎪			
Soldat persence 2 ⎬ Cost £ 2„ 12 Sterling			
Preceives du ⎪ with usual Advance is	6	10	//
Sentiment 3 ⎪			
Contes Moreaux 4 ⎭			
Ouvres de Mollairs 10 Vol: lent Barth	4	//	//
Boyers Royal French & English Dictionary	2	8	//
70 Odd Vol: of other Books,			
mostly broken setts say worth each 2/	7	//	//
New York Curr.^y £	50	18	//

House Furniture & Utensils

Item	£	s	d
A warming pan	1	"	"
a Dozen of China cups & Saucers	1	4	"
a large Iron Pott	1	"	"
a small Ditto	"	16	"
an Old Carpet	1	"	"
3 Cristal Salt Cellars @ 3/	"	9	"
a pair of Cards	"	12	"
a Small Butter Tub	"	5	"
a Glass Lanthorn	"	16	"
a Large China punch Bowl	1	12	"
A Neat Arm Chair cost	6	"	"
16 Common Chairs @ 4/	3	4	"
3 Neat Japaned Servers	8	"	"
a Glass or flint mugg	"	8	"
2 large red Tea Potts @ 12/	1	4	"
10 drinking glasses @	1	1	4
a Looking Glass	1	"	"
20 Coffe cups different Sizes @ 3/	3	"	"
1 White Tea pott	"	4	"
3 cream Juggs @ 3/	"	9	"
2 large white Stone Juggs @ 6/	"	12	"
1 Doz: more Cups & Saucers	1	4	"
2 pair Andirons one at the Captains	4	"	"
A Mettle Stove at Mr. Clowe's	8	10	"
A Large washing Copper Kittle	6	10	"
2 Camp Bedsteads	2	"	"
a Stabunk	"	10	"
a large Bread Chest	1	4	"
2 Large Common Chairs @ 6/	"	12	"
5 Wooden Chairs @ 6/	1	10	"
Some Maps say worth	1	10	"
a Travelling Case several Appartments	"	16	"
a Tea Table Broke	"	8	"
2 Cloaths Brushes @ 2/	"	4	"
a Common Table with a Drawer	"	16	"
1 Large Iron Stove Cost to Mr. Clowes	18	"	"
another Ditto worth	15	"	"
a Lanthorn	"	4	"
A Small desk & Book Case Cost to Mr. Clowes	8	"	"
a Large painted Sugar Canester Ditto	1	12	"
A Tea Chest without Canisters	1	"	"
A Blue travelling Chest of Drawers	4	"	"
2 Compleat House Beds with everything belonging to them	50	"	"
a Small Table Carpet	"	16	"
2 large Tumbler glasses @ 3/	"	6	"
A Chinia pint mugg	"	6	"
3 Small Chinia Bowls @ 5/	"	15	"
4 Small White Stone Bowles @ 2/	"	8	"
6 Ditto Delph Ditto @ 1/6	"	9	"
2 Pewter Tankards @ 6/	"	12	"

Item	Price	£	s	d
1 Pint Ditto		"	6	"
5 Pewter Basons	@ 5/	1	5	"
2 Copper Coffe Potts		"	16	"
Vinegar, Oil &.c. Bottles		"	8	"
1 large Soop & 5 Table Silver Spoons		15	"	"
Small Tea Spoons & Tongs		2	"	"
A pair of Japan'd Candlesticks		"	6	"
2 pair old Brass Ditto	@ 4/	"	8	"
2 Copper Tea Kittles		1	12	"
1 Doz. Silver tiped Knives & Forks		3	"	"
9 Common Knives and forks		"	16	"
3 Quart Decanters	@ 8/	1	4	"
2 Pint Ditto	@ 6/	"	12	"
a flint Sugar dish		"	8	"
2 Small Looking glasses	@ 16/	1	12	"
a Small Camp Table		1	4	"
an old Japan'd Server		"	16	"
a Coffee Pott Queensware		"	10	"
a pair of Brass Top Tonges & Shovell		"	16	"
6 pair of Sheets	@ 40/	12	"	"
32 Towels	@ 3/	4	10	"
4 Table Cloths	@ 10/	2	"	"
a Leather Feather Bed		3	"	"
a Small Cotton Ditto very fine		3	"	"
a Racoon Skin Blankett		"	12	"
Window Curtins		1	4	"
A Pewter Turine Cost		2	10	"
6 Wooden Bowles	@ 3/	"	18	"
2 Stone Butter Boats	@ 5/	"	10	"
a Stone peper Box		"	3	"
16 Plates Queens Ware	@ 2/	1	12	"
4 Dishes Ditto different Sizes	@ 7/	1	8	"
1 large Oval Pewter dish		"	16	"
a Fire Screen cost		1	4	"
a Fish Kittle		3	"	"
4 Brass Ditto in use	@ 16/	3	4	"
An Iron Pott & Kittle at the Farm		2	"	"
2 Iron Potts in the Kitchin		1	12	"
a Mettle Dutch Oven		"	16	"
4 Gridirons	@ 8/	1	12	"
an Iron Ladle		"	5	"
5 Smoothing Irons with the Stand	@ 6/	1	10	"
a Frying pan		"	16	"
a Large Iron Fire Shovell		"	8	"
a Bread Toster		"	4	"
a Crook		"	16	"
a Chafing dish		"	12	"
A White fish hanging Gridiron		"	4	"
a Hanging Spitt		"	12	"
2 Dough Troughs		2	"	"
a Sceive		"	4	"
a Bakers Kittle		"	12	"
a Dough Knife		"	4	"
2 Cloths to turn the bread on		1	4	"

a Pitch Pott		"	10	"
5 Water Bucketts	@ 10/	2	10	"
2 Crooks at the Farm		1	12	"
a Copper Chocolate Pott		"	6	"
a Childs Skillett		"	6	"
a Pestell & Mortar		"	16	"
a Choping Knife		"	12	"
2 Stone Chamber Potts	@ 6/	"	12	"
2 Mice Traps at the Captains		"	6	"
3 Milk pails	@ 4/	"	12	"
2 Churns	@ 16/	1	12	"
1 Large wash Tubb		2	"	"
1 Less Ditto		1	4	"
2 Stone Juggs with Pickles	@ 3/	"	6	"
2 Bottle fashon Ditto	@ 3/	"	6	"
a Large Firr Table		1	"	"
an Oval Walnutt Ditto		1	"	"
a Smaller oval Blk Birch Ditto		"	16	"
a Broken Camp Table		"	10	"
2 pair of Snuffers	@ 6/	"	12	"
a Bread Toaster		"	3	"
2 Small Tubbs	@ /6	"	12	"
a Coffee Mill		1	"	"
New York Curr:^y £		274	2	4

Merchandize &.c.

7 Yards of Strouds	@ 16/	5	12	"
16 Ells of wollen Check	@ 6/	4	16	"
2 Yards of white Molton	@ 7/	"	14	"
12 Yards of Cotton	@ 6/	3	12	"
4 Yards of Rateen	@ 16/	3	4	"
2 pair of white Molton Legings	@ 8/	"	16	"
4 Small Check Shirts	@ 4/	"	16	"
2 pair of Worsted Stockings	@ 12/	1	4	"
10 Small white Shirts	@ 4/	2	"	"
4 pair of Milled Hose	@ 8/	1	12	"
2 Milled Scarlett Caps	@ 8/	"	16	"
6 pair of Shoes	@ 16	4	16	"
1 peice Embossed Serge almost whole		7	10	"
1 Ditto white Flannell almost Ditto		5	7	6
13 Common Cotton Handkerchiefs	@ 2/	1	6	"
1 Common Spotted Ditto		"	2	"
6 Pewter Basons @ 3/		"	18	"
½ Doz: fire Steels @ 6^d		"	3	"
13 pair of Mittins @ 4/		2	12	"
a Rateen Capot		2	10	"
13 peices of Narrow binding	@ 4/	2	12	"
4 papers of Ink powder	@ 2/	"	8	"
14 horn Combs		"	14	"
1½ pound of fine thread	@ 16/	1	4	"
6 Bottles of Essence peperment	@ 4/	1	4	"

Item	Rate	£	s	d
1 Gro: of Jewes harps		3	"	"
6 Yards of small red Tape	@ 4.ᵈ	"	2	"
1½ of Vermillion	@ 16/	1	4	"
1 pair of womans Shoes		"	16	"
8 pair of Leather Breeches	@ 20/	8	"	"
3 Common Hats	@ 8/	1	4	"
2 Capots De Molton	@ 30/	3	"	"
8 pounds of Snuff	@ 10/	4	"	"
1½ peice Ribbond	@ 24/	1	4	6
2½ peices of Tape	@ 6/	"	15	"
false Silver works		3	"	"
a Small white Shirt		"	7	"
5 Yards fine sort of twil'd Linen	@ 10/	2	10	"
a Large Canoe Sail		2	10	"
4 Account Books	@ 16/	3	4	"
4 Small Ditto	@ 6/	1	4	"
2 Rhemes of Paper		3	"	"
4 Quire of large Paper	@ 4/	"	16	"
2 pounds of Tacks	@ 16/	1	12	"
6½ Doz: of horn Buttons	@ 1/	"	6	6
2 Bottles of Turlington	@ 6/	"	12	"
2 Gunn Locks	@ 6/	"	12	"
4 Sticks of Twist	@ 1/6	"	6	"
15 Blanketts 2½ points	@ 16/	12	"	"
1 Ditto 3 Ditto		"	18	"
2 pound of large brass Wire	@ 6/	"	12	"
4½ pounds of Emery	@ 2/	"	9	"
1 pound of Black lead I believe Antimoney	@ 6/	"	6	"
2 pound of Verdigrace & ½ ℔ Allom		"	5	"
1½ pound of Brimstone in powder	@ 4/	"	6	"
½ pound green paint		"	6	"
5 Cupboard Locks	@ 4/	1	"	"
3 pair of HL Hinges	@ 4/	"	12	"
6 pounds of Attalence	@ 3/	"	18	"
30 Gimblets	@ 6ᵈ	"	15	"
2 pound of Blue	@ 8/	"	16	"
a pair of Table Hinges & Screws		"	4	"
1 Bottle of Lintseed Oil		"	5	"
1 Pound Puttey & ½ ℔ blue paint		"	14	"
8 pounds of best green Tea	@ 30/	12	"	"
2 Calf Skins for uppers	@ 16/	1	12	"
1 Bottle of Sweet Oil		"	4	"
2 Jarrs Lintseed Oil 6 Gˢ & Jarrs		5	"	"
170 ℔ of Nails different Sorts	@ 3/	25	10	"
30 ℔ˢ of Peril Barley	@ 1/	1	10	"
41 panes of glass	@ 2/	4	2	"
2 ℔ of Raisins	@ 3/	"	6	"
26 ℔ˢ of Sturgeon twine	@ 3/6	4	11	"
½ a Keg of Clover Seed		3	"	"
15 ℔ of Common green Tea	@ 16/	12	"	"
2½ Gro: of Corks	@ 8/	1	"	"

Item	Rate	£	s	d
1 Ball of Candle Weak say worth		"	4	"
5 ℔ of Bohea Tea	@ 12/	3	"	"
13 ℔ of Mold Candles	@ 3/	1	19	"
63 Bags of Linen	@ 3/	9	12	"
6 pair of Indian Shoes	@ 2/6	"	15	"
a Small Copper Kettle		"	12	"
10 ℔ of grease	@ 2/	1	"	"
1½ Bushell of Barley	@ 8/	"	12	"
33 pounds of Oakam		1	13	"
33 Doz: of Pipes	@ 3/	5	2	"
21 ℔.ˢ of Tallow	@ 2/	2	2	"
1 pair of small Scales and brass weights		2	"	"
23 ℔.ˢ of Salt Butter	@ 2/	2	6	"
17 ℔.ˢ of fresh Ditto	@ 3/	2	11	"
6 ℔.ˢ of Cheese	@ 2/	"	12	"
2 Gall: of Cherry Brandy	@ 3/0	3	"	"
¾ of a large Keg of Liquor		4	16	"
about 2 Gallons of Shrub	@ 32/	3	4	"
½ Keg of Rum Say		3	"	"
about 3 Quarts of Port wine	@ 4/	"	12	"
1 quarter Cask of Mallaga wine		20	"	"
½ a Cask of Beef worth about		6	"	"
153 new Cags of which 60 of mine	@ 6/	18	"	"
13 Kegs that has been in use	@ 5/	3	5	"
138 Bushels of Detroit Corn	@ 20/	138	"	"
about 11 Bushels of Arbra Croch Corn	@ 12/	6	12	"
1 Bag of Beans		"	16	"
1 Bushell of Oats		"	9	"
3 Kegs of Porter	@ £ 4	12	"	"
1½ Barrell of Salt	@ £ 8	12	"	"
5 Barrells of Lime	@ 30/	7	10	"
1½ Barrell of Ashes	@ 30/	2	5	"
½ Barrell of Tarr		4	"	"
2 peices of Common Linen	@ 75/	7	10	"
1½ Ditto of Calimanco	@ 80/	6	"	"
1 Ditto of Calico		4		
3 Files and 6 Rasps		1	7	"
3 Steel Tobacco Boxes	@ 3/	"	9	"
2 papers of Pins		"	4	"
3 peices of Calico	@ 70/	10	10	"
25 papers of Tobacco	@ 1/	1	5	"
4 Bunches of Salmon Twine	@ 4/	"	16	"
44 Pounds of cutt Tobacco	@ 4/	8	16	"
2 Kegs of Detroit Butter 158½ ℔:	@ 3/	23	15	6
93 ℔. of Hoggs Lard	@ 2/	9	6	"
3 peices of Sail Duck	@ 120/	18	"	"
4 Ditto of Osinbrigs	@ 220/	44	"	"
4 Kegs Salt Butter 262 ℔:	@ 2/	26	4	"
3 Boxes Soap 362	@ 3/	54	6	"
3 Ditto Sper:ᵃ Candles 86 ℔.ˢ	@ 7/	30	16	"
about 80 ℔.ˢ of Paint	@ 4/	16	"	"
2 Ice Cutters	@ 2	"	4	"
a Tubb with gum say 12 ℔:	@ 1/4	"	16	"

Item	Rate	£	s	d
6 pound of Beaver Stones	@ 6/	1	16	"
a Large new Shead or Tent Russia Sheeting		3	"	"
110 ℔: of drest Skins	@ 3/	16	10	"
12 ℔: of Beaver	@ 12/	7	4	"
31 Red Skins	@ 6/	9	6	"
4 bad Otters	@ 10/	2	"	"
1 Carraboe Skin in the Hair		1	"	"
2 Orinal Skins in the Ditto	@ 12/	1	4	"
a Orinal Skin Shirt & a Wolf Skin		1	2	"
2 Bear Skins & 3 Orinal S: pose		3	"	"
10 Racoon Skins	@ 2/6	1	5	"
1 Small Keg about 30 ℔: Powder	@ 3/	4	10	"
5 Half Beaver Hats	@ 20/	5	"	"
11 Brown Martens	@ 12/	6	12	"
6 Foxes	@ 4/	1	4	"
8 Kegs of Red wine	@ 128/	51	4	"
92 Kegs of British Brandy	@ 128/	588	16	"
17 Hhds. with I. Rum each 65 Gallons	@ £ 65/	1105	"	"
5 Kegs Ab: of Ditto Remd: in 3 Hhds.	@ £ 8	40	"	"
about 1½ Gallons of French Brandy	@ 32/	2	8	"
1 Quarter Cask of Spirits		36	"	"
½ a Barrell of Port		14	"	"
1 Quarter Cask of White wine Vinegar		20	"	"
1 Barrell of Mollasses		24	"	"
1 Ditto of Coffe Suppose 150 ℔:	@ 2/	15	"	"
19 Barrells of British Brandy 606 Gall:	@ 16/	484	8	"
1 Barrell of York Rum 36 Gallons	@ 18/	32	8	"
Suppose 200 ℔: of Iron	@ 2/	20	"	"
about 80 ℔: of Steel	@ 2/8	10	13	4
1 Barrell of brown Suggar 320 ℔:	@ 1/4	21	6	8
1 Quarter Cask of Port wine		32	"	"
1 Keg of Pepper 57 ℔	@ 4/	11	8	"
1 Teirce of Loaf Sugar 250 ℔	@ 3/	37	10	"
157 ℔: of Ditto Loose	@ 3/	23	11	"
about 100 ℔: of Gumm	@ 1/	5	"	"
13 Bunches of Watap		"	13	"
6 covering Barks	@ 8/	2	8	"
11 Roles mending Bark	@ 12/	6	12	"
1 Keg of W: India Rum		8	"	"
2 Kegs Powder in the Magazine		20	"	"
Cash in Curr: Bills		93	10	"
16 Yards of Russia Sheeting	@ 5/	4	"	"
18 Spotted Jacketts at	30/	27	"	"
3 Double Rateen Jacketts	@ 40/	6	"	"
9 pair of Cotton Trowsers	@ 16/	7	4	"
39 Cotton Shirts	@ 16/	31	4	"
3 Check Ditto	@ 16/	2	8	"
4 Doz: of Worsted Caps	@ 24/	4	16	"
23 Common Handkerchiefs	@ 2/	2	6	"
650 Flints	@ 4/	1	6	"

8½ ℔ of Net thread	@ 6/	2	11	"
2 Crooked Knives	@ 2/	"	4	"
6 Padlocks	@ 4/	1	4	"
7 Augers	@ 4/	1	8	"
3 pints of Sweet Oil	@ 3/	"	9	"
58 ℔ of Ball	@ 1/4	3	17	4
89 ℔ of Chocolate	@ 4/	17	16	"
45 ℔ of more Soap	@ 3/	6	15	"
26 Cod Lines	@ 10/	13	"	"
18 ℔ of Pepper	@ 5/	4	10	"
20 ℔ of brass Kettles	@ 5/	5	"	"
4 pair of Shoe Buckles at	4/	"	16	"
15 Dozen of worms	@ 2/	1	10	"
3 Barrells of Vinegar making	@ £ 6	18	"	"
230 ℔ of Role Tobacco	@ 4/	46	"	"
225 ℔ of Carrot Tobacco	@ 3/	33	15	"
197 ℔ of Gunn Powder	@ 3/	29	11	"
of Flour				
of Pork				
1 more Quarter cask of Port wine		32	"	"
1 Quarter Cask of White wine or Maderia		32	"	"
New York Curr.ʸ		3841	7	4

Dr Ballance

1776 Dec: 31.ˢᵗ		montreal money		N: York Curr:ʸ		
To amount brought over in						
New York Currency £				5197	17	"
To M.ʳ Robert Aird due me		10	10			
To M.ʳ M.ᶜ Gulpin Ditto				57	"	2
To M.ʳ M.ᶜ Carty Ditto				10	7	
To Mons:ʳ Cha:ˢ Chaboulliez Ditto		2485				
To Mess:ʳˢ Auge Masher &c Ditto		12				
To Mons:ʳ La Mote Ditto		1273				
To Mess:ʳˢ Reaume in C.° Ditto		135				
To my half Share Adv:ᵉ in						
Fish with M.ʳ B:				67	7	6
To M.ʳ Edward Pollard Due me				60	"	"
To my half Share Adv.ᵉ to Millwakei		9026	6½			
To Mess:ʳˢ Pillette Due me		4				
To Mons:ʳ Geautuz Due me		114				
To Mons:ʳ Mumforton Ditto		142				
To the Barracks here Ditto				103	18	"
To M.ʳ Ainse Ditto		511	18			
				914	5	"
				6410	14	8

Description			£	s	d
To Mons:ʳ Du Gay Ditto 51„16 pel: is	103	12			
To Mons:ʳ Bellcour Ditto	231				
To Mons:ʳ Courotte Ditto	12				
To Mʳ Hanson Ditto	66	10			
To Mons:ʳ La Fantezee Ditto 154„10 peltry is	309				
To Mons:ʳ Remour Quenell Ditto 4„5	8	10			
To Mons:ʳ J B Hamalin Ditto 37„10	75				
To due me by Soldiers as per their Book			31	19	
To Cᵗ De Peyster for 18 Kegs Rum & a Barrell pitch lent			190	"	"
			53	13	8
		£	6686	7	4
To due me by my Engagees	3886	14			
To Col: Caldwell due me for 75 Kegs of Rum destroyed on lake Erie			450	"	"
To Shipping as per Inventery			900	"	"
To Houses & Lands as per Ditto			1068	"	"
To Slaves as per Ditto			390	"	"
To Cattle Ditto			323	12	8
To Carriages & Harness Ditto			103	16	1
To Toolls &c Ditto			168	5	7
To my Own Necessaries Ditto			96	2	9
To Books & writing implements Ditto			50	18	"
To House Furniture &c Ditto			274	2	4
To Merchandize &.c. Ditto			3841	7	4
			259	3	1½
New York Curr.ʸ		£	14611	15	2½

Trifling & dubious Debts Vizᵗ:

Description			£	s	d
To Le due in the North due me 80 pel. ----					
To Bodwin Ditto 49„10 &			2	10	"
To Beausollile Ditto 8„10 &				13	4
To Beslille Smyth Ditto 3					
To Mʳ Bourrissa Senior Ditto			7	5	—
To my ¼ Share due our old C.º in the North	2960	15			
To Mʳ Bruce half his Note 1000„0 pel					
To Mʳ Bertrand 41„0					
To Clutrez due me 121„14					
To Langlois 35 0 &			3	—	—
To Mʳ Burginnen			1	12	"
To Sorrell			2	15	5
To Du Cheneau Couchois & Galliard 78„15					

Contra

	Montreal money		N: York Curr:[y]		

1776
Dec.: 31.:[st]

	Montreal money		N: York Curr:[y]		
Amount brought forward in N. York Curr:[y] £			4035	10	5½
By Mons.:[r] Shenduler due him	9	10			
By the Great N.W. C:[o] Ditto	315				
By Mess.:[rs] Todd & M:[c] Gill Ditto			1446	14	8¾
By Mons.:[r] Cerrie Ditto	1646		131	7	4
		£	5613	12	6¼
By half Hodefries wages	300	"			
By ½ Coursells Ditto	300	—			
By 2/3 Mirans Ditto	466	—			
By ½ Traverseys Ditto	250	—			
By ½ La Fantizies Ditto	300	—			
By ½ Feltons Ditto	300	—			
By ½ Chelous Ditto	300	—			
By ½ Ned Shehays Ditto	300	—			
By M.:[r] Solomon for Prov.:[s] to Return say			75	—	—
By M.:[r] M:[c] Beath D:[o] & Rum to return			123	—	—
By Mons.:[r] Letems Ditto			8	—	—
By Mess.:[rs] M:[c] Tavish & Co. for Prov.:[s] to return			150	16	—
By Mons.:[r] La Mote and C:[o] Ditto			14	"	—
By M.:[r] Fleming Ditto Commissary			17	—	—
			167	15	—
By Stock for the neat of my Estate			6168	11	6¼
		£	8443	3	8¼
			14611	15	2½

222

Inventery of John Askin his
Estate taken the 31 of December 1778

		[N.Y.C.]		
		[£]	[S]	[D]
Shiping &c.ca				
a large Keel Boat with Oars Sails &c.ca		60		
a Common Batea[u]		12		
£ 4- a Small fish [ ]		10		
	£	82		
H[ouses Lands &]:ca				
		300		
		120		
		150		
		100		

*[Manuscript is torn and the remainder
of this page is missing]*

Cattle		[£]	[S]	[D]
3 £ 80	2 Good Milch Cows		60	
2 £ 100	3 fatt Oxen		120	
	2 Horsses		35	
x	a large Sow		10	
x	2 Medling Sows		12	
x	a Boar		6	
1+ £ 5	a Smaller Pig		3	
11 +	20 fowles @ 8/		8	
		£ 254		

Carrages Harness &:[ca]   x

		£	s	d
£ 20	a four Wheeled Carrage x	24		
	a Carriole x	5		
	a small D:[o]	1	4	
	2 large Wood Slays well Shod	13	6	8
	[ ] Wood Cart well Shoad	12		
	[ ] Chair Harness	8		
	Womans Saddle Bridle &:[ca]	8		
	fine Saddle Bridle Whip & Holsters cost in London £ 6„11„6	19	14	6
	a pair of Saddle Baggs		16	
	old Pistol Holsters		8	
	a Wheel Barrow Iron Spindle		16	
	a Sedan Chair	5		
	a logg Slay well Shod	3		
	a Common Harness	6		
£ 4	a Covered 4 Wheeled Carrage x	6		
	£	113	5	2

Tools &:[ca]

		£	s	d
	a Weighing Beam Cost £ 3 Ster[g]:	9		
£ 5	a smaller Ditto 1„4	3	12	
	a Double Screw or Jack Cost £ 4„15„6	14	6	6
	a Com:[n] Weighing Beam old at y:[e] Bakers	2	8	
	a Machine to cut Oates	4		
	a Brush Scythe	1		
x	2 Hand & 1 Tennent Saw	2		
	a frame Wood Saw		12	
	2 pair of Grooving Plains	2		
	a large Mortizing Chizell		16	
	a Garden Hoe		6	
x	a Spade & a Shovell	1		
	a Sett of Cast Weights	6		
	a pair of Horse fetters	1	4	
	a Curry Comb & 2 Hay forks	1		
	a Wattering Pott		12	
	a Pepper Mill	1		
	a B[urn]ing Iron my Name		10	
	a Steel Stamp my D:[o]		10	
	a Proof Bottle		4	
	a Turkey Whett Stone		6	
	half a Dimond Pencill		18	
	a Sett of Copper Measures	4		
	3 logg Chains	4		
	a pair of Bellows	2		
	2 large Anvills	16		
	a Vice	2		
	a large Sledge	1	10	

			@	£	s	d
		a pair of Pinchers			6	
		a small Sledge		1		
		1 Hoof pairer			8	
		2 Screw Plates & Taps		2		
x		a Machine for grinding Razers		1		
		a Small Bench Vice		1	4	
		a Half Busshell Measure			14	
		2 Doggs for Sawyers			10	
	£ 8	Coopers Tools for		6		
		a Compass Saw			10	
x		a Square			4	
x		2 Shingle Splitters	@ 12/	1	4	
x		a New Drawing Knife			12	
		a Stone Hammer			16	
		1 Trowell			6	
		1 Mallott			2	
x		3 Hoes	@ 8/	1	4	
		2 pair of Snow Shoes	@ 16/	1	12	
		1 Scraper			4	
	4	2 funnells	@ 4/		8	
		2 Whip Saws for		1	10	
		2 Cow Bells			10	
x		20 Bar.¹ of Coal	@ 6/	6		
		3 Smyths Hammers	@ 16/	2	8	
		4 p:ʳ of Smyths Tonges	@ 20/	4		
		1 p:ʳ of Pinchers			10	
		a Shoeing Hammer			6	
x		1 Hoof pairer			6	
		3 files	@ 5/		15	
		2 Vales or Bench Irons	@ 40/	4		
		1 [Sergeant] or Wood Presser		2		
		2 Handsaws	@ 12/	1	4	
		1 Tennent Saw			16	
		1 Adze			8	
		2 Augers	@ 4/		8	
	2	1 Iron Rake			16	
x		1 Ice Cutter			12	
			£	129	7	6

My Own Necessaries &:ᶜᵃ

				£	s	d
	£ 50	1 Double Barrelled Gunn & a pair of Dble Barrelled Pistols		60		
		1 fine fusil		16		
		1 Gold Watch x		30		
x		a Case of Holster Pistols Cost £ 3″13″6 Ster:		10		6
		a leather powder flask x			16	
		1 Tin Powder flask			5	
		1 Shott Belt with Brass Top			12	
		1 Neat Hanger & Pistol		4		
		a Knife Bayonett x		1	4	

		£	s	d
	a fine Pockett Compass	2		
	a Spy Glass	5		
	2 Razors with a Case		16	
	1 p. of fine Sheats	1	4	
	1 Pistol tinder Box		8	
	an Umbrella		16	
	Pinchers & Curling Tongues		12	
	a Stand or Rack for Gunns	1	4	
	Gunn Hammers & turn Screws		16	
	a Worked Pockett Book x	1	4	
	1 Sett of Mathematical Instrumn.	6	6	
	1 Sliding Rule		18	
	fiddle Strinks for	2	8	
1 £ 10,,8	2 fiddles Cost	20	16	
x	1 fine long Silver Mounted Gunn	60		
	1 Magnafying Glass x	1		
	1 Compleat Razor Case	2		
	£	230	5	6

Books & Writeing Implements

		£	s	d
	a Writing Desk	4		
	a Small Table Desk		16	
	a pewter & Lead Ink Stand		10	
	1 Sand & Pounce Box		6	
	a Square Trunk with Papers	1		
	a large painted Chest for Papers	4		
	1 Red leather Case for papers		12	
	1 Ass kin Memord. Book		16	
x	1 Slate & Pencil		10	
	Mayers Book Keeping		12	
[M. F]	The American Negociator 1 Vol:		16	
x	Windgates Arithmetic 1 D.		10	
	Algebra by Simpson 1 Vol:	1	4	
[M. Brs]	Chambers Dictionarys 2 Vols	6		
	The Dictionary of Arts & Sciences 5 Vol	6		
x	Ouvers de Grassiotte 2 Vol			
	Bellisaire 1 D.			
	Hommes de Qualite 2 D.			
	Soldat persence 2 D. Cost in London £ 2,,12 Ster.	7	16	
	Preuves de Sentiment: 3 D.			
2-- £ 6	Contes Moreaux 4 D.			
	Ouvers de Molliars 10 D.	4		
	Le Dictionaire Royal	2	8	
	[Madame] Bon 10 Vol	2		
	16 News Plays @ 5/	4		
	Elementes of Navagation 1 Vol	1	2	6
	Observations on Lightning		10	6
	a fine Prayer Book		18	
	The Spectator 8 Vol. x	4	4	
	The Memoirs of Sullay 9 Vols:	4	15	

	Item	£	s	d
	146 N.ᵒˢ of Magazins	10	19	
	a large Box to hold Books	1	4	
	a large Bible with Cutts			
	x my brother has this bible	8	14	
	a New Dictionary	3	3	
	a Hair Trunk with Papers	2		
	The Earl of Chesterfields Letters 4 Vol	3	4	
	The Whole Duty of Man 1 Vol:		12	6
	About 120 Odd Vols @ 2/	12		
	£	101	2	6

Furniture & Utensils

	Item	£	s	d
	1 Warming Pann	1		
	2 Brass Skilletts @ 15/	1	10	
	1 large Cheina Bowl	1	12	
	1 Neat Square Table	2		
	1 large Silver Soop Spoon x gave to [Addie]	4		
	2 Silver Porrengers	18		
	a large Common dineing Table	1		
	1 Oval Table		16	
	1 Neat folding Camp Table	2		
	a worse Ditto		16	
	1 Kitchen Table		8	
Burnted]	1 Camp Table		8	
	1 large painted Sugar Canester lock	2		
	1 large Tin Ditto		12	
x	2 Copper Tea Kittles	1	10	
	1 small Cheina Tea Canester		6	
	1 Small Plated Tea Pott & Sugar dish	3		
	2 Japaned Candlesticks x		8	
	2 large Queens Wour Juggs		16	
x	1 Quart Mugg D.ᵒ		6	
	a Pepper Box		2	
	1 Butter Plate		4	
	1 fine large Arm Chair	6		
x	my Own Bed with Curtins &.ᶜᵃ x	24		
	4 Watter Bucketts x @ 8/	1	12	
	a fine New fashioned Lamp	2		
	3 looking Glasses @ 12/	1	16	
	1 fire Schreen		12	
	2 p.ʳ of Andirons Brass tops x	3		
x	1 large Chest of Drawyers Cost	10		
	1 Clock	40		
	a Womans Desk & Book Case	8		
	1 large Mettle Stove	20		
[M.ʳ C]	1 small D.ᵒ Ditto	8		
	1 Iron plate Stove	8		
	1 Mettle Duch Oven		16	
	1 Copper Coffey Pott		8	
	1 Mortar & Pestol		16	

227

			@	£	s
		2 frying Panns	@ 12/	1	4
		4 Smoothing Irons x	@ 6/	1	4
		1 Stand for Smoothing Irons			6
		1 large Washing Kittle		5	
		1 large Driping Pann		1	4
		4 large & small Gridirons		2	
		1 large pewter Dish			16
		1 Sallad Dish			6
		1 large pewter Turine		2	10
		1 small Carpett		1	
		1 pair of Wool Cards			12
		1 large Japaned Tea Board		5	
		1 Midling Tea Board		3	
		1 smaller Ditto		2	
		1 flint Sugar dish			8
		2 large Com:n Arms Chairs			16
3		2 Cloths Brushes			6
		1 Tea Chest & Cannesters x		1	4
		1 Blue Travling Chest of Drawyers x		4	
		1 fish Kittle		3	
		1 Choaping Knife			10
		1 Chamber Pott			8
		2 very large Coolers		2	10
x		2 mice Traps			4
C		18 White Plates	@ 3/	2	14
C		6 Tea Potts	@ 5/	1	10
		1 Coffey Mill x			4
		2 Sauce panns	@ 12/	1	4
C		11 small stone dishes	@ 4/	2	4
C		some putty pans			16
C		12 Brass Casks	@ 4/	2	8
-		1 Baskett			6
C		26 Wings		1	6
C		9 Wooden dishes	@ 4/	1	16
C		2 Basons	@ 8/		16
		2 Iron Tea kittles	@ 24/	2	8
C		9 large 18 Small Silver Spoons x & [1/S: T.]		37	10
		2 hand & 1 Houfe Bell		1	10
		2 Setts of Tongues &:ca x	@ 32/	3	4
2		1 Iron Laddle			8
		2 lanterns	@ 6/		12
		2 Brass Kittles x	@ 16/	1	12
C		3 small Copper D:o to y:e men	@ 20/	3	
		1 Sett of New Chiena		8	
		1 New Serving Tay		1	4
C	8	10 Table Cloths	@ 24/	12	
C	4	5 pairs of Sheats	@ 40/	10	
C		20 Towels	@ 6/	6	
		2 Mahagney Knife Cases x		10	16
		2 Doz: pairs of Green Ivory Handled Kn:		11	8
		1 Doz: pairs of desert Knives &:ca		4	4
		1 Box with 2 Setts of Cheina		3	15
x		1 large Silver Coffey Pott x		78	17

			£	s	d
	2 gilt [Rummers]		20	17	6
x	1 Silver Bottle C[ ] x		11	10	9
x	2 Silver Salt Sellars x		11	17	
	2 p.rs of Silver Salt Shovells x		2	2	
	12 Oval Glasses for Salts x		2	14	
x	1 Small Coper Coffey Pott			4	
	2 plated Candlesticks x		4		
	2 p.r of Brass Candlesticks	@ 20/ x	2		
C	1½ Doz: Pictures x	@ 20/	18		
C	5 Window Curtins		12		
C	[ ] Other Bed Curtins &:ca		20		
C	15 Chairs	@ 4/	3		
C	1 Common Camp Table			16	
	1 p.r of Tongues & Shovell			16	
C	4 Quart Decanters	@ 10/	2		
C	2 p.r Com.n Salt Sellers	@ 6/		12	
C	2 Mustard Potts	@ 2/		4	
	1 Pint Decanter			6	
	3 large tin Canisters		1	4	
C	8 Com.n Knives & 15 forks		1		
	1 Knife Box x			8	
C	3 Tea Potts	@ 6/		18	
C	5 large White Cups & Sawcers	@ 2/		10	
C	5 Glasses	@ 3/		15	
C	3 Tumblers	@ 5/		[15]	
C	1 Small White Bowl			[5]	
C	1 Sugar Dish			3	
C	1 Butter			3	
C	10 Cups & Sawcers all for			16	
C	3 Milch Potts	@ 2/		6	
	The Childrens Bed Compleat		8		
	1 Clostool		1	4	
	1 fountain for Washing Hands		1	4	
	1 Pewter Chamber Pott			12	
C	6 Iron Potts in Use	@ 16/	4	16	
x	10 Axes in Use	@ 16/	8		
C	8 Queens Wair Dishes	@ 6/	2	8	
	1 Bread Toaster			16	
C	4 Midling Sized pewter dishes	@ 10/	2		
C	8 Pewter Plates	@ 2/		16	
	£		578	14	3

Merchandize &:ca

			£	s	d
	5 p.r of Leather Breeches	@ 20/	5		
	4 p.r of knitt Mittens	@ 5/	1		
	6 Blanketts 2½ points	@ 16/	4	16	
	3 Ditto 3 Ditto	@ 24/	3	12	
	2 p.r milled Hoss	@ 12/	1	4	
	5 Indian Shirts	@ 14/	3	10	
	3 p.r Cotton Trowsers	@ 16/	2	8	

Item	Rate	£	s	d
3 pᵣ Russia Sheeting Trowsers	@ 20/	3		
4 Rateen Jacketts	@ 32/	6	8	
1 Spotted Jackett		1	10	
1 Blue Coat		1	12	
1 Blankett Coat		2		
17¾ yᵈ flannell	@ 5/	4	9	
5 Double Worsted Caps	@ 5/	1	5	
7 Single Caps	@ 4/	1	8	
6 Red silk Hankf:	@ 10/	3		
8¼ yᵈˢ Bed tick	@ 4/	1	13	
7¾ yᵈˢ of Striped flannell	@ 7/	2	13	3
6½ yᵈˢ of Sail Cloth	@ 6/	1	16	
16 yᵈˢ of Strouds	@ 16/	12	16	
1 yᵈ of Blue Coating			16	
11¾ ℔s of Casteel Soap	@ 4/	2	7	
Abᵗ 10 Peices of [furniture]	@ 8/	4		
1 Indian Shott Pouch			6	
1 [Attalence] Collar			12	
16¾ ℔s of Nett Chord	@ 4/	3	7	
10¼ ℔s of Nett thread	@ 7/	3	11	9
½ ℔ of Sail thread			5	
Abᵗ 130 ℔s of Chocolate	@ 6/	39		
13½ ℔s Sper: Candles	@ 8/	5	8	
18 ℔s of Tallow Candles	@ 4/	3	12	
14 ℔s of peper	@ 8/	5	12	
7 ℔s of Salt petter	@ 8/	2	16	
385 ℔s of Nails	@ 3/	57	7	6
10 ℔s white Paint	@ 6/	3		
30 ℔s of putty	@ 5/	7	10	
40 ℔s of Coffey	@ 3/	6		
5½ ℔s of Chalk	@ 2/		11	
5¾ ℔s Blk lead	@ 4/	1	3	
10 ℔s of Brimstone	@ 6/	3		
12 ℔s of Ball	@ 2/	1	4	
18 ℔s of Deck Nails	@ 2/	1	16	
11 Padlocks & Hasps	@ 6/	3	6	
4½ ℔s of Beads	@ 4/		18	
6 Doz: of Gimbletts	@ 10/	3		
1½ ℔s of Vermillion	@ 16/	1	4	
3 Handsaws	@ 16/	2	8	
1 Iron Ladle			8	
7 New Augers	@ 6/	2	2	
11¼ ℔s of Sturgon Twine	@ 5/	2	16	3
3 Doz large Needles	@ 3/		9	
3½ Doz of Awls	@ 2/		7	
40 files of Difᵗ Sorts	@ 3/	6		
½ ℔ of Whip Chord			16	
5 pᵣ of Smoothing Irons	@ 10/	2	10	
2 pewter Basons	@ 8/		16	
10 New funnells	@ 2/	1		
4 Cupboard locks	@ 4/		16	
18 loaves Sugar Abᵗ 200 Wᵗ	@ 4/	40		
8 Gunns that have Served	@ 30/	12		

Item	Rate	£	s	d
3 Calf Skins	@ 24/	3	12	
21½ ℔s of Soal leather	@ 6/	6	9	
2 Common Kittles	@ 20/	2		
Ab! 120 ℔s Indian Sugar in 3 Barks		8		
6 Doz: of Gunn Worms	@ 2/		12	
Ab! 150 flints			12	
54 ℔s of Shott	@ 2/	5	8	
2 Elk Skins	@ 10/	1		
1 large fine Door lock		1	10	
1 Small New Chizil			4	
5 old Gunn locks	@ 4/	1		
Ab! 6 ℔s of Grease	@ 4/	1	4	
8½ ℔s Brass Wire	@ 5/	2	2	6
1 Black Deerskin			10	
60 Bags	@ 3/	9		
2 New Account Books		4	10	
half of 3 Cheese		2		
1 Razor Case Cost		2		
2 p!s of Ox hide Shoes	@ 6/		12	
2½ Doz: of Thimbles	@ 3/		7	6
1 Bever Skin			8	
1 p! of Mogizins			5	
13 ℔s Oakam	@ 2/	1	6	
Ab! 20 ℔s of Tarr	@ 3/	3		
1 large Sail of Russia Sheeting		4		
Mock Silver Works Supose Worth		2		
114 Busshells of Corn	@ 20/	114		
2 Bar!s of Lime	@ 30/	3		
2 Bar!s of Salt	@ £ 12	24		
28 Kegs Butter & Grease	@ £ 10	280		
6 Bar!s of Montreal Pork	£ 20	120		
9 C! flour	@ 80/	36		
Ab! 700 ℔s of [Grease]		50		
7 Roles of Bark	@ 8/	2	16	
1 New Adze			16	
13 Peices of Strouds	@ £ 12	156		
6 Ditto of Multon	@ £ 7	42		
10 Gro: of Gartering	@ 24/	12		
12 ℔s Sturgon twine	@ 4/	2	8	
16 ℔s Nett thread	@ 8/	6	8	
34 Nett lines	@ 6/	10	4	
20 Codlines	@ 12/	12		
14 ℔s of good thread	@ 10/	7		
5 double peices of Ribon	@ 32/	8		
5 Peices of Linnen	@ £ 5	25		
12 Doz: of Scalping Knives	@ 8/	4	16	
1 !:! Gunn flints		2	10	
668 ℔s Shott & Ball	@ 2/	66	16	
18 y!ds of Calico	@ 8/	7	4	
4 peices of Calimanco	@ 90/	18		
1 Doz: [Hans] so pretty		1		
170 Blanketts 2½ points	@ 16/	102		
10 Blanketts of 1 point	@ 6/	3		

Item	Rate	£	s	d
12 Blanketts of 3 Points	@ 20/	12		
1 Gro: of bed lace		2		
34 ℔s of Vermillion	@ 16/	27	4	
½ ℔ of fine thread		1		
8 Kegs of Powder 450 ℔s	@ 6/	135		
78 ℔s of Brass Kittles	@ 6/	23	8	
41 ℔s of Copper Kittles	@ 10/	20	10	
18 N W Gunns	@ 80/	72		
1 Doz: of Mustard		4		
24 large Axes	@ 16/	19	4	
Bath [Coating] & trimings		8		
Tobacco here & at Detroit Unsold y.ᵉ half is Ab.ᵗ 1200 ℔s @ 8/		480		
Watch Glasses for		1		
6 Empty Jarrs	@ 3/		18	
Sundrys on their Way from England Am.ᵗ after deducting for what I have Recv.ᵈ of them £ 1133„4„5 Half.ˣ :		1813	3	10
Sundry Liquors on their way from Montreal Not Arrived first Cost per A/.ᶜ is £ 990„8„6 Halfx		1584	13	7
Some Pitch, Tarr, Cordage Liquor & Powder belonging to a former Cargo on the way & not Arrived here say		150		
Some School Boys Books		2	5	
285 Bags Corn at Chaboyagan		285		
22 loaves dble Refined Sugar say 160 ℔s	@ 5/	40		
Brown Sugar Ab.ᵗ 60 ℔s	@ 2/	6		
Broken loaf Sugar Ab.ᵗ 30 ℔s	@ 4/	6		
Ab.ᵗ 50 ℔s Com.ⁿ Soap	@ 2/	5		
Ab.ᵗ ½ a Keg Spirits		5		
Ab.ᵗ 1 Keg Butter		6		
1 Busshell of Beans		1		
Ab.ᵗ 10 ℔s of Honey	@ 8/	4		
Ab.ᵗ 8 ℔s of Pruins & Raisons	@ 4/	1	12	
21 Spotted Jacketts	@ 24/	25	4	
13 Rateen Jacketts	@ 30/	19	10	
16 p.ˢ of Russia Trowsers	@ 16/	12	16	
32 Peices of Gartering	@ 6/	9	12	
11 Russia Sheeting Shirts	@ 16/	8	16	
9 Doz: of Mittens	@ 40/	18		
1 Cotton Shirt			16	
2 p.ˢ of Cotton trowsers	@ 16/	1	12	
28 Worsted Caps	@ 3/	7	4	
15 Bottles of Turlington	@ 8/	6		
2 Bever Blanketts	@ 80/	8		
200 Kegs of Rum & Spirits	@ £ 10	2000		
3 Kegs of Wine	@ £ 8	24		
6 Kegs Montreal Pork	@ £ 6	36		
2/3 of a Bar.ᵗ of D.º		16		
1 Keg of Montreal Salt		4		
1 Bar.ᵗ of Muscavado Sugar		30		

30 ℔s of Green Tea	@ 30/	45			
77 ℔s of half Inch Roap	@ 1/4	5	2	8	
1 Bar: of Coffey say		24			
1 Keg of Coffey say		6			
Ab: 230 ℔s Carrott Tobacco	@ 8/	92			
Ab: 10 G: Madiera	@ 40/	20			
1 Bar: Vinegar Ab:		10			
Ab: 2 G: of Sweet Wine	@ 30/	3			
Ab: 4 G: of Vinegar	@ 16/	3	4		
1½ G: Molasses	@ 20/	1	10		
70 ℔s Role Tobacco	@ 8/	2	16		
1 Bar: & Bag of Apples		2	5		
22 flacons of sweet Ayle	@ 6/	6	12		
4 half Axes	@ 6/	1	4		
5 Tomeyhalks	@ 4/	1			
1 Box of Mould Candles		10			
1 Box & 5 Bricks of Casteel Soap		18			
Ab: 120 ℔s	@ 3/				
3 funnells	@ 4/		12		
Ab: 35 ℔s of Common Soap	@ 2/	3	10		
2 Brass Casks	@ 5/		10		
28 ℔s of Brass Kittles	@ 5/	7			
20 ℔s of Red paint	@ 3/	3			
8 ℔s Bever Stones	@ 6/	2	8		
70 Gunn flints say			6		
4½ Doz: of Gunn Worms	@ 2/		9		
8 Plates of Stove Iron say	@ 16/	6	8		
Ab: 400 ℔s Iron in Bars	@ 2/	40			
Ab: 30 ℔s of Steel	@ 3/	4	10		
46 ℔s of Copper Kittles	@ 9/	20	14		
Am: in N: Y: Cur: £		8763	9	10	

D: Ballance

1778 Dec: 31:		[Montreal Money]		New York Cur		
To Mess:s McBeath & Write due me		918	5			
To M: La Voine Barthe privatt A/:		834	5			
To M: Henry Bostwick				231	3	7
To the N W C:		1417	5			
To Maj: De Peyster for y: Crown				385	15	4
To Mess:s Barthe & C:		38998	10			
To Adv: to y: French River my part		9066	1			
To Adv: to Detroit Exclu:						
y: Tobacco		3007	10			
To Adv: to Sagana		3885				
To the Barracks due me				101	3	7½
To Cash in Specie				154	16	
To M: Fleming due me				74	14	
To L: Clowes due me				87	11	

			£	s	d
To Lt Bennett due me			47	4	4
To the Commissary General due me			107	8	10
To Mr Howard due me	1761	8			
To Messrs Grant & Solomon	1650				
To Messrs Abbott & Finchley			28	8	
To Messrs David Mc Cray & Co	180				
To Messrs Holmes & Grant	618				
To Capt Robertson			666	2	6
To Mr Gallouway			123	18	4
To Mr Burggy			167	13	2
	62336	4	4155	15	—
To Messrs Chaboulliez Bourrisa &ca	1934	7			
To Mons Rhode due me	553				
To Mons Cursot due me	765				
To Vessells in Co my share is			956	16	3
To Mr J: B: Barthe privatt A/c	273				
To Capt Grant due me			13	1	
To Mr Jno Stedman due me			3	8	3
To Mons Cotte due me	54				
To Mr Jehu Hay due me			2	16	
To Mr Mc Comb Iron 183 ℔s			18	2	
To Mons Biron due me	393				
To Mons Cerré due me	88	10			
To Mons Orillatt due me	79	7			
To Doc Mitchell due me			7	1	10
To Mons J B Campau due me	141	14			
To Mr B: Lyons due me			309	19	8
To Mr Jos Ainsse due me			200	6	10
To Mons Curotte	12		286	5	
	4293	18			
N: York Cur:		£	8129	10	6½

1778

		£	s	d	
To Sundry Debts due me	£	8129	10	6½	
To Vallue in Boats &ca per A/c		82			
To Value in Housses Lands &ca		1494	13	4	
To Value in Slaves		350			
To Value in Cattle		254			
To Value in Carrages & Harness		113	5	2	
To Value in Tools		129	7	6	
To Value in my Own Necessarys Exclusive of Clothing		230	5	6	
To Value in Books &ca		101	2	6	
To Value in Furniture		578	14	3	
To Value in Merchandize		8763	9	10	
New York Cur:	£	20226	8	7½	

To Ball.ᵉ from the Other Side			12882	17	1¾
To Mʳ M.ᶜGulpin due me			375	11	
To Mʳ Thoˢ Bentley due me	4809.6		320	12	5
To Monsʳ Du Rocher due me	188:15		12	11	8
To Monsʳ [Bellesur]	85:10		6		8
To Monsʳ J:B: Hamalin	130:0		8	13	4
204090 Livers est Equal à		£	13606	6	2¾

The Doubtfull & Bad Debts
are wrote on the Other side

Contra

1778
Dec: 31.ˢᵗ

By Messʳˢ Todd & Mᶜ Gill due them £ 2581„7„11¼ Haf.ˣ			4130	4	8¼
By Major De Peyster due him			1053	4	10
By Mʳ Mᶜ [Farlin] due him			852	15	2
By Mʳ Park due him			148	14	9½
By Nicholas Miran due him			155	4	4
By Major De Peyster for Sundrys			30	6	6
By Messʳˢ Mᶜ Donnald & Walker			66	1	2
By Mʳ Joˢ Sangunett 4 Canoes	600				
By Monsʳ Gullion 1 Keg Grease say			10		
By 20 Canoes I have Chᵈ			266	13	4
By McTavish & Bannerman			51	16	
By Ensigⁿ Brooks			33	14	
By Mʳ Frobisher	100				
By Mʳ Perinault	158				
By Current Bills made			109		
By Mʳ Hamalin	209				
By Monˢ Augˢ Chaboulliez	32	10			
By Mʳ Wᵐ Edgar			10	8	
By Mʳ Paul La[Croin]	432	10			
By Messʳˢ Jmˢ & Jnº MᶜGill			9	6	8
By Messʳˢ Dow & Young			13	6	8
By Monsʳ Chandlair	9	10			
	1541	10	102	15	4
		£	7043	11	5¾
By Provisions Supose			300		
By Am.ᵗ of debts N: York Cur:		£	7343	11	5¾
Ballance being the Neat of my Estate Exclusive of the following Debts which are Dubious			12882	17	1¾
New York Cur:		£	12882	17	1¾

Dubious & Bad Debts due John Askin Viz:

Clutiez	121„14			
M.[r] [Harinson] [or]				
La Croin	66„10			
Monsr Carrignon the Am.[t]				
in Acc.[t] book for 1778				
Remon Quenell 4: 5 Pl:	8: 10			
Monsr Burginnon		1	12	
Sorrell Engagé		2	15	5
Henry Williams		5	10	2
Coll: Caldwell for the				
Crown he is Dead		450		
Mr Dodge		2	7	4

There is also some Debts in a
Small Book with my mens
Accounts due me by
  Monsr La [Fantozie]
  Monsr Bertrand   These I believe good
  Monsr Toumande

Note on the Sources

The most extensive manuscript collection pertaining to Michilimac-kinac during the American Revolution war years is the Haldimand Papers in the British Museum, London. Frederick Haldimand served as Governor-General of Canada from 1778 until 1784. His papers contain official correspondence to and from the commandant, officers, citizens, and government officials at Michilimackinac. In the Mac-kinac Island State Park Commission collections are microfilmed copies of many of the Michilimackinac documents. David Armour collected many of these while researching in the British Museum in 1974. During our study we consulted Additional Manuscripts 21684, 21686, 21730, 21745, 21756, 21757, 21758, 21771, 21772, 21779, 21801, 21804, 21805, 21817, 21832, 21833, 21841, 21845, 21850, 21852, 21854, 21876, and 21886.

There is also a large collection of Haldimand Papers in the Public Archives of Canada, Ottawa. A calendar of this collection appears in the *Report on Canadian Archives* for the years 1881-1889. Most of the material relevant to Michilimackinac has been published in the *Michigan Pioneer and Historical Collections,* Vols. 9, 10, 11, 12, 19, and 20. Some also appear in the *Wisconsin Historical Collections,* Vols. 7, 11, 12, and 18.

Other useful documents in the Public Archives of Canada include the "Consolidated Returns of Indian Trade Licenses, 1777-1790," which list the names of each trader who took out a license to send merchandise westward. The number of canoes and quantities of mu-nitions and liquor increase and decrease in relationship to war-time conditions. This record also reveals the huge quantity of gunpowder, lead, and fusils that was traded to Indians. Two other collections that give understanding to the period are the Louis Joseph Ainsse Papers and the Lawrence Ermatinger Papers.

While in Great Britain, Armour also visited the Public Record Office and examined War Office Records, Admiralty Records, Treasury Of-fice Records, and Audit Office Records. He also looked for Michilimackinac documents and artifacts at the Army Museum, Ogilby Trust, the National Army Museum, and the National Maritime Museum, all in London, the City of Liverpool Museums, and the Ewart Public Library and the Dumfries Burgh Museum in Dumfries, Scotland. Pertinent documents and illustrations were copied.

In the Burton Historical Collection, Detroit Public Library, records and letters of prominent traders provide valuable insights into the business and civilian life at Michilimackinac. The most useful are the John Askin Papers. In 1928 Milo M. Quaife edited a two volume edition of these published by the Detroit Library Commission. Other collections are the papers of Jean Baptiste Barthe, A. Frazier, Alexander Macomb, William Edgar, William Macomb, Peter Pond, John Porteous, and Thomas Williams. In the Alexander Harrow Papers is the Logbook of the Sloop *Welcome*. This log also contains entries for the *Dunmore, Angelica,* and *Gage*.

The Thomas Gage Papers contain extensive Michilimackinac correspondence for the years 1764-1775. This collection is in the William L. Clements Library, University of Michigan, Ann Arbor.

At the Toronto Public Library are the accounts of David McCrea & Co. of Michilimackinac with William and John Kay, Quebec Papers, Volume III, 75, pages 170-241. They cover the years 1777-1788 with detailed accounts of Indian trade goods furnished McCrea from 1777 to 1780.

Documents in the James D. Doty Papers at the State Historical Society of Wisconsin, Madison, provided unexpected data on civil government at Michilimackinac. Doty was a prominent lawyer, judge, and politician in territorial Michigan and Wisconsin. Fortunately he was interested in history and interviewed long time residents of Michilimackinac and recorded documents and recollections which dated back to the Revolution. On July 18, 1834 he copied orders and ordinances dictated by Patrick Sinclair in 1779 and 1780. The original of this was owned by Michael Dousman on Mackinac Island. His "Memorandum of Travels in Northern Michigan and Wisconsin, July 10-August 2, 1822" contains useful comments about the Revolutionary War Years. Doty wrote a "History of the Northwest" which included an extract of a letter from Dr. David Mitchell, dated Feb. 15, 1819, giving a description of Michilimackinac in 1779. The original of this manuscript is in the Huntington Library.

Several published sources provide data regarding Michilimackinac and the fur trade during the American Revolution. Peter Pond's *Journal* appears in the *Wisconsin Historical Collections*, vol. 18, pp. 314-354. *Alexander Henry's Travels and Adventures in the Years 1760-1776* (Chicago, 1921) and *John Long's Voyages and Travels in the Years 1768-1788* (Chicago, 1922), both edited by Milo M. Quaife, are first hand accounts of the trials and tribulations experienced by these wilderness businessmen. They also comment extensively on Indian culture and the natives role in the trade. The best information regarding both the real and feared ramifications resulting from the breaking out of hostilities in the east was gathered from Wallace W. Stewart, ed. *Documents Relating to the North West Company* (New York, 1968, originally published 1934).

Although rebel political and military leaders seldomed referred to Michilimackinac specifically as a target of their policies or campaigns, they sought to conquer it as part of their effort to wrest control of the West from Great Britain. Peter Force, ed. *American Archives*, 4th & 5th Series, (Washington, D.C., 1839-48); Worthington Chauncey Ford, ed., *Journals of The Continental Congress, 1774-1789,* 34 vols. (Washington 1904-37); and Edmund C. Burnett, ed., *Letters of Members of The Continental Congress,* 8 vols. (Gloucester, Mass., 1963) are all valuable sources for discovering American strategy and thinking. Two useful sources regarding the activities of George Rogers Clark are *Clark's Memoirs* (Ann Arbor, 1966, originally published as part of W. H. English's *Conquest of the Country Northwest of the River Ohio,* 1896), and the *George Rogers Clark Papers,* which were edited by James Alton James and appear as Vols. 8 and 19 in the *Illinois Historical Collections.* Clarence Alvord edited two other volumes in this series which are pertinent to the study — Vol. 2, *Cahokia Records, 1778-1790* and Vol. 5, *Kaskaskia Records, 1778-1790.*

Beginning in 1959 the Mackinac Island State Park Commission and the Museum, Michigan State University began archaeological excavations on the site of Fort Michilimackinac. This program continues to the present and the hundreds of thousands of artifacts provide the researcher with many glimpses into life at this eighteenth century outpost. Throughout the years a number of reports detailing and analyzing these findings have been published. The most comprehensive of these is Lyle M. Stone's, *Fort Michilimackinac 1715-1781: An Archaeological Perspective on the Revolutionary Frontier* (East Lansing, 1974). Other reports of interest include:

Armour, David A., *Made in Mackinac: Crafts at Fort Michilimackinac, Mackinac History,* Vol. I, No. 8 (Mackinac Island, 1966).

Brown, Margaret Kimball, "Glass from Fort Michilimackinac: A Classification for Eighteenth Century Glass," *The Michigan Archaeologist,* Vol. 17, Nos. 3 & 4 (September-December, 1971).

Cleland, Charles E., "Comparison of the Faunal Remains from French and British Refuse Pits at Fort Michilimackinac: A Study in Changing Subsistence Patterns," *Canadian Historic Sites; Occasional Papers in Archaeology and History,* No. 3 (Ottawa, 1970), pp. 7-23.

Dunnigan, Brian Leigh, *Milestones of the Past: Military Buttons and Insignia from Mackinac, Mackinac History,* Vol. II, No. 3 (Mackinac Island, 1975).

Hamilton, T. M., *Firearms on the Frontier: Guns at Fort Michilimackinac; Reports in Mackinac History and Archaeology,* No. 5 (Mackinac Island, 1976).

Heldman, Donald P. and William L. Minnerly, *The Powder Magazine at Fort Michilimackinac: Excavation Report; Reports in Mackinac History and Archaeology,* No. 6 (Mackinac Island, 1977).

Heldman, Donald P. *Excavations at Fort Michilimackinac, 1976; The Southeast and South Southeast Row Houses* (Mackinac Island, 1977).

Maxwell, Moreau S. and Louis H. Binford, *Excavation at Fort Michilimackinac, Mackinac City, Michigan; 1959 Season* (East Lansing, 1961).

Miller, J. Jefferson, II and Lyle M. Stone, *Eighteenth-Century Ceramics from Fort Michilimackinac* (Washington, D.C., 1970).

Petersen, Eugene T., *Clay Pipes: A Footnote to Mackinac's History, Mackinac History,* Vol. I, No. 1 (Mackinac Island, 1963).

Petersen, Eugene T., *Gentlemen on the Frontier: A Pictorial Record of the Culture of Michilimackinac* (Mackinac Island, 1964).

Stone, Lyle M., *Archaeology at Fort Michilimackinac, Mackinac History,* Vol. I, No. 9 (Mackinac Island, 1967).

During the past few years a concerted effort has been made to collect pictorial documents which shed light on life at the Straits during the American Revolution. In Great Britain the Merseyside County Museum in Liverpool houses the collection of Indian items which Arent Schuyler De Peyster brought back from Canada. Original eighteenth century Indian objects are very rare. The London repositories of the British Museum, Public Record Office, National Army Museum and Courtauld Institute of Art all furnished valuable iconographic material. Mr. F. E. G. Bagshawe also supplied the splendid portrait of Sir John Caldwell in Indian garb. From Seville, Spain came the map of St. Louis which is housed in the Archivo General de Indias.

Since Michilimackinac was part of Canada during the Revolution it is not surprising that the libraries of Canada contain an abundance of pictures. The Public Archives of Canada, the National Gallery of Canada in Ottawa, The Royal Ontario Museum, the Art Gallery of Ontario, and the McCord Museum in Montreal all graciously furnished a number of items.

Other materials were scattered throughout the United States. The drawings of Peter Rindisbacher housed in the West Point Museum were invaluable in depicting Great Lakes Indians. The Friedrich von Germann drawings of British soldiers stationed in Canada were graciously provided by the New York Public Library. Other drawings and portraits were secured from the Library of Congress, the Fogg Art Museum at Harvard, the Clements Library in Ann Arbor, the Chicago Historical Society, Indiana State Museum, Indiana Historical Society, New York Historical Society, the Virginia State Library, the Boston Public Library and the Burton Historical Collection of the Detroit Public Library. Objects were specially photographed by the Neville Public Museum in Green Bay and the Museum of Michigan State University.

Our research would not have been possible without the assistance provided by the staff of the institutions mentioned. Thank you.

Special appreciation is due to Mr. E. J. Priestley of the Merseyside County Museums in Liverpool, England, who uncovered innumerable bits of information about the King's Eighth Regiment. He also arranged to photograph the museum's rich collection of De Peyster Indian materials. A grant from the Michigan American Revolution Bicentennial Commission obtained with the assistance of its Director Howard Lancour made it possible for David Armour to conduct research in England and Scotland.

Laura Eiseler accurately typed the several drafts of the book. Many helpful criticisms and comments were provided by the readers of the manuscript: Richard Hathaway, Head of the Michigan Unit of the Michigan State Library; Eugene T. Petersen, Marian Petersen, and Donald Heldman of the Mackinac Island State Park Commission staff.

Notes

I. Arent Schuyler De Peyster Arrives at Michilimackinac

[1]Captain Arent Schuyler De Peyster to General Thomas Gage, 16 July 1774, Thomas Gage Papers, Clements Library, University of Michigan, Ann Arbor.

[2]Gage to Captain John Vattas, 26 Dec. 1773, *Wisconsin Historical Collections* (hereafter *WHC*), Vol. 12, p. 38.

[3]Arent Schuyler De Peyster, *Miscellanies by an Officer*, (Dumfries, 1813), Vol. I, p. 64.

[4]Moreau S. Maxwell and Lewis H. Binford, *Excavation at Fort Michilimackinac, Mackinac City, Michigan, 1959 Season*, (East Lansing, 1961), pp. 61-65.

[5]Donald P. Heldman and William L. Minnerly, *Fort Michilimackinac Archaeological Investigations 1974 and 1975,* Archaeological Completion Report Series, Number 7, (Washington, D.C., 1976). Donald P. Heldman and William L. Minnerly, *The Powder Magazine at Fort Michilimackinac: Excavation Report, Reports in Mackinac History and Archaeology, Number 6* (Mackinac Island, 1977).

[6]Vattas to Gage, 13 July 1774, Gage Papers.

[7]David A. Armour, ed., *Attack at Michilimackinac: Alexander Henry's Travels and Adventures in Canada and the Indian Territories Between the Years 1760 and 1764,* (Mackinac Island, 1971; originally published 1809), pp. 49-70.

[8]De Peyster to Gage, 16 July 1774, Gage Papers.

[9]Vattas to Gage, 1 June 1774, *Ibid.*

[10]*Ibid.*

[11]Vattas to Gage, 26 June 1774, *Ibid.*

[12]Vattas to Gage, 13 July 1774, *Ibid;* Milo M. Quiafe, ed., *Alexander Henry's Travels and Adventures in the Years 1760-1776,* (Chicago, 1921), pp. 210, 217, 224-26.

[13]Vattas to Gage, 1 June 1774, Gage Papers; Vattas to Lieutenant Colonel Samuel Cleaveland, 1 June 1774, W.O. 55/1537, Public Record Office; C. S. Colleton to Cleaveland, 3 June 1774, *Ibid.*

[14]Vattas to Gage, 13 July 1774, Gage Papers.

II. The Natives and the Fur Trade

[1]David A. Armour, "Beads in the Upper Great Lakes: A Study in Acculturation," (unpublished paper done for the Grand Rapids Public Museum, 1976), pp. 25-45.

[2]De Peyster to Gage, 16 July 1774, Gage Papers.

[3]*Ibid.*

[4]"Number of Indians Resorting to Michilimackinac," 10 Sept. 1782, ADD 21758, 150, Haldimand Papers (hereafter ADD), British Museum, also in *Michigan Pioneer and Historical Collections* (hereafter *MPHC*), Vol. 10, pp. 635-36; "List of Goods given in a Present to the Ottawas of Arbrecroche & Kishkacon equally divided in the Fall of 1778," ADD 21757, 79, also in *MPHC*, Vol. 9, p. 655.

[5]De Peyster, *Miscellanies by an Officer*, p. 30, n. 4.

[6]Peter Pond, "Journal, 1740-1775," *WHC,* Vol. 18, p. 328; Several useful studies of Great Lakes Indians are: Frances Densmore's, *Chippewa Customs,* (Minneapolis, 1970; originally published 1929); W. Vernon Kinietz's, *The Indians of the Western Great Lakes, 1615 – 1760,* (Ann Arbor, 1972; originally published 1940); George Irving Quimby, *Indian Life in The Upper Great Lakes, 11,000 B.C. to A.D. 1800,* (Chicago, 1960) and *Indian Culture and European Trade Goods,* (Madison, 1966).

[7]Armour, "Beads," p. 43; Jonathan Carver, *Travels through the Interior Parts of North America, in the Years 1766, 1767, and 1768,* (reprinted 1956; originally published 1781), pp. 302-3; Emma H. Blair, ed., *Indian Tribes of the Upper Mississippi and the Great Lakes Region,* 2 vols., (Cleveland, 1912), Vol. II, pp. 161, 191.

[8]See David A. Armour's biographies of Matchekewis and La Fourche in *Dictionary of Canadian Biography.*

[9]"List of Goods given, . . ." ADD 21757, 79, also in *MPHC,* Vol. 9, p. 655.

[10]Quimby, *Indian Life in the Upper Great Lakes,* p. 128.

[11]De Peyster, *Miscellanies by an Officer,* pp. 90-92; Mary Belle Shurtleff, *Old Arbre Croche,* (1963), p. 8.

[12]David Mitchell, Extract of a letter dated 15 Feb. 1819 recorded in James D. Doty, "The History of the Northwest," microfilmed copy in James Duane Doty Papers in State Historical Society of Wisconsin; Pond, p. 328.

[13]Pond, pp. 327-28, 341–2.

[14]Lieutenant Governor Henry Hamilton to the Earl of Dartmouth, 2 Sept. 1776, *MPHC,* Vol. 10, pp. 267-68.

[15]David McCrae & Co. of Mackinac Their Account with William and John Kay of Montreal, 17 June 1778, *Quebec Papers,* Volume B, 75 p. 176, Toronto Public Library.

[16]Pond, pp. 341-42.

[17]"Abstracts and Index of Indian Trade Licenses, 1763-1776; sample of licenses," 1774, Public Archives of Canada, microfilmed copy in Minnesota Historical Society.

[18]John Long, *John Long's Voyages and Travels in the Years 1768-1788,* (Chicago, 1922; originally published 1791), pp. 50-52.

[19]Armour, *Attack,* pp. 7-8

[20]*John Long's Voyages,* pp. 50-52.

[21]"Abstracts and Index of Indian Trade Licenses, . . ."; the Forrest Oakes Account Book, 29 July 1765-2 Feb. 1780, in the Lawrence Ermatinger Papers (M.G. 19, A 2, Series 1, Volume 3), Public Archives of Canada, contain accounts detailing the contents of bales and cases transported in the fur trade.

[22]*John Long's Voyages,* pp. 72-76, 121-22, 129-32; Quaife, *Henry's Travels,* pp. 303-4.

[23]"Memorandums Relative to Trade in the Upper Country," *MPHC,* Vol. 10, pp. 272-74.

[24]Pond, pp. 342-46.

[25]De Peyster to Cleaveland, 24 Sept. 1774, W.O. 55/1537, Public Record Office.

III. The Community

[1]De Peyster to Gage, 5 May 1775, Gage Papers.

[2]Thomas Simes, *A Military Course for the Government and Conduct of a Battalion Designed for their Regulations in Quarter, Camp or Garrison,. . .,* (London, 1777), pp. 136-37; Brian Leigh Dunnigan, *King's Men at Mackinac: The British Garrisons, 1780-1796,* (Mackinac Island, 1973), p. 11.

[3]Vol. 139, Proclamations, Gage Papers.

[4]De Peyster, *Miscellanies by an Officer,* pp. 109-10.

[5]*Ibid.,* pp. 38-40.

[6]Thomas Williams Petty Ledger, 1775-1779, p. 7, Thomas Williams Papers, Burton Historical Collection, Detroit Public Library.

[7]Simes, pp. 219-21.

[8]John Caldwell to Father, 24 Sept. 1779, Bagshawe MSS B 3/13/115, John Rylands Library (Manchester).

[9]John Askin to John Hay, 27 April, 1778; Milo M. Quaife, ed., *The John Askin Papers,* Vol. I, 1747-1795, (Detroit, 1928), p. 68.

[10]Askin, "Inventory of My Estate," 31 Dec. 1776, Public Archives of Canada, M6 19 A 3.

[11]*Ibid.*

[12]David A. Armour, "The Women at Michilimackinac," *Mackinac History*, Vol. I, No. 10, (Mackinac Island, 1967), p. 4.

[13]Askin to Sampson Fleming, 28 April 1778, *Askin Papers*, Vol. I, p. 79; Askin's "Diary," 19, 20 April 1774, 7, 11, 13 April 1775; *Ibid.*, pp. 50, 54-55; Charles E. Cleland, "Comparison of the Faunal Remains from French and British Refuse Pits at Fort Michilimackinac: A Study in Changing Subsistence Patterns," *Canadian Historic Sites: Occasional Papers in Archaeology and History, No. 3*, (Ottawa, 1970), pp. 7-23.

[14]Askin's "Diary," 3 May 1774, *Askin Papers*, Vol. I, p. 51.

[15]Askin to Thomas McMurray, 28 April 1778, *Askin Papers*, Vol.I, pp. 68–69.

[16]"Medicine Sold at Michilimackinac," 1767, John Porteous Papers, Burton Collection; Invoice of Goods to David McCrae and Co. From William & John Kay, 1 April 1779, *Quebec Papers*, Vol. B, 75, p. 211.

[17]John Porteous, 16 Aug. 1767, Porteous Papers; Pond, p. 328.

[18]De Peyster to Gage, 5 May 1775, Gage Papers.

[19]Lyle M. Stone, *Fort Michilimackinac 1715-1781: An Archaeological Perspective on the Revolutionary Frontier*, (East Lansing, 1974), pp. 207-9; De Peyster to Gage, 5 May and 14 May 1775, Gage Papers.

[20]Askin's "Diary," 24 April to 25 May 1775, *Askin Papers*, Vol. I, pp. 55-56.

[21]"Abstracts and Index of Indian Trade Licenses, 1763-1776; samples of licenses," 1775. The licenses for 1775 show the trade canoes carrying to Michilimackinac quantities of goods totaling approximately:

1,150 kegs and barrels of rum and wine	38 cases of axes and ironware
38,000 pounds of gunpowder	73 bales of kettles–brass, copper and tin
44,000 pounds of ball and shot	200 bales of tobacco
1,051 fusils [trade muskets]	130 kegs of pork and lard
730 bales of dry goods	16 barrels of salt
6 bags of wheat and flour	

[22]*Ibid*; Harold A. Innis, *The Fur Trade in Canada*, (New Haven, Conn., 1962) p. 194.

[23]De Peyster to Gage, 16 June 1775, *Ibid.*

[24]Askin's "Diary," 19 April 1774 to 30 Nov. 1774, 7 Jan. 1775 to 18 Nov. 1775, *Askin Papers*, Vol. I, pp. 50-58.

[25]*Ibid.*

[26]John Porteous, 16 Aug. 1767, Porteous Papers.

[27]De Peyster to Gage, 16 June 1775, Gage Papers.

[28]Simes, pp. 7-12, details of funeral services given.

[29]Mackinac Register, 23 June 1775, *WHC*, Vol. 18, pp. 488-89, (original in St. Ann's Church, Mackinac Island).

[30]Mackinac Register, 27 June 1775, 9 July 1775, 10 July 1775, *WHC*, Vol. 19, pp. 75-77.

[31]*John Long's Voyages*, p. 177.

[32]Pond, pp, 342-46.

IV. The Rebellion Reaches Michilimackinac

[1]Askin's "Diary," 27 Sept. 1775, *Askin Papers*, Vol. I, p. 57.

[2]Mackinac Register, 3 Oct. 1775, *WHC*, Vol. 19, p. 77.

[3]Pierre Gibault to Bishop Briand, 4 Dec. 1775, "Letters to Bishop Briand," American Catholic Historical Society *Records*, XX, (1909), pp. 423-24.

[4]Hamilton to Dartmouth, 29 Aug. to 2 Sept. 1776, *MPHC*, Vol. 10, pp. 264-70.

[5]A brief but informative account of Detroit and the American Revolution is Philip P. Mason's *Detroit, Fort Lernoult, and the American Revolution*, (Detroit, 1964).

[6]A good recent history of military activity during the American Revolution is Don Higginbotham's *The War of American Independence: Military Attitudes, Policies, and Practice, 1763-1789*, (New York, 1971). A short account is Howard H. Peckham's *The War of Independence: A Military History*, (Chicago, 1958).

[7]John Adams to James Warren, 7 June 1775, Edmund C. Burnet, ed., *Letters of Members of the Continental Congress,* (Gloucester, Mass., 1963), Vol. I, pp. 113-14.

[8]*Adams* to Warren, 18 Feb. 1776, *Ibid.,* pp. 354-55.

[9]General George Washington to General Philip Schuyler, 5 Nov. 1775, Peter Force, ed., *American Archives,* 4th Series, No. III, p. 1368.

[10]John Hancock to Lewis Morris and James Wilson, 15 Sept. 1775, *Ibid.,* p. 717; George Ross to Wilson, 15 Sept. 1775, *Letters of the Members of the Continental Congress,* Vol. I, p. 197; Richard Smith's "Diary," 13 Sept. 1775, *Ibid..* pp. 193-94.

[11]Worthington C. Ford, ed., *Journals of the Continental Congress, 1774-1789,* Vol. 4, pp. 182, 200, 215-19; Copy of a Paper of Intelligence from Montreal received at Quebec, in General Carleton's Letter, 14 May, 1776, MG 11, "Q" Series, Vol. 12, pp. 22–23, Public Archives of Canada.

[12]*Mackinac Register,* 15 March, 1776, *WHC,* Vol. 19, pp. 77–78.

[13]Simon McTavish to William Edgar, 12 May 1776, W. Stewart Wallace, ed., *Documents Relating to the North West Company,* (New York, 1968; originally published in 1934), pp. 48-49.

[14]McTavish to Edgar, 9 June 1776, *Ibid.,* pp. 49-50.

[15]Macomb Account Book, 1776-1781, 23 May 1776, Macomb, Edgar and Macomb Papers, Burton Collection, pp. 49-51; James Bannerman to Edgar, 10 June 1776, *Documents Relating to the North West Company,* pp. 51-52.

[16]Bannerman to Edgar, 23 June 1776, *Ibid.,* pp. 52–53.

[17]McTavish to Edgar, 9 June 1776, *Ibid.,* pp. 49-50.

[18]"Ordre a M. Ainsse de prendre le commendement des Nations d'Outaois, 17 June 1776," Louis Joseph Ainsse Papers, 1673-1874, Item No. 56, Public Archives of Canada.

[19]De Peyster to Charles Langlade, 4 July 1776, *WHC,* Vol. 18, pp. 355-56.

[20]General Guy Carleton to De Peyster, 25 June 1776, *MPHC,* Vol. 10, p. 261, also in *WHC,* Vol. 11, p. 174.

[21](Carleton) to De Peyster, 19 July 1776, *MPHC,* Vol. 10, p. 263.

[22]"Abstracts and Index of Indian Trade Licenses, 1763-1776; sample of licenses," 1776.

[23]Bannerman to Edgar, (?) July 1776, *Documents Relating to the North West Company,* pp. 54-55.

[24]McTavish to Edgar, 15 Aug. 1776, *Ibid.,* p. 56.

[25]Bannerman to Edgar, (?) July 1776, *Ibid.,* pp. 54-55.

V. British War Policy Takes Shape

[1]Thomas Anbury, *With Burgoyne from Quebec,* ed. by Sidney Jackman, (Toronto, 1963), pp. 66-68; Abrams Chapman to William Edgar, 30 June 1776, William Edgar Papers, Burton Collection.

[2]McTavish to Edgar, 22 Sept. 1776, *Documents Relating to the North West Company,* p. 57.

[3]*Ibid.,* 4 Oct. 1776, p. 58.

[4]Isaac Todd to Edgar, 12 Sept. 1776, Edgar papers.

[5]Gage to Carleton, 3 June 1775 and 5 Sept. 1775, Gage Papers.

[6](Carleton) to De Peyster, 6 Oct. 1776, *WHC,* Vol. 12, pp. 40-41, also in *MPHC,* Vol. 10, p. 270.

[7]Carleton to Hamilton, 6 Oct. 1776, *MPHC,* Vol. 9, p. 344.

[8]Carleton to Hamilton, 2 Feb. 1777, *Ibid.,* pp. 345-46.

[9]Lord Germain to Carleton, 26 March 1777, *WHC,* Vol. 11, pp. 175-77.

[10]A fine collection of essays regarding the Spanish in Louisiana appears in John Francis McDermott, ed., *The Spanish in the Mississippi Valley, 1762-1804,* (Urbana, Ill., 1974). Also useful are William E. Foley's *A History of Missouri,* Vol. I, 1673 to 1820, (Columbia, Mo., 1971), and Abraham P. Nasatir's "The Anglo-Spanish Frontier in the Illinois Country during the American Revolution, 1779-1783," in *Journal of Illinois State Historical Society,* Vol. 21, (October , 1928), pp. 291-358.

[11]Abraham P. Nasatir, "Ducharme's Invasion of Missouri, an Incident in the Anglo-Spanish Rivalry for the Indian Trade of Upper Louisiana," *Missouri Historical Review,* Vol. 24, (October, 1929), pp. 3-25, (January, 1930), pp. 238-60, (April, 1930), pp. 420-39.

[12]"Abstracts and Index of Indian Trade Licenses, 1763-1776" for 1775 and "Consolidated Returns of Indian Trade Licenses, 1777-1790" for 1777, 1778, 1779, Canada MSS G, Public Archives of Canada. For additional information see David A. Armour's biography of Jean Marie Du Charme in the *Dictionary of Canadian Biography*.

[13]Spanish Account of Western Nations in 1777, *WHC*, Vol. 18, pp. 358, 364-68, (manuscript in General Archives of the Indies, Seville, pressmark 'Papeles procedientes de la Isla de Cuba').

[14]De Peyster, (extract of a letter), Feb. 1777, *MPHC*, Vol. 10, p. 271.

[15]De Peyster to (Carleton), 12 April 1777, *WHC*, Vol. 12, p. 41.

[16]De Peyster to Carleton, 4 June 1777, *MPHC*, Vol. 10, p. 275; De Peyster to Carleton, 6 June 1777, *WHC*, Vol. 7, p. 406, also in *MPHC*, Vol. 10, pp. 275-76.

[17]Black Bird was called Siggenauk by his own people, Le Tourneau by the French, and El Heturno by the Spanish; Robert G. Carroon, "Milwaukee and the American Revolution," *Historical Messenger* of the Milwaukee County Historical Society, (Winter, 1973), p. 118.

[18]De Peyster to Carleton, 6 June 1777, *WHC*, Vol. 7, p. 406, also in *MPHC*, Vol. 10, pp. 275-76.

[19]De Peyster to (Carleton), 13 June 1777, *MPHC*, Vol. 10, pp. 276-77.

[20]Carleton's speech to Indians upon River Bouquet, 21 June 1777, Carleton Papers, State Historical Society of Wisconsin, copies of documents in Q Series, Public Archives of Canada.

[21]Paul Trap, "Charles Langlade in the American Revolution,"unpublished manuscript, copy in Mackinac Island State Park Commission's Collections, pp. 10-21.

[22]Hamilton to General Frederick Haldimand, 6 July 1781, photostat in Henry Hamilton Papers, Burton Collection (original in British Museum, ADD MSS 21,783 F. 48); John Hay, "Return of Parties of Indians sent from Detroit against the Rebells after the 2d July 1777," W.O. 28/10, Public Record Office.

[23]Circular sent to Hamilton, n.d., *MPHC*, Vol. 9, p. 345.

[24]John Dodge to Thomas Williams, 24 July 1777, Williams Papers, Burton Collection; Thomas Bentley to Daniel Murray, 1 Aug. 1777, ADD 21845, 6-7, also in *MPHC*, Vol. 19, p. 326; Bentley's statement, 1 Aug. 1777, ADD 21845, 10-11, also in *MPHC*, Vol. 19, p. 328; Hamilton, "Declaration," 15 Aug. 1777, *MPHC*, Vol. 19, p. 327; Bentley's petition, 6 Oct. 1777, ADD 21845, 12-13, also in *MPHC*, Vol. 19, pp. 331-32. For a more detailed account of the activities of Thomas Bentley see Clarence W. Alvord's *The Illinois Country, 1673-1818*, (Chicago, 1965; originally published in 1922), pp. 308-28.

[25]Carleton to unaddressed, 22 May 1777, *MPHC*, Vol. 9, p. 348.

[26]State of the Naval Department at Detroit, 27 Oct. 1777, ADD 21,804, 24-27, Frederick Haldimand Papers, British Museum; Vessels on Upper Lakes, 1759-1778, *WHC*, Vol. 11, p. 199.

[27]Vessels on Lake Erie, 1779, ADD 21,804, 166.

[28]State of the Naval Department at Detroit, 27 Oct. 1777, ADD 21,804, 25.

[29]*Ibid.*

[30]Dodge to Williams, 24 July 1777, Williams Papers, Burton Collection.

[31]"Consolidated Returns of Indian Trade Licenses, 1777-1790," for 1777. Merchants brought approximately the following quantities of goods to Michilimackinac in 1777:

    2,218 kegs of rum and brandy

     336 kegs of wine

    1,282 fusils

   47,750 pounds of gunpowder

   58,425 pounds of shot and ball

   £58,400 total value of the whole

[32]Carleton to De Peyster, 14 July 1777, *MPHC*, Vol. 10, p. 279, also in De Peyster, *Miscellanies by an Officer*, Vol. I, p. 234.

[33]David A. Armour, "A White Beaver for the Colonel," *Michigan Natural Resources*, (July-August, 1973), pp. 11-13.

VI. Trade Flourishes

[1]Askin to John Hay, 27 April 1778, *Askin Papers*, Vol. I, p. 68; Askin to Alexander Grant, 28 April 1778, *Ibid.*, p. 77; Samuel Robertson to Haldimand, 1780, ADD 21757, 562-565, also in *MPHC*, Vol. 9, pp. 622-3.

[2]Askin to Charles Patterson, 17 June 1778, *Askin Papers,* Vol. I, p. 135.

[3]Askin to Todd and McGill, 22 June 1778, *Ibid.,* p. 142; Askin to Sampson Fleming, 28 April 1778, *Ibid.,* p. 79.

[4]Askin to Todd and McGill, 14 June 1778, *Ibid.,* p. 128.

[5]De Peyster, *Miscellanies by an Officer,* Vol. I, p. 73.

[6]Askin to Todd and McGill, 8 May 1778, *Askin Papers,* Vol. I, p. 84.

[7]Askin to Todd and McGill, 28 May 1778, *Ibid.,* p. 102.

[8]Askin to Hay, 27 April, 1778, *Ibid.,* p. 68.

[9]Askin to Alexander Henry, 23 June 1778, *Ibid.,* p. 145; Askin to Grant, 28 April 1778, *Ibid.,* p. 78; Askin to Hay, 27 April 1778, *Ibid.,* p. 67.

[10]Agreement with Mess[rs] Will[m] & John Kay, 6 April 1778, Quebec Papers, Vol. B, 75, pp. 168-9.

[11]Askin to Charles Chaboillez, 18 May 1778, *Askin Papers,* Vol. I, pp. 95-96.

[12]James Andrews, Mason Bolton, Zach Thompson, Alexander Grant, "Memorandums relative to the Naval Department on the Upper Lakes, 13 May 1778, ADD 21,804, 66-67.

[13]Askin to McGill, Frobisher, Patterson, etc., 28 April 1778, *Askin Papers,* Vol. I, pp. 74-75; Askin to Grant, 28 April 1778, *Ibid.,* pp. 76-77.

[14]Askin to Todd and McGill, 8 May 1778, *Ibid.,* p. 84; Askin to North West Company, 8 May 1778, *Ibid.,* p. 83.

[15]Askin to Jean Baptiste Barthe, 18 May 1776, *Ibid.,* p. 90.

[16]De Peyster to Carleton, 30 May 1778, ADD 21757, 3-5, ADD 21756,2, also in *MPHC,* Vol. 9, p. 366.

[17]Askin to Grant, 28 April 1778, *Askin Papers,* Vol. I, pp. 76-77.

[18]Askin to McGill, Frobisher, Patterson, et al., 28 April 1778, *Ibid.,* p. 74.

[19]Askin to Nathaniel Day, 8 May 1778, *Ibid.,* p. 81.

[20]Askin to James Sterling, 8 May 1778, *Ibid.,* p. 80.

[21]Askin to Sterling, 28 April 1778, *Ibid.,* p. 71.

[22]Askin to Chaboillez, 18 May 1778, *Ibid.,* pp. 95-96.

[23]Askin to Barthe, 6 June 1778, *Ibid.,* p. 114.

[24]Askin to Barthe, 18 May 1778, *Ibid.,* pp. 90-94.

[25]Askin to Barthe, 24 May 1778, *Ibid.,* pp. 99-100; Askin to Barthe, 29 May 1778, *Ibid.,* p. 103.

[26]Askin to Todd and McGill, 8 May 1778, *Ibid.,* pp. 85-86.

[27]To De Peyster without signature, 6 Oct. 1777, *MPHC,* Vol. 10, p. 280.

[28]Memorandum to Carleton, 20 Jan. 1778, *MPHC,* Vol. 19, pp. 337-39.

[29]Askin to Barthe, 29 May 1778, *Askin Papers,* Vol. I, p. 103.

[30]De Peyster to John Pattison, 15 April 1778, ADD 21757, 68, also in *MPHC,* Vol. 10, p. 284.

[31]De Peyster to Carleton, 29 June 1778, ADD 21757, 27-28, ADD 21756, 2-3, also in *MPHC,* Vol. 9, p. 367.

[32]De Peyster to Haldimand, 16 Sept. 1778, ADD 21757, 61-62, also in *MPHC,* Vol. 9, p. 371.

[33]Askin to Beausoleil, 18 May 1778, *Askin Papers,* Vol. I, p. 98.

[34]"Major De Peyster on Account of the Crown Dr. to Charles Paterson & Co.," 15 Sept. 1778, ADD 21757, 118, also in *MPHC,* Vol. 9, p. 652.

[35]De Peyster to Haldimand, 16 Sept. 1778, ADD 21757, 61-62, also in *MPHC,* Vol. 9, p. 371; For more information on Grand Portage see Nancy L. Woolworth's "Grand Portage in the Revolutionary War," *Minnesota History,* (Summer, 1975), pp. 198-208.

[36]Askin to Edward Pollard, 4 June 1778, *Askin Papers,* Vol. I, p. 107; Askin to Fleming, 4 June 1778, *Ibid.,* p. 105.

[37]Askin to Richard Dobie, 15 June 1778, *Ibid.,* p. 131.

[38]11 June 1778, *Journals of the Continental Congress, 1774-1789,* Vol. 11, pp. 587-89; The Board of War to George Washington, 19 May 1778, *Letters of the Members of the Continental Congress,* Vol. 3, pp. 257-58.

[39]Askin to Madam Chaboillez, 15 June 1778, *Askin Papers,* Vol. I, pp. 129-30.

[40]Askin to Charles Chaboillez, 6 June 1778, *Ibid.*, p. 115.

[41]Askin to Chaboillez, 17 June 1778, *Ibid.*, p. 151; Askin to Chaboillez, 30 June 1778, *Ibid.*, p. 153; Askin to Barthe, 30 June 1778, *Ibid.*, pp. 156-57.

[42]Askin to Fleming, 4 June 1778, *Ibid.*, p. 105; Askin to Sterling, 5 June 1778, *Ibid.*, pp. 108-9.

[43]Askin to Todd and McGill, 22 June 1778, *Ibid.*, p. 142; Askin to Todd and McGill, 29 June 1778, *Ibid.*, pp. 151-52.

[44]Askin to Todd and McGill, 23 June 1778, *Ibid.*, pp. 143-44.

[45]Askin to Barthe, 6 June 1778, *Ibid.*, p. 114; Askin to Todd and McGill, 14 June 1778, *Ibid.*, p. 128; Askin to Todd and McGill, 29 June 1778, *Ibid.*, p. 152.

[46]Askin to North West Company, 2 July 1778, *Ibid.*, pp. 159-60.

[47]Askin to Barthe, 26 June 1778, *Ibid.*, pp. 148-49.

[48]"Consolidated Returns of Indian Trade Licenses, 1777-1790," for 1778. The merchants brought approximately the following quantities of goods to Michilimackinac in 1778:

> 2,155 kegs of rum and brandy
>   301 kegs of wine
> 1,492 fusils
> 55,775 pounds of gunpowder
> 71,350 pounds of shot and ball
> £74,310 total value of whole

[49]Askin to Benjamin Frobisher, 15 June 1778, *Askin Papers,* Vol. I, pp. 134-35.

[50]Askin to Fleming, 10 May 1778, *Ibid.*, pp. 86-87; Nathaniel Day, Return of Provisions forwarded to the upper posts to July 14, 1778, ADD 21852, 10.

[51]Askin to Philip DeJean, 4 June 1778, *Askin Papers,* Vol. I, pp. 105-6.

[52]Askin to Barthe, 8 June 1778, *Ibid.*, p. 119.

[53]Askin to Patterson, 17 June 1778, *Ibid.*, p. 135.

[54]Askin to Beausoleil, 18 May 1778, *Ibid.*, p. 98.

[55]"Bill of sale," 15 July 1775, *Ibid.*, pp. 58-59.

[56]De Peyster to Carleton, 30 May 1778, ADD 21757, 3-5, ADD 21756, 2, also in *MPHC*, Vol. 9, p. 365; Askin to Barthe, 29 May 1778, *Askin Papers,* Vol. I, p. 103.

[57]De Peyster to Traders, 10 May 1778, *WHC*, Vol. 18, pp. 368-69.

[58]De Peyster to Carleton, 29 June 1778, ADD 21757, 27-28, ADD 21756, 2-3, also in *MPHC*, Vol. 9, p. 366.

[59]Askin to Barthe, 26 June 1778, *Askin Papers,* Vol. I, pp. 148-49; Askin to Hay, 17 June 1778, *Ibid.*, p. 136; De Peyster to Carleton, 29 June 1778, ADD 21757, 27-28, ADD 21756, 2-3, also in *MPHC*, Vol. 9, p. 366; Gautier's recruits, 3 June 1778, *WHC*, Vol. 11, pp. 110-11.

[60]John Campbell to Capt. LeMaistre, 22 June 1778, W.O. 28/10, Public Record Office.

[61]Accounts Drawn for the Posts in the Upper Country, 1778, T. 64/115, Public Record Office; De Peyster, "Draft," 20 July 1778, *MPHC*, Vol. 12, p. 311-12.

[62]"State of pay due to the Officers, Interpreters and Others in the Indian Department from 1 January to 31st May 1778 both days Inclusive," W.O. 28/10, Public Record Office.

[63]De Peyster to Carleton, 29 June 1778, ADD 21757, 27-28, ADD 21756, 2-3, also in *MPHC*, Vol. 9, pp. 366-67.

[64]"Petition for Missionary at Michilimackinac," to Carleton, 23 July 1778, ADD 21757, 33, also in *MPHC*, Vol. 10, pp. 286-87; "Subscription . . . for the maintenance of the Missionary," 25 July 1778, ADD 21757, 37-38, also in *MPHC*, Vol. 10, pp. 288-90.

[65]De Peyster to Haldimand, 24 July 1778, ADD 21756, 22, ADD 21757, 35, also in *MPHC*, Vol. 9, p. 367.

VII. Fire in Illinois

[1]Richard McCarty to John Askin, 7 June 1778, ADD 21757, 7, also in *Illinois State Historical Collections,* Vol. 5, pp. 44-46.

[2]De Peyster to Haldimand, 15 Aug. 1778, ADD 21756, 4-5, ADD 21757, 47, also in *Illinois State Historical Collections,* Vol. 5, p. 46, and *MPHC*, Vol. 9, p. 368.

[3]George Rogers Clark, *Clark's Memoir*, from W. H. English's *Conquest of the Country Northwest of the River Ohio*, (Ann Arbor, 1966; originally published in 1896), p. 492.

[4]De Peyster to Haldimand, 31 Aug. 1778, ADD 21756, 5, ADD 21757, 55, also in *MPHC*, Vol. 9, pp. 369-70.

[5]Haldimand to De Peyster, 30 Aug. 1778, ADD 21756, 23 ADD 21757, 53, also in *MPHC*, Vol. 9, pp. 353-54.

[6]Haldimand to Hamilton, 26 Aug. 1778, *MPHC*, Vol. 9, p. 402.

[7]Hamilton to Lt. Gov. Cramahé, 17 Aug. 1778, *MPHC*, Vol. 9, pp. 463-64.

[8]Hamilton to Haldimand, 16 Sept. 1778, *MPHC*, Vol. 9, p. 475.

[9]Hamilton to Haldimand, n.d., *MPHC*, Vol. 9, p. 466.

[10]Louis Chevallier to De Peyster, 20 July 1778, *MPHC*, Vol. 10, p. 286.

[11]Hamilton to Haldimand, n.d., *MPHC*, Vol. 9, p. 465.

[12]Richard Henry Lee to Thomas Jefferson, 10 Aug. 1778, *Letters of Members of the Continental Congress*, Vol. 3, pp. 364-65.

[13]E. Foy to De Peyster, 28 Aug. 1778, ADD 21756, 22-23, ADD 21757, 51, also in *MPHC*, Vol. 19, p. 350.

[14]De Peyster to Haldimand, 7 Oct. 1778, ADD 21756, 6-7, ADD 21757, 69-70, also in *MPHC*, Vol. 9, p. 373.

Any presents given to La Fourche and his men were in addition to the following list of goods given to the Ottawa of L'Arbre Croche and Kishkacon in the fall of 1778. The Ottawa had received an even larger quantity in the spring.

[15]8 ps Strouds	24 ps Tape
2 ps - Moultons	8 dozen knives
5 pairs 1 pt Blankets	30 pounds paint
10 pairs 2 ditto	12 Bricks of Tobacco
62 pairs 2½ ditto	9 kegs of Rum-10
12 pairs 3 ditto	Some flints, steels, screws, awls, combs, L[ooking]
4 Barrels Powder × 1 for this year	Glasses, needles, thread, Ribbon & Trinkets
4 Bags of Shot × 2 ditto	40 loaves
4 Bags of Ball × 2 ditto	2 Barrels of Pork × no provisions
120 Shirts	2 Barrels of flour for the year 1780
30 Bed Gowns	Flowered Flannel 1 piece

This account is in ADD 21757, 79, also in *MPHC*, Vol. 9, p. 655.

[15]De Peyster to Haldimand, 21 Sept. 1778, ADD 21757, 7-8, ADD 21757, 63-64, also in *MPHC*, Vol. 9, p. 372.

[16]Chevallier to De Peyster, 15 Sept. 1778, ADD 21757, 59-60, also in *MPHC*, Vol. 19, p. 353.

[17]De Peyster to Haldimand, 16 Sept. 1778, ADD 21756, 5-6, ADD 21757, 61-62, also in *MPHC*, Vol. 9, p. 370.

[18]De Peyster to Haldimand, 24 Oct. 1778, ADD 21756, 7-8, ADD 21757, 73-74, also in *MPHC*, Vol. 9, pp. 374-75.

[19]De Peyster to Haldimand, 29 Jan. 1779, ADD 21756, 9, ADD 21757, 80, also in *MPHC*, Vol. 9, pp. 377-78.

VIII. Fearful Times

[1]Mackinac Register, 1 Jan. 1778, *WHC*, Vol. 18, pp. 490-91.

[2]*Ibid.*

[3]*WHC*, Vol. 11, p. 100, fn. 1.

[4]De Peyster to Haldimand, 29 May 1779, *MPHC*, Vol. 19, pp. 425-26.

[5]Chevallier to Haldimand, 28 Feb. 1779, *MPHC*, Vol. 19, p. 375.

[6]De Peyster to Haldimand, 29 March 1779, ADD 21756, 9-10, ADD 21757, 84, also in *MPHC*, Vol. 9, pp. 378-79.

[7]De Peyster to Haldimand, 2 May 1779, ADD 21756, 10-11, ADD 21757, 92, also in *MPHC*, Vol. 9, p. 379.

[8]Mason Bolton to Haldimand, 24 March 1779, *MPHC,* Vol. 9, pp. 428-29.

[9]Lernoult to (?), 26 March 1779, *MPHC,* Vol. 9, pp. 429-30.

[10]Bannerman to Edgar, 22 April 1779, *Documents Relating to the Northwest Company,* p. 61.

[11]Haldimand to De Peyster, 6 May, 1779, ADD 21756,24, ADD 21757, 94, also in *MPHC,* Vol. 9, pp. 357-58.

[12]Haldimand to Campbell, 8 April 1779, *MPHC,* Vol. 19, pp. 387-88.

[13]Haldimand to De Peyster, 6 May 1779, ADD 21756, 24, ADD 21757, 96, also in *MPHC,* Vol. 19, p. 402.

[14]De Peyster to Haldimand, 2 May 1779, ADD 21756, 10-11, ADD 21757, 92, also in *MPHC,* Vol. 9, pp. 379-80.

[15]De Peyster to Haldimand, 13 May 1779, ADD 21756, 11-12, ADD 21757, 98-99, also in *MPHC,* Vol. 9, p. 380.

[16]De Peyster to Campbell, 13 May 1779, ADD 21,771, 90, also in *MPHC,* Vol. 19, p. 411.

[17]Charles Gautier to De Peyster, 19 April 1779, ADD 21757, 90-91, also in *MPHC,* Vol. 19, pp. 397-98.

[18]De Peyster to Campbell, 13 May 1779, ADD 21,771, 90, also in *MPHC,* Vol. 19, p. 411.

[19]Haldimand to De Peyster, 25 Dec. 1778, ADD 21756, 23-24, ADD 21757, 77-78, also in *MPHC,* Vol. 9, p. 356.

[20]De Peyster to Haldimand, 13 May 1779, ADD 21756, 11-12, ADD 21757, 98-99, also in *MPHC,* Vol. 9, p. 381.

[21]*Ibid.*

[22]De Peyster to Haldimand, 1 June 1779, ADD 21756, 12-13, ADD 21757, 106-7, also in *MPHC,* Vol. 9, pp. 382-83; De Peyster to Haldimand, 14 June 1779, ADD 21756, 13-14, ADD 21757, 110-11, also in *MPHC,* Vol. 9, pp. 384-85.

[23]Haldimand to Bolton, 10 June 1779, *MPHC,* Vol. 19, pp. 429-30.

[24]Brehm to De Peyster, 30 May, 1779, *MPHC,* Vol. 9, pp. 412-13.

[25]De Peyster to Haldimand, 14 June 1779, ADD 21756, 13-14, ADD 21757, 110-11, also in *MPHC,* Vol. 9, p. 384.

[26]De Peyster to Haldimand, 27 June 1779, ADD 21756, 16, ADD 21757, 134-35, also in *MPHC,* Vol. 9, pp. 388-89.

[27]De Peyster to Haldimand, 14 June 1779, ADD 21756, 13-14, ADD 21757, 110-11, also in *MPHC,* Vol. 9, pp. 383-84; "Proceedings of the Weekly Court of Justices," Montreal, 21 March 1780, ADD 21845, 543.

[28]De Peyster to Haldimand, 2 May 1779, ADD 21756, 10-11, ADD 21757, 92, also in *MPHC,* Vol. 9, p. 380.

[29]De Peyster to Haldimand, 14 June 1779, ADD 21756, 13-14, ADD 21757, 110-11, also in *MPHC,* Vol. 9, p. 385.

[30]De Peyster to Haldimand, 1 June 1779, ADD 21756, 12-13, ADD 21757, 106-7, also in *MPHC,* Vol. 9, p. 383.

[31]Haldimand to De Peyster, 13 July 1779, ADD 21756, 28, ADD 21757, 176, also in *MPHC,* Vol. 9, p. 364; Nathaniel Day, Return of Provisions forwarded to the upper posts to Sept. 1779, ADD 21852, 116.

[32]Haldimand to De Peyster, 3 July 1779, ADD 21756, 26–27, ADD 21757, 152–53, also in *MPHC,* Vol. 9, p. 362.

[33]Haldimand to De Peyster, 13 July 1779, ADD 21756, 28, ADD 21757, 176, also in *MPHC,* Vol. 9, p. 364; Haldimand to (?), 23 July 1779, *MPHC,* Vol. 9, p. 426.

[34]De Peyster's expenses directed to Haldimand, 1779, T. 64/115, Public Record Office.

[35]De Peyster to Haldimand, 21 July 1779, ADD 21756, 18, ADD 21757, 178-79, also in *MPHC,* Vol. 9, pp. 390-91.

[36]*John Long's Voyages,* pp. 177-80.

[37]De Peyster to Brehm, 20 June 1779, ADD 21756, 15, also in *MPHC,* Vol. 9, pp. 386-87; De Peyster's Accounts, 29 June 1779, A01/376/1, 9, Public Record Office.

[38]"Monthly Return of the different Posts upon Lakes Garrisoned by the King's 8th Reg. &c &c.," 1 July 1779, W.O. 17/1573, Public Record Office.

[39]Bolton to Haldimand, 8 Feb. 1779, *MPHC,* Vol. 19, p. 372; Haldimand to De Peyster, 25 Dec. 1778, ADD 21756, 23-24, ADD 21757, 77-78, also in *MPHC,* Vol. 9, p. 355.

IX. De Peyster Takes the Offensive

[1]De Peyster to Captain Richard Lernoult, 20 June 1779, *MPHC*, Vol. 19, p. 437.

[2]De Peyster to Haldimand, 27 June 1779, ADD 21756, 16, ADD 21757, 134-35, also in *MPHC*, Vol. 9, p. 389.

[3]De Peyster to Langlade, 1 July 1779, *WHC*, Vol. 18, pp. 375-76.

[4]De Peyster to Bolton, 6 July 1779, *MPHC*, Vol. 19, p. 448; De Peyster to Major Nairne, Commander at Montreal, *MPHC*, Vol. 9, p. 390; "Fourniture fait a differentes personnes-12, 722 livres, 6 juillet, 1779," Louis Joseph Ainsse Papers, 1673-1874, Item No. 68, Public Archives of Canada.

[5]De Peyster to Haldimand, 9 July 1779, ADD 21756, 18, ADD 21757, 170, also in *MPHC*, Vol. 9, p. 390.

[6]Hingwapooshees and the Delaware Council to Col. Daniel Brodhead, 17 June 1779, *WHC*, Vol. 23, pp. 362-64.

[7]De Peyster, *Miscellanies by an Officer*, pp. 15-37.

[8]*Ibid.*, pp. 93-94.

[9]"Consolidated Returns of Indian Trade Licenses, 1777-1790," for 1779; Haldimand to De Peyster, 20 May 1779, ADD 21756, 25, ADD 21757, 102, also in *MPHC*, Vol. 9, p. 359.
The merchants brought approximately the following quantities of goods to Michilimackinac in 1779:

> 1,060 kegs of rum and brandy
> 90 kegs of wine
> 800 fusils
> 20,000 pounds of gunpowder
> 26,000 pounds of ball and shot
> £36,955 total value of the whole

[10]R. M. to De Peyster, 14 June 1779, *MPHC*, Vol. 9, p. 360.

[11]"Articles relative to the establishment of a General Store at Michilimackinac," ADD 21757, 226-29, also in *MPHC*, Vol. 10, pp. 305-7.

[12]Charles Grant to Haldimand, 24 April 1780, *Report on Canadian Archives*, 1888, p. 61.

[13]"Necessary part of the councils" held by Thomas Bennett with the Potawatomies at St. Joseph, 3 Aug. 1779, *MPHC*, Vol. 10, pp. 348-53.

[14]Bennett to De Peyster, 9 Aug. 1779, ADD 21757, 188, also in *MPHC*, Vol. 9, pp. 392-93.

[15]De Peyster to Haldimand, 9 Aug. 1779, ADD 21756, 19, ADD 21757, 186, also in *MPHC*, Vol. 9, pp. 391-92.

[16]Bennett to Lernoult, 15 Aug. 1779, *MPHC*, Vol. 19, pp. 455-56.

[17]Bennett's report, 1 Sept. 1779, ADD 21757, 230-31, also in *MPHC*, Vol. 9, pp. 395-96.

[18]"Statement of Goods," n.d., ADD 21758, 326, also in *MPHC*, Vol. 10, p. 366; Among the goods confiscated from Du Sable were:

		Livre
1 New Canoe decorated with plumes		600
1 Covered Kettle weighing 15 lbs at 10c		150
1 Large axe for use		20
10 Minots of parched corn		500
3 Minots flour		150
15 lbs of Gum @ 2		30
500 lbs of Flour and four sacks		1000
220 lbs of Grease and three Barrels		660
10 Barrels of Rum containing each 20 pts		5280
3 Bundles of Fishing lines	15	45
4 Bear Skins	15	60
2 Cotton Shirts	18	36
2 prs French Shoes & Buckles	30	60
1 Barrel of Sugar		90
1 Horn full of Powder		12
1 Sponge		12
		8705

[19]De Peyster, *Miscellanies by an Officer*, Vol. I, p. 244.

[20]Bennett's report, 1 Sept. 1779, ADD 21757, 230-31, also in *MPHC*, Vol. 9, p. 395.

[21]George Rogers Clark to Thomas Jefferson, 29 April 1779, H. A. Washington, ed., *The Writings of Thomas Jefferson . . .* , (Washington, D.C., 1853), Vol. I, pp. 222-24.

[22]Clark, *Memoirs,* pp. 553-54.

[23]Clark to Jefferson, 23 Sept. 1779, ADD 21757, 250-51, also in *MPHC,* Vol. 19, pp. 466-67.

[24]Haldimand to De Peyster, 3 July 1779, ADD 21757, 150, also in *Miscellanies by an Officer,* Vol. I, p. 244.

[25]*Ibid.,* pp. 15-37.

[26]Traders of Michilimackinac to Todd and McGill, 20 Sept. 1779, *Ibid.,* pp. 236-39.

[27]De Peyster to Michilimackinac Traders, 20 Sept. 1779, *Ibid.,* pp. 240-41.

X. Patrick Sinclair Assumes Command

[1]An informative biographical sketch of Patrick Sinclair is Hamish Bain Eaton's "Patrick Sinclair of Lybster and the Great Lakes," (an unpublished manuscript, copy in Mackinac Island State Park Commission Collection).

[2]Deed given at Detroit, 27 July 1768, Patrick Sinclair Papers, Burton Collection.

[3]"Commission to Patrick Sinclair as Lieutenant Governor and Superintendent of Michilimackinac," 7 April 1775, *MPHC,* Vol. 24, pp. 3-4.

[4]"Instructions for Captain Patrick Sinclair, . . ." ADD 21757, 568-69, also in *MPHC,* Vol. 9, pp. 516-18.

[5]Sinclair to Haldimand, 27 July 1779, ADD 21757, 184, also in *MPHC,* Vol. 9, p. 518; Haldimand to Sinclair, 17 Aug. 1779, ADD 21757, 192, also in *MPHC,* Vol. 9, p. 519; Sinclair to Haldimand, 19 Aug. 1779, ADD 21757, 202, also in *MPHC,* Vol. 9, p. 520; Haldimand to Sinclair, 20 Aug. 1779, ADD 21757, 206-7, also in *MPHC,* Vol. 9, p. 521; Haldimand to Sinclair, 19 Aug. 1779, ADD 21757, 198, also in *MPHC,* Vol. 9, p. 521.

[6]Sinclair to Haldimand, 7 Oct. 1779, ADD 21757, 260, also in *MPHC,* Vol. 9, p. 523.

[7]Sinclair to Brehm, 15 Oct. 1779, ADD 21757, 268-69, also in *MPHC,* Vol. 9, p. 527; Species of Stores, 30 Sept. 1779, Laboratory Stores, 30 Sept. 1779, ADD 21817, 42-56.

[8]Sinclair to Brehm, 7 Oct. 1779, ADD 21757, 262-67, also in *MPHC,* Vol. 9, p. 524.

[9]*Ibid.,* pp. 525-27.

[10]*Welcome,* Logbook, 16 Oct. 1779, Alexander Harrow Papers, Burton Collection.

[11]Sinclair to Brehm, 29 Oct. 1779, ADD 21757, 276-78, also in *MPHC,* Vol. 9, p. 530.

[12]"Remarks on Board his Majesty's Sloop Felicity by Samuel Robertson on Piloting her on Lake Michigan," 21 Oct. 1779-5 Nov. 1779, *WHC,* Vol. 11, pp. 203-12.

[13]Copies of Sinclair's orders, 22 Oct., 28 Oct., 1 Nov. 1779, Doty Papers.

[14]Sinclair to Brehm, 7 Oct. 1779, ADD 21757, 262-67, also in *MPHC,* Vol. 9, p. 526.

[15]De Peyster, 18 Sept. 1780, ADD 21758, 326.

[16]Sinclair to Brehm, 29 Oct. 1779, ADD 21757, 276-78, *MPHC,* Vol. 9, p. 531; Sinclair's orders, 28 Oct. 1779, Doty Papers.

[17]Sinclair to Brehm, 29 Oct. 1779, ADD 21757, 276-78, also in *MPHC,* Vol. 9, pp. 531-32.

[18]*Welcome,* Logbook, 3 Nov. 1779.

[19]*Ibid.,* Nov. 1779; David Mitchell, 15 Feb. 1819, extract of a letter in James D. Doty, "The History of the Northwest," Doty Papers.

[20]Alexander Grant to Bolton, 6 Jan. 1780, *MPHC,* Vol. 19, p. 496; Sinclair to Brehm, 29 Oct. 1779, ADD 21757, 276-78, also in *MPHC,* Vol. 9, p. 531.

XI. Target: St. Louis

[1]Sinclair to Brehm, 29 Oct. 1779, ADD 21757, 276-78, also in *MPHC,* Vol. 9, p. 530.

[2]Sinclair to Brehm, 15 Feb. 1780, ADD 21757, 284-91, also in *MPHC,* Vol. 9, pp. 541-42.

[3]Lord Germain to Haldimand, 17 June 1779, The Papers of Lord George Sackville Germain, Clements Library.

[4]Sinclair to Brehm, 15 Feb. 1780, ADD 21757, 284–91, also in *MPHC*, Vol. 9, p. 542.

[5]Sinclair to Haldimand, 15 Feb. 1780, ADD 21757, 292, also in *MPHC*, Vol. 9, p. 544; Sinclair to De Peyster, 15 Feb. 1780, *MPHC*, Vol. 19, pp. 500–501.

[6]Sinclair to Brehm, 15 Feb. 1780, ADD 21757, 284–91, also in *MPHC*, Vol. 9, p. 542.

[7]Sinclair to Haldimand, 15 Feb. 1780, ADD 21757, 292, also in *MPHC*, Vol. 9, p. 544.

[8]Sinclair's orders, 4 Jan. 1780, Doty Papers.

[9]Sinclair to Haldimand, 17 Feb. 1780, ADD 21757, 298, also in *MPHC*, Vol. 9, pp. 546–47.

[10]Pierre Prevost to George Rogers Clark, 20 Feb. 1780, *WHC*, Vol. 18, pp. 404–6.

[11]Sinclair to Brehm, 15 Feb. 1780, ADD 21757, 284–91, also in *MPHC*, Vol. 9, pp. 538–39.

[12]*Ibid;* Sinclair to De Peyster, 15 Feb. 1780, *MPHC*, Vol. 19, pp. 499–500. For an in depth study of early architecture and construction on Mackinac Island see Brian Leigh Dunnigan's "The Post of Mackinac, 1779–1812," (an unpublished thesis submitted to the State University of New York College at Oneonta at its Cooperstown Graduate Programs).

[13]Sinclair to senior naval officer, 15 Feb. 1780, *MPHC*, Vol. 19, p. 499.

[14]Sinclair to Brehm, 29 Oct. 1779, ADD 21757, 276–78, also in *MPHC*, Vol. 9, pp. 532–33.

[15]Sinclair to Brehm, 15 Feb. 1780, ADD 21757, 284–91, also in *MPHC*, Vol. 9, p. 538.

[16]*Ibid.,* pp. 540–41.

[17]Provisions issued at Michilimackinac, 25 Sept. 1779 to 24 April 1780, *MPHC*, Vol. 9, p. 655.

[18]Sinclair's orders, 23 Jan. 1780, Doty Papers.

[19]Sinclair to Brehm, 15 Feb. 1780, ADD 21757, 284–91, also in *MPHC*, Vol. 9, p. 540.

[20]Sinclair to Haldimand, 15 Feb. 1780, ADD 21757, 294–95, also in *MPHC*, Vol. 9, pp. 545–46.

[21]Madame Bourassa Langlade to priest at Montreal, 16 Jan. 1780, *WHC*, Vol. 18, pp. 403–4.

[22]Sinclair to Haldimand, 15 Feb. 1780, ADD 21757, 294–95, *MPHC*, Vol. 9, pp. 545–46.

[23]Pierre Durand, "Statement of work," 5 March 1780, *MPHC*, Vol. 10, pp. 365–66.

[24]J. B. Barthe Invoice Book, 1778–1780, 13 Sept. 1779, Jean Baptiste Barthe Papers, Burton Collection; John Askin, "Inventory . . . .," 31 Dec. 1776.

[25]Durand, "Statement of work," 5 March 1780, *MPHC*, Vol. 10, pp. 365–66.

[26]"Monthly Return of the different Posts upon the upper Lakes Garrisoned by the King's or 8th Regt," 1 Jan. 1780, W.O. 17/1574, Public Record Office.

[27]De Peyster to Bolton, 10 March 1780, *MPHC*, Vol. 19, pp. 501–2; De Peyster to Sinclair, 12 March 1780, ADD 21757, 304–5, also in *MPHC*, Vol. 9, pp. 580–81.

[28]Louis Chevallier to Unaddressed, 13 March 1780, ADD 21757, 306, also in *MPHC*, Vol. 10, pp. 380–81.

[29]Sinclair to Bolton, 4 June 1780, *MPHC*, Vol. 19, pp. 529–30.

[30]Sinclair to Haldimand, 29 May 1780, ADD 21757, 362–63, also in *MPHC*, Vol. 9, pp. 548–49.

[31]Sinclair to Haldimand, 29 May 1780, ADD 21757, 360, also in *MPHC*, Vol. 9, p. 554.

[32]Provisions that Askin turned over to Mitchell, 24 April 1780, ADD 21757, 323–26, also in *MPHC*, Vol. 9, p. 656.

[33]Sinclair to Haldimand, 15 Feb. 1780, ADD 21757, 294-95, also in *MPHC*, Vol. 9, p. 545.

[34]Sinclair to Haldimand, 8 July 1780, ADD 21757, 406–7, also in *MPHC*, Vol. 9, pp. 576–78; Papers concerning Samuel Robertson, 1780, ADD 21757, 408, also in *MPHC*, Vol. 9, pp. 618–19.

[35]Christian Burgy, 28 April 1780, ADD 21757, 336, also in *MPHC*, Vol. 9, p. 620; Robertson to Clowes, 27 April 1780, ADD 21757, 328, also in *MPHC*, Vol. 9, p. 619; Robertson to Haldimand, 1780, ADD 21757, 562–65, also in *MPHC*, Vol. 9, pp. 624–25; Sinclair to Haldimand, 8 July 1780, ADD 21757, 406–7, also in *MPHC*, Vol. 9, pp. 577–78.

[36]"Coroner's Account," 24 May 1780, ADD 21757, 356, also in *MPHC*, Vol. 9, p. 657.

[37]Robertson to Clowes, 27 April 1780, ADD 21757, 328, also in *MPHC*, Vol. 9, p. 619.

38Robertson to Haldimand, 1780, ADD 21757, 562–65, also in *MPHC*, Vol. 9, pp. 625–26.

39Phillips to Clowes, 27 April 1780, ADD 21757, 332, also in *WHC*, Vol. 12, p. 49; Clowes to Bolton, 4 June 1780, ADD 21757, 373, also in *MPHC*, Vol. 9, p. 621.

40Sinclair to Haldimand, 29 May 1780, ADD 21757, 362–63, also in *MPHC*, Vol. 9, pp. 548–49.

41De Peyster to Haldimand, 17 May 1780, *MPHC*, Vol. 10, pp. 395–96.

42Louise Phelps Kellogg, *The British Régime in Wisconsin and the Northwest*, (reprinted New York, 1971; Madison, 1935), pp. 167–68.

43Sinclair to Bolton, 4 July (?) 1780, *WHC*, Vol. 11, p. 154; Sinclair to Haldimand, 8 July 1780, ADD 21757, 404-5, also in *MPHC*, Vol. 9, pp. 558-59. An excellent account of the Battle of St. Louis is John Francis McDermott, "The Myth of the 'Imbecile Governor; — Captain Fernando de Leyba and the Defense of St. Louis in 1780," in McDermott, ed., *The Spanish in the Mississippi Valley, 1762–1804*, pp. 314–91.

44Sinclair to Haldimand, 29 May 1780, ADD 21757, 364–65, also in *MPHC*, Vol. 9, p. 553.

45Captain John Mompesson to Unaddressed, 15 April 1781, *MPHC*, Vol. 10, p. 467.

46Sinclair to Bolton, 4 June 1780, *MPHC*, Vol. 19, pp. 529–30.

47Sinclair to Haldimand, 29 May 1780, ADD 21757, 362–63, also in *MPHC*, Vol. 9, pp. 548–49.

48*Ibid.*, Sinclair to Bolton, 4 June 1780, *MPHC*, Vol. 19, 529.

49Sinclair to Haldimand, 29 May 1780, ADD 21757, 364–65, also in *MPHC*, Vol. 9, pp. 553–54.

50Brehm to Sinclair, 17 April 1780, ADD 21757, 318–21, also in *MPHC*, Vol. 9, p. 537.

51Traders Memorial to Haldimand, 11 May 1780, *MPHC*, Vol. 9, pp. 550–52.

52J. B. Barthe Invoice Book, 1778-80, J. B. Barthe Papers, Burton Collection; Sinclair to Brehm, 29 May 1780, ADD 21757, 366–67, also in *MPHC*, Vol. 9, p. 552.

53"Consolidated Returns of Indian Trade Licenses, 1777–1790," for 1780; The traders brought approximately the following quantities of goods to Michilimackinac in 1780:

    1,390 kegs of rum and brandy
      120 kegs of wine
      814 fusils
  25,800 pounds of gunpowder
  35,000 pounds of ball and shot
  £45,660 total value of the whole

54Charles Grant to Haldimand, 24 April 1780, *MPHC*, Vol. 19, p. 510.

55Haldimand to De Peyster, 12 Feb. 1780, *MPHC*, Vol. 9, p. 634.

56De Peyster to Haldimand, 8 June 1780, *MPHC*, Vol. 10, pp. 399–400, also in *WHC*, Vol. 12, pp. 49–51.

57Brehm to Sinclair, 17 April 1780, ADD 21757, 318–321, also in *MPHC*, Vol. 9, p. 536.

58"Indian Presents for Michilimackinac," 13 May 1780, *MPHC*, Vol. 19, pp. 517–18.

59Traders petition to Sinclair, 27 April 1780, ADD 21757, 334, also in *MPHC*, Vol. 9, 549–50.

60Stone, *Fort Michilimackinac 1715–1781*, p. 323.

61Sinclair to Haldimand, 29 May 1780, ADD 21757, 360, also in *MPHC*, Vol. 9, p.554.

62Clowes to Bolton, 4 June 1780, ADD 21757, 373, also in *MPHC*, Vol. 9, p. 621.

63Sinclair to Haldimand, 29 May 1780, ADD 21757, 360, also in *MPHC*, Vol. 9, p. 554.

64John Campbell to Robert Mathews, 24 July 1780, *MPHC*, Vol. 19, p. 547; Agreement to furnish corvés, 24 June 1780, *MPHC*, Vol. 10, p. 405; Sinclair to Haldimand, 8 June 1780, *MPHC*, Vol. 9, p. 556.

65William Grant to Unaddressed, 21 June 1780, ADD 21757, 566, also in *MPHC*, Vol. 9, pp. 557–58; Traders' opinions regarding move to island, 21 June 1780, ADD 21757, 382, also in *MPHC*, Vol. 9, pp. 556–57.

66Sinclair's orders, 26 May 1780, Doty Papers.

67Sinclair to Brehm, 8 July 1780, ADD 21757, 413–14, also in *MPHC*, Vol. 9, p. 579; Brehm to Sinclair, 17 April 1780, ADD 21757, 318–21, also in *MPHC*, Vol. 9, pp. 534–35.

⁶⁸Brehm to Sinclair, 10 Aug. 1780, ADD 21757, 455–56, also in *MPHC*, Vol. 9, p. 564.

⁶⁹Sinclair to Haldimand (?), n.d., *MPHC,* Vol. 10, p. 390.

XII. Turmoil at Michilimackinac

¹Sinclair to Haldimand, 8 July 1780, ADD 21757, 404–5, also in *MPHC*, Vol. 9, pp. 558–59.

²"The Information of William Brown, a carpenter taken Prisoner at Pencour," ADD 21757, 570–71.

³Haldimand to Bolton, 18 June 1780, *MPHC*, Vol. 19, pp. 535–36; Haldimand to MacLean, 1780, *MPHC*, Vol. 19, p. 512; Sinclair to Haldimand, 8 July 1780, ADD 21757, 415, also in *MPHC*, Vol. 9, p. 560.

⁴Brehm to Sinclair, 17 April 1780, *MPHC*, Vol. 9, p. 534; Sinclair to Bolton, 4 July (?) 1780, *MPHC*, Vol. 19, p. 529.

⁵Clowes to Bolton 23 Aug. 1780, ADD 21757, 489–90, also in *MPHC*, Vol. 9, pp. 607–8.

⁶Clowes Report of an inquiry into Lt. Mercer's behavior, 3 July 1780, ADD 21757, 396–97; Mercer to Unaddressed, July 1780, ADD 21757, 389–90, also in *MPHC*, Vol. 9, pp. 595–97.

⁷Joseph Frobisher and William Grant post bond, 3 July 1780, ADD 21757, 392–93, also in *MPHC*, Vol. 9, pp. 620–21; Robertson to Haldimand, 1780, ADD 21757, 562–65, also in *MPHC*, Vol. 9, pp. 626–27.

⁸Sinclair to Brehm, 2 Aug. 1780, ADD 21757, 451–52, also in *MPHC*, Vol. 9, p. 569.

⁹Joseph Louis Ainsse to Haldimand, 5 Aug. 1780, ADD 21757, 533–36, also in *MPHC*, Vol. 10, pp. 434–37; Census of St. Joseph, 1780(?), ADD 21757, 573, *MPHC*, Vol. 10, pp. 406–7; Chevallier to Haldimand, 9 Oct. 1780, *MPHC*, Vol. 10, pp. 438–40.

¹⁰Ainsse to Sinclair, 30 June 1780, ADD 21757, 385, also in *MPHC*, Vol. 10, p. 406.

¹¹Ainsse to Haldimand, 5 Aug. 1780, ADD 21757, 533–36, also in *MPHC*, Vol. 10, pp. 434–37; Sinclair to Haldimand, 2 Aug. 1780, ADD 21757, 451–52, also in *MPHC*, Vol. 9, p. 569.

¹²Chevallier to Haldimand, 9 Oct. 1780, *MPHC*, Vol. 10, pp. 438–40.

¹³Expenses incurred by Ainsse, 6 Aug. 1780, ADD 21757, 529, also in *MPHC*, Vol. 10, p. 415; Ainsse to Haldimand, 5 Aug. 1780, ADD 21757, 533–36, also in *MPHC*, Vol. 10, pp. 434–37.

¹⁴De Peyster to Bolton, 6 July 1780, *MPHC*, Vol. 19, p. 540.

¹⁵Sinclair to Brehm, 8 July 1780, ADD 21757, 413–14, also in *MPHC*, Vol. 9, pp. 578–79.

¹⁶De Peyster to Haldimand, 1 Oct. 1780, ADD 21757, 526–27, also in *MPHC*, Vol. 9, pp. 615–16.

¹⁷*Welcome,* Logbook, 11 July 1780; *Welcome,* cargo and passengers, 29 July 1780, ADD 21757, 430, also in *MPHC*, Vol. 9, p. 657.

¹⁸Alexander Harrow to Alexander Grant, 31 July 1780, ADD 21757, 447–48, also in *MPHC*, Vol. 9, pp. 601–2.

¹⁹Harrow to Normand McKay, 30 July 1780, ADD 21757, 428, also in *MPHC*, Vol. 9, pp. 602–3.

²⁰Sinclair to McKay, 21 July 1780, ADD 21757, 421, also in *MPHC*, Vol. 9, p. 605.

²¹*Welcome,* Logbook, 30 July 1780, Harrow to Grant, 31 July 1780, ADD 21757, 447–48, also in *MPHC*, Vol. 9, pp. 601–2.

²²*Welcome,* Logbook, 24 July, 3 Sept., 4 Dec., 7 Dec., 1779; Sinclair to De Peyster, n.d., ADD 21757, 355, also in *MPHC*, Vol. 9, p. 600; Grant to Bolton, 6 Jan. 1780, *MPHC*, Vol. 19, p. 496; De Peyster to Bolton, 13 Aug. 1780, ADD 21757, 461–62, also in *MPHC*, Vol. 9, p. 598; Sinclair to James Guthrie, 31 July 1780, ADD 21757, 445, also in *MPHC*, Vol. 9, p. 605.

²³De Peyster to Bolton, 13 Aug. 1780, ADD 21757, 461–62, also in *MPHC*, Vol. 9, p. 599.

²⁴"The Humble Petition of 2 Companies of the Kings or 8th Regiment of Foot in Garrison at Michilimackinac," 30 July 1780, ADD 21757, 443–44, also in *MPHC*, Vol. 9, pp. 587–88.

[25]Daniel Mercer to De Peyster, 1 Aug. 1780, ADD 21757, 449, also in *MPHC*, Vol. 9, p. 597.

[26]Mercer to Unaddressed, July 1780, ADD 21757, 389–90, also in *MPHC*, Vol. 9, pp. 595–97.

[27]Sinclair to Brehm, 23 Aug. 1780, ADD 21757, 499–500, also in *MPHC*, Vol. 9, p. 611.

[28]Sinclair to Brehm, 3 Aug. 1780, ADD 21757, 453–54, also in *MPHC*, Vol. 9, pp. 572–73.

[29]Sinclair to Haldimand, 2 Aug. 1780, ADD 21757, 451–52, also in *MPHC*, Vol. 9, p. 570.

[30]Jean Marie Calvé to Haldimand, 23 Aug. 1780, ADD 21757, 493, also in *MPHC*, Vol. 10, pp. 421–22.

[31]Sinclair to Haldimand, 22 Aug. 1780, ADD 21757, 483–84, also in *MPHC*, Vol. 9, pp. 570–1.

[32]Sinclair to Haldimand, 15 Feb. 1780, ADD 21757, 294–95, also in *MPHC*, Vol. 9, 545.

[33]Sinclair to Haldimand, 22 Aug. 1780, ADD 21757, 483–84, also in *MPHC*, Vol. 9, pp. 570–71.

[34]Askin to Nathaniel Day, 29 July 1780, *MPHC*, Vol. 19, pp. 551–52.

[35]De Peyster to Bolton, 13 Aug. 1780, ADD 21757, 461–62, also in *MPHC*, Vol. 9, p. 599.

[36]Sinclair to Haldimand, 22 Aug. 1780, ADD 21757, 480–81, also in *MPHC*, Vol. 9, p. 591.

[37]Sinclair to Brehm, 23 Aug. 1780, ADD 21757, 499–500, also in *MPHC*, Vol. 9, pp. 611–12.

[38]Clowes to Bolton, 23 Aug. 1780, ADD 21757, 489–90, also in *MPHC*, Vol. 9, pp. 607–8.

[39]Clowes, "Letters from the Officer of the Day," 22 Aug. 1780, ADD 21757, 482; Sinclair to Haldimand, 22 Aug. 1780, ADD 21757, 480–81, also in *MPHC*, Vol. 9, p. 591.

[40]Mompesson to Haldimand, 22 Aug. 1780, ADD 21757, 470–71, also in *MPHC*, Vol. 9, p. 589.

[41]Mompesson to Mathews, 22 Aug. 1780, ADD 21757, 468, also in *MPHC*, Vol. 9, p. 590.

[42]Sinclair to Haldimand, 22 Aug. 1780, ADD 21757, 480–81, also in *MPHC*, Vol. 9, p. 591.

[43]Sinclair to Brehm, 23 Aug. 1780, ADD 21757, 499–500, also in *MPHC*, Vol. 9, p. 610.

[44]De Peyster to Haldimand, 31 Aug. 1780, *MPHC*, Vol. 10, p. 423.

[45]Merchants approval of Sinclair, 22 Aug. 1780, ADD 21757, 478, also in *MPHC*, Vol. 10, p. 421.

[46]Clowes to De Peyster, 26 Aug. 1780, ADD 21757, 503, also in *MPHC*, Vol. 9, p. 612.

[47]Thomas Shirley to Sir John Caldwell, 6 Feb. 1785, Bagshawe MSS B 3/37/154, John Rylands Library.

[48]Merchants petition Mompesson, 5 Sept. 1780, ADD 21757, 511, also in *MPHC*, Vol. 9, pp. 614–15.

[49]Mompesson to Mathews, 10 Sept. 1780, ADD 21757, 514–15, also in *MPHC*, Vol. 9, pp. 612–13.

[50]Mompesson to Sinclair, 15 April 1781, ADD 21758, 25, also in *MPHC*, Vol. 10, p. 467.

[51]De Peyster to Bolton, 18 Sept. 1780, *MPHC*, Vol. 19, p. 574.

[52]Mompesson to De Peyster, 20 Sept. 1780, *MPHC*, Vol. 19, p. 575.

[53]Haldimand to Sinclair, 21 Aug. 1780, ADD 21757, 464, also in *MPHC*, Vol. 9, pp. 573–74.

[54]Haldimand to Sinclair, 10 Aug. 1780, ADD 21757, 457–58, also in *MPHC*, Vol. 9, pp. 566–67.

[55]*John Long's Voyages*, pp. 185–91.

[56]De Peyster to Haldimand, 1 Oct. 1780, ADD 21757, 526–27, also in *MPHC*, Vol. 9, pp. 615–16.

[57]De Peyster to Sinclair, 17 Sept. 1780, ADD 21757, 522, also in *MPHC*, Vol. 9, p. 617.

[58]"Memorial of the Merchants of Michilimackinac to be presented to His Excellency General Haldimand," n.d., *MPHC*, Vol. 10, p. 367.

[59]De Peyster to Haldimand, 31 Aug. 1780, *MPHC*, Vol. 10, p. 424.

[60]John Campbell to Mathews, 10 Aug. 1780, *MPHC*, Vol. 19, pp. 556–57; Sinclair to Haldimand, 8 July 1780, ADD 21757, 417, also in *MPHC*, Vol. 9, p. 561.

[61]De Peyster to Bolton, 18 Sept. 1780, *MPHC*, Vol. 19, p. 574.

[62]Harrow to Grant (?), 21 Aug. 1780, ADD 21757, 463, also in *MPHC*, Vol. 9, pp. 606–7.

[63]*Welcome*, Logbook, 31 July 1780.

[64]Haldimand to Sinclair, 21 Aug. 1780, ADD 21757, 466, also in *MPHC*, Vol. 9, pp. 621–22.

[65]R. Mathews to Sinclair, 9 Oct. 1780, ADD 21757, 549, also in *MPHC*, Vol. 9, p. 576.

[66]Haldimand to Bolton, 12 Sept. 1780, *MPHC*, Vol. 19, pp. 570–71.

[67]Haldimand to Sinclair, 12 Sept. 1780, ADD 21757, 516–17, also in *MPHC*, Vol. 9, p. 575.

[68]Haldimand to Sinclair, 10 Aug. 1780, ADD 21757, 457–58, also in *MPHC*, Vol. 9, p. 567; John Schank to Grant, 10 Aug. 1780, ADD 21805, 16, also in *MPHC*, Vol. 19, p. 555; Haldimand to Sinclair, 1780, ADD 21757, 591, also in *MPHC*, Vol. 9, p. 574.

[69]*Ibid.*

[70]De Peyster to Bolton, 28 Oct. 1780, *MPHC*, Vol. 19, pp. 578–79; De Peyster to Brig. Gen. H. Watson Powell, 13 Nov. 1780, *MPHC*, Vol. 19, p. 580.

[71]"Monthly Return . . . ," 1 Oct. 1780, W.O. 17/1574, Public Record Office.

[72]Powder at Michilimackinac, 1 Oct. 1780, *MPHC*, Vol. 19, p. 576; Ordnance at Michilimackinac, 31 March 1780, *MPHC*, Vol. 10, pp. 388–89.

[73]*Welcome*, Logbook, 3 Nov. and 9 Nov. 1780.

[74]*Ibid.*, 8 Nov. 1780.

[75]*Ibid.*, 2 Dec. and 4 Dec. 1780.

[76]*Ibid.*, 10 Dec., 11 Dec., and 22 Dec. 1780.

XIII. War Costs Rise

[1]*Welcome*, Logbook, 1 Jan. 1781.

[2]*Ibid.*, 27 Jan. 1781.

[3]Haldimand to De Peyster, 6 Jan. 1781, *MPHC*, Vol. 9, p. 641; De Peyster to Powell, 13 Nov. 1780, *MPHC*, Vol. 19, p. 581.

[4]De Peyster to Haldimand, 8 Jan. 1781, *MPHC*, Vol. 10, pp. 450–51; Sinclair to Powell, 1 May 1781, *MPHC*, Vol. 19, p. 632; Sinclair to Brehm, 12 May 1781, ADD 21758, 42–43, *MPHC*, Vol. 10, p. 480.

[5]Sinclair to Langlade (?), 30 Jan. 1781, *WHC*, Vol. 18, pp. 415–17.

[6]José de Galvez to Bernardo Galvez, 15 Jan. 1782, *WHC*, Vol. 18, pp. 430–32; Nelson Vance Russell, *The British Regime in Michigan,* (Northfield, Minnesota, 1939), pp. 210–14.

[7]Francisco Cruzat to B. Galvez, 19 Dec. 1780, *WHC*, Vol. 18, pp. 413–15.

[8]*Welcome*, Logbook, 12 Feb. 1781.

[9]*Ibid.*, 4 Jan. and 9 Jan. 1781.

[10]Mompesson to De Peyster, 30 April 1781, ADD 21758, 35–36, also in *MPHC*, Vol. 9, pp. 631–32; *Welcome*, Logbook, 21 March 1781.

[11]*Welcome*, Logbook, 3 April – 25 April 1781.

[12]Garrison Order, 28 April 1781, ADD 21758, 62, also in *MPHC*, Vol. 10, p. 477.

[13]Henry R. Schoolcraft, *Personal Memoirs . . . . ,* (Philadelphia, 1851), pp. 445–46.

[14]*Welcome*, Logbook, 25 April 1781; Sinclair to Brehm, 12 May 1781, ADD 21758, 42–43, also in *MPHC*, Vol. 10, p. 480.

[15]Deed to Mackinac Island, 12 May 1781, Clements Library; Sinclair to Powell, 6 June 1781, *MPHC*, Vol. 19, p. 638.

[16]*Welcome*, Logbook, 24 May 1781.

[17]Sinclair to Powell, 6 June 1781, *MPHC*, Vol. 19, p. 638; Sinclair to Unaddressed, 31 July 1781, ADD 21758, 81, also in *MPHC*, Vol. 10, pp. 502–3.

[18]Sinclair to Unaddressed, 8 July 1781, ADD 21758, 67, also in *MPHC*, Vol. 10, p. 495.

[19]Sinclair to Unaddressed, 31 July 1781, ADD 21758, 81, also in *MPHC*, Vol. 10, p. 503.

[20]Sinclair to Powell, 6 June 1781, *MPHC*, Vol. 19, p. 638.

[21]Mathews to Campbell, 25 Aug. 1781, *MPHC*, Vol. 19, p. 657.

[22]Haldimand to Sinclair, 1781, ADD 21758, 110–11, *MPHC*, Vol. 10, pp. 477–78.

[23]Memorial of Montreal merchants, 19 April 1781, *MPHC*, Vol. 19, pp. 620–21.

[24]"Consolidated Returns . . . ," 1781. The traders brought approximately the following quantities of goods in 1781:

```
 1,824  kegs of rum and brandy
   294  kegs of wine
   543  fusils
20,250  pounds of gunpowder
27,800  pounds of ball and shot
₤38,224 total value of the whole
```

[25]Haldimand to Powell, 11 April 1781, *MPHC*, Vol. 19, p. 618.

[26]Haldimand to Sinclair, 31 May 1781, *WHC*, Vol. 12, pp. 56–57, also in *MPHC*, Vol. 10, p. 486.

[27]Sinclair to Haldimand, 12 May 1781, *WHC* Vol. 12, p. 56.

[28]Haldimand to Powell, 23 June 1781, *MPHC*, Vol. 19, pp. 641–42.

[29]"Memorial of the Merchants of Michilimackinac," n.d., ADD 21758, 364, also in *MPHC*, Vol. 10, p. 367.

[30]M.E.M. to Ensign McDougall, 23 May 1781, and M.E.M. to Amos Langdon, 5 July 1781, Macomb Letterbook, August 11, 1780–July 5, 1781, Macomb Papers, Burton Collection.

[31]Lernoult to Powell, 22 June 1781, *MPHC*, Vol. 19, pp. 640–41; Haldimand to De Peyster, 24 June 1781, *MPHC*, Vol. 10, p. 491.

[32]"Outlines of a Reformation of Expenses in the Indian Department given by C. H., private," ADD 21758, 360–62, also in *MPHC*, Vol. 10, pp. 555–57.

[33]Haldimand to De Peyster, 24 June 1781, *MPHC*, Vol. 10, pp. 491–92.

[34]Haldimand to Powell, 24 June 1781, *MPHC*, Vol. 10, pp. 492–93.

[35]"Return of the Number & Denomination of People victualled at Michilimackinac Island between the 25th March & the 24 April, 1781," ADD 21758, 30–31, also in *MPHC*, Vol. 10, p. 470.

[36]Sinclair to Powell, 6 June 1781, *MPHC*, Vol. 19, p. 638.

[37]Sinclair to Powell, 15 June 1781, *MPHC*, Vol. 19, p. 638.

[38]"Government," 10 June 1781, A. Frazier Accounts, A. Frazier Papers, Burton Collection. This purchase by Sinclair was permissible because it was for canoes and provisions. The cost and quantity of merchandise acquired by Sinclair from Meldrum was:

59 Bags Indian corn 66/8	196	13	4
5 Kegs Grease 60 lb. 300 lb 8/	120		
10 Canoes 13/6/8	133	6	8
20 Rolls Bark 8/	8		
200 lb Gum 2/8	26	13	4
30 Bunches Watap 2/	3		
1 large Canot	40		
25 lb Grease	10		
	₤537	13	4

[39]Sinclair to Unaddressed, 31 July 1781, ADD 21758, 77, also in *MPHC*, Vol. 10, pp. 503–4.

[40]Sinclair to Haldimand, 26 Sept. 1781, ADD 21758, 94, also in *MPHC*, Vol. 10, pp. 514–15.

[41]"Invoice of Indian Presents . . . ," 31 Aug. 1781, *MPHC*, Vol. 19, pp. 658–60.

[42]"Account of Bills drawn for His Majesty's Service, . . . ," 1781, T. 64/115, Public Record Office; *MPHC*, Vol. 20, pp. 210–11.

[43]Sinclair to Haldimand, 22 Oct. 1781, ADD 21758, 104, also in *MPHC*, Vol. 10, pp. 529–30.

[44]"Account of Bills drawn for His Majesty's Service, . . . ," 1781; "Dr. to George Meldrum for Sundries furnished Engineer department," 11 Aug. 1781, A. Frazier Accounts; Engineer stores received from Traders, 1 Nov. 1781, *MPHC*, Vol. 10, pp. 533–34.

[45]*Angelica*, Logbook, 7 Aug., 8 Aug., and 19 Aug. 1781, Harrow Papers, Burton Collection.

[46]Thomas Aubrey to Haldimand, 30 July 1781, *MPHC*, Vol. 10, p. 502.

[47]Haldimand to Powell, 24 June 1781, *MPHC*, Vol. 19, p. 643.

[48]*Dunmore*, Logbook, 4 Sept. and 5 Sept. 1781, Harrow Papers.

[49]De Peyster to Powell, 17 March 1781, *MPHC*, Vol. 19, p. 601; Haldimand to Powell, 20 April 1781, *MPHC*, Vol. 19, p. 624.

[50]Joseph Howard to Haldimand, 24 Sept. 1781, *MPHC*, Vol. 19, pp. 622–23; Joseph Sayer for Joseph Howard, 6 Aug. 1781, ADD 21758, 87, also in *MPHC*, Vol. 10, p. 505.

[51]John Kay and David McCrae to Haldimand, 13 Nov. 1780, ADD 21757, 555–56, also in *MPHC*, Vol. 10, pp. 446–48.

[52]Joseph Baptiste Parent to Haldimand, 28 April 1781, *MPHC*, Vol. 19, pp. 630–31.

[53]Normand McLeod, Alexander Saunders, and John Martin to Haldimand, 21 Aug. 1781, *MPHC*, Vol. 19, pp. 654–55.

[54]De Peyster to Powell, 10 Oct. 1781, *MPHC*, Vol. 19, pp. 664–65; Sinclair to Powell, 2 Nov. 1781, *MPHC*, Vol. 19, p. 671.

[55]Thomas Finchley to De Peyster, 10 Oct. 1781, *MPHC*, Vol. 19, pp. 665–66.

[56]Sinclair to Powell, 2 Nov. 1781, *MPHC*, Vol. 19, p. 671.

XIV. Exit Patrick Sinclair

[1]De Peyster to Alexander McKee, 3 April 1782, *MPHC*, Vol. 10, pp. 565–66.

[2]Sinclair to Haldimand, 29 April 1782, ADD 21758, 126, also in *MPHC*, Vol. 10, p. 572–73.

[3]Sinclair to Haldimand, 9 March 1782, ADD 21758, 114, also in *MPHC*, Vol. 10, pp. 552–53.

[4]Sinclair to Haldimand, 9 March 1782, ADD 21758, 116, also in *MPHC*, Vol. 10, pp. 553–54.

[5]Sinclair to Haldimand, 5 July 1782, ADD 21758, 144, also in *MPHC*, Vol. 10, pp. 596–97.

[6]Sinclair to Haldimand, 12 June 1782, ADD 21758, 134, also in *MPHC*, Vol. 10, p. 585.

[7]Haldimand to Unaddressed, 6 May 1782, *MPHC*, Vol. 10, p. 573.

[8]Mathews to De Peyster, 5 Aug. 1782, *MPHC*, Vol. 10, p. 623.

[9]Memorandums-John Coates, 19 June 1782; William Grant, 19 June 1782, Matt Lessey & Co., 19 June 1782, and "Return of Indian Corn received into the Indian Store . . . ," 20 June 1782, ADD 21758, 136–37, also in *MPHC*, Vol. 19, pp. 292–94.

[10]"Number of Indians Resorting to Michilimackinac," 10 Sept. 1782, ADD 21758, 150, also in *MPHC*, Vol. 10, pp. 635–36.

[11]Sinclair to Campbell, 16 July 1782, *MPHC*, Vol. 20, p. 31.

[12]De Peyster to Powell, 16 May 1782, *MPHC*, Vol. 20, p. 19

[13]Grant to Powell, 24 Jan. 1782, *MPHC*, Vol. 20, p. 2.

[14]Sinclair to Haldimand, 25 June 1782, ADD 21758, 138, also in *MPHC*, Vol. 10, p. 595.

[15]Sinclair to Haldimand, 28 June 1782, ADD 21758, 142, also in *MPHC*, Vol. 10, pp. 595–96.

[16]Kellogg, *The British Regime in Wisconsin*, . . . , pp. 183–85.

[17]De Peyster to Alexander McKee, 6 Aug. 1782, *MPHC*, Vol. 20, p. 37.

[18]Sinclair to Haldimand, 5 July 1782, ADD 21758, 144, also in *MPHC*, Vol. 10, pp. 596-97.

[19]Michilimackinac merchants and inhabitants to Haldimand, 13 July 1782, ADD 21758, 146, also in *MPHC*, Vol. 10, p. 599.

[20]J. Fairbairn Smith, *Sesquicentennial Commission: U.S.A. Bicentennial 1776–1976; Presenting Graphic View of Michigan Masonic Tracing Board*, (1976), p. 13.

[21]"Consolidated Returns, . . . ",1782. The traders brought approximately the following quantity of merchandise to Michilimackinac in 1782:

> 991 kegs of rum and brandy
> 336 kegs of wine
> 794 fusils
> 23,547 pounds of gunpowder
> 42,900 pounds of shot and balls
> £55,940 total value of the whole

[22]Haldimand to Campbell, 15 Aug. 1782, *MPHC*, Vol. 20, pp. 42–43.

[23]Lieutenant Colonel Henry Hope to Haldimand, 19 Oct. 1782, ADD 21758, 178–82, also in *MPHC*, Vol. 10, pp. 656–57.

[24]Indian Department payroll, 16 Sept. 1782, ADD 21758, 148, also in *WHC*, Vol. 12, pp. 60–61, and *MPHC*, Vol. 10, p. 636.

[25]Hope to Haldimand, 19 Oct. 1782, ADD 21758, 178–82, also in *MPHC*, Vol. 10, p. 658.

[26]*Ibid.*, pp. 658–59.

[27]Lieutenant Richard Hockings, Condition of Fort Michilimackinac, 20 Sept. 1782, ADD 21758, 160–63, also in *MPHC*, Vol. 10, p. 645.

[28]Hope to Haldimand, 21 Sept. 1782, ADD 21758, 164, also in *MPHC*, Vol. 10, p. 645.

[29]Haldimand to Sinclair, 21 Oct. 1782, ADD 21758, 184, also in *MPHC*, Vol. 10, p. 661.

[30]Hope to Captain Daniel Robertson, 20 Sept. 1782, ADD 21758, 157–59, also in *WHC*, Vol. 12, pp. 61–64, and *MPHC*, Vol. 10, pp. 638–40.

[31]"Return of Carpenters employed in the Naval Department . . . ," 19 Sept. 1782, ADD 21758, 156, also in *MPHC*, Vol. 10, p. 638.

[32]Engineer's Account, 18 Sept. 1782, ADD 21758, 154, also in *MPHC*, Vol. 10, p. 637.

[33]Dunnigan, *King's Men at Mackinac*, p. 17.

[34]Clowes to Haldimand, 26 Sept. 1784, ADD 21758, 340; Sinclair, Certification of Clowes' property, 20 Aug. 1782, ADD 21758, 341.

[35]Powell to Haldimand, 17 Aug. 1782, *MPHC*, Vol. 20, p. 45.

XV. The Coming of Peace

[1]Daniel Robertson to Mathews, 20 April 1783, ADD 21758, 226, also in *MPHC*, Vol. 11, p. 358.

[2]Richard Wright to Thomas Williams & Co., Williams Papers, Burton Collection.

[3]Russell, *The British Regime in Michigan . . .* , pp. 227–29.

[4]Robertson to Mathews, 20 April 1783, ADD 21758, 226, also in *MPHC*, Vol. 11, p. 358.

[5]Robertson to McBeath, 26 April 1783, ADD 21758, 230, also in *MPHC*, Vol. 11, pp. 360–61.

[6]Robertson to Mathews, 10 Feb. 1783, ADD 21758, 216, also in *MPHC*, Vol. 11, p. 341.

[7]Robertson to Mathews, 9 Aug. 1783, ADD 21758, 252, also in *MPHC*, Vol. 11, pp. 379–82.

[8]"Consolidated Returns . . . ," 1783. The traders brought approximately the following quantity of merchandise to Michilimackinac in 1783:

> 1,647 kegs of rum and brandy
> 193 kegs of wine
> 742 fusils
> 34,490 pounds of gunpowder
> 40,650 pounds of shot and ball
> £66,790 total value of the whole

[9]Haldimand to Sir John Johnson, 26 May 1783, *MPHC*, Vol. 20, p. 124.

[10]Abraham Cuyler to Mathews, 17 July 1783, *MPHC*, Vol. 20, p. 145.

[11]Robertson to Brig. General Allen MacLean, 10 July 1783, ADD 21758, 244, also in *MPHC*, Vol, 11, pp. 375–76; Robertson to Mathews, 27 June 1783, ADD 21758, 240, also in *MPHC*, Vol. 11, p. 369; Robertson to Brehm, 6 July 1783, ADD 21758, 242–43, also in *MPHC*, Vol. 11, p. 374.

[12]Robertson to Mathews, 9 Aug. 1783, ADD 21758, 252, also in *MPHC*, Vol. 11, p. 379.

[13]Robertson to Mathews, 7 Sept. 1783, ADD 21758, 255–56, also in *MPHC*, Vol. 11, p. 384.

[14]De Peyster to Haldimand, 15 July 1783, *MPHC*, Vol. 20, p. 143; Robertson to Brehm, 6 July 1783, ADD 21758, 242–43, also in *MPHC*, Vol. 11, p. 374.

[15]Robertson to Mathews, 29 Oct. 1783, ADD 21758, 272–73, also in *MPHC*, Vol. 11, p. 374.

[16]Schoolcraft, *Memoirs . . . ,* pp. 478–79.

[17]Michilimackinac landowners to Robertson, 27 Oct. 1783, ADD 21758, 270, also in *MPHC*, Vol. 11, pp. 393–95.

[18]A. Dundas to Lernoult, 15 Nov. 1782, W.O. 28/2, Public Record Office.

[19]Robertson to Claus, 7 Sept. 1783, ADD 21758, 254, also in *WHC*, Vol. 12, pp. 66–67, and *MPHC*, Vol. 11, p. 383.

Index

275

Soldier drawings by Dirk Gringhuis

The Authors

David A. Armour, Deputy Director of the Mackinac Island State Park Commission, was born in Grove City, Pennsylvania, where he graduated from the local high school. Having attended the University of London he received a B.A. from Calvin College (1959), and a M.A. (1960) and Ph.D. (1965) from Northwestern University. He taught Colonial American history at the University of Wisconsin, Milwaukee, for four years before accepting his present position in 1967. Dr. Armour is the author of a number of books and articles and from 1968-1973 was editor of *Historical Archaeology*, the annual publication of the Society for Historical Archaeology.

Keith R. Widder is the Curator of History for the Mackinac Island State Park Commission. He has researched extensively and written numerous pieces about the history of the straits of Mackinac region. Prior to coming to Mackinac in 1971, he taught American history. He graduated from Wheaton College (A.B.) in 1965 and the University of Wisconsin, Milwaukee, (M.A.) in 1968. He is a native of Sheboygan, Wisconsin.

MICHILMACINA

The Bas